RAISE YOU FIVE

RAISE YOU FIVE

Essays & Encounters 1964–2004

Volume One

Barry Callaghan

McArthur & Company
Toronto

First published in Canada in 2005 by
McArthur & Company
322 King St., West, Suite 402
Toronto, Ontario
M5V 1J2
www.mcarthur-co.com

This paperback edition published in 2006 by
McArthur & Company

Library and Archives Canada Cataloguing in Publication

Callaghan, Barry, 1937-
Raise you five / Barry Callaghan.

Contents: v. 1. Essays, 1964-2004
ISBN 1-55278-490-8 (v. 1 : bound)
ISBN 1-55278-567-X (v. 1 : pbk.)

I. Title.

PS8555.A49R34 2005 C814'.54 C2005-900582-3

The publisher would like to acknowledge the financial support of the Government of Canada through the Book Publishing Industry Development Program, The Canada Council for the Arts, and the Ontario Arts Council for our publishing activities. We also acknowledge the Government of Ontario through the Ontario Media Development Corporation Ontario Book Initiative.

Interior Design by Michael P. M. Callaghan
Cover Design by Tania Craan
Printed in Canada by Webcom

10 9 8 7 6 5 4 3 2 1

For Claire, who sings the song

Special thanks to *Marilyn Di Florio*
for her longtime commitment and assistance

Should we have stayed at home,
wherever that may be?

Elizabeth Bishop

CONTENTS

On the Prowl on Rue Morgue Avenue ⇜ xiii
True Stories ⇜ 1
Ponce in Puerto Rico ⇜ 14
What Darkness Is For ⇜ 17
Country Stomps ⇜ 34
A Glass of Water Freely Given ⇜ 36
Shearing ⇜ 51
David Annesley ⇜ 52
W.H. Auden: Where the Decent Outnumber the Swine ⇜ 60
Din Don Din ⇜ 66
Goya ⇜ 68
In the Eye of the Dung Beetle ⇜ 69
The Axeman Cometh: Nikita Khrushchev ⇜ 77
Mermaid: A True Story ⇜ 84
The Master and Margarita ⇜ 86
Letter from Marina G.: Leningrad, 1979 ⇜ 94
A Little B-Ball with Rabbit: John Updike ⇜ 97
Couples: Plowing Through Acres of Pudenda ⇜ 106
Marie-Claire Blais ⇜ 112
Black Light ⇜ 116
The Butler's Boot and the Kitchen Sink ⇜ 122
Alan Sillitoe: Pip in Our Time ⇜ 130
Counting My Steps: Jakov Lind ⇜ 134
Stephen Leacock: Out in No Man's Land ⇜ 142
Beckett: I Can't Go On, I'll Go On ⇜ 156
Steinbeck Dead: 1969 ⇜ 164
Samuel Beckett at the Café Français ⇜ 168
W.W.E. Ross: After the Battle, the Dawn ⇜ 174
Your Point Is Nine in Polar Darkness ⇜ 186

First Ice ∽ 195
Steps: Jerzy Kosinski ∽ 196
Arid Attitudes: Hugh MacLennan ∽ 200
Harold Pinter: *The Homecoming* ∽ 205
A Face in the Mirror: The Poetry of French Canada ∽ 209
Portnoy, Son of a Jewish Joke ∽ 215
Margaret Laurence: England, 1965 ∽ 219
Soul on Ice: Eldridge Cleaver ∽ 226
No Exit: Expo '67 ∽ 231
Trudeau and Quebec: 1967 ∽ 239
Kébékanto of Love ∽ 248
Hemingway: *In Our Time* ∽ 251
Understanding Me, Deah: Marshall McLuhan ∽ 259
The Eyes Have It ∽ 263
The Eyes Have It ∽ 267
Norman Mailer and Mario Lanza ∽ 268
Hear the Clopping of the Horses ∽ 273
Stalin Shrugged ∽ 284
"Star, Star, Star, Oh My God" ∽ 287
Trudeau: The 1968 Campaign ∽ 291
Eruption of Rage Against the Second Rate ∽ 306
Davies' Dour Angels: *Fifth Business* ∽ 310
A Beggar in Jerusalem: Elie Wiesel ∽ 313
Desolation Row: New York ∽ 317
Claude Monet's Magpie: A Sonnet ∽ 346
Song My: My Lai ∽ 347
On the Line With the Old Brigade ∽ 355
Points of Rebellion: Justice William O. Douglas ∽ 359
Moving ∽ 363
The Heart of the World: Yehuda Amichai ∽ 364

ON THE PROWL ON RUE MORGUE AVENUE

In 1964, I was sitting in a Jarvis Street beer hall known by radio script writers and actors and summer stock vaudevillians as the Neverclean. It was really the Everene Hotel but to them it was the Neverclean. Some drinkers in that hall also belonged to the Non-Entity Club, called the Non-Entity club because next door to the Neverclean there was a restaurant and a bar that actually was named the Celebrity Club. Members of that Club did not tug their forelock sheepishly when they said Celebrity because many of them were celebrities who worked in television. The CBC television dance and news studios were just across the street.

More than a few actors and writers staggered to work across that busy street, dead drunk, fly open or wearing one high-heel shoe.

Those were innovative but somewhat slap-happy days. At CBC radio, there was the impish announcer who delighted in setting fire to the bottom of news announcers' scripts while they were trying to read them on air, and there was the theatre critic at the *Toronto Star* who wrote his columns in longhand in a coded script that only one elderly man could decipher, while the man who handicapped thoroughbred horses was legally blind; on CBC television, a national news announcer told his crew (and the nation) to stop giving him goddamn cues, a federal cabinet minister and former war hero beat a reporter about the ears with his cane, and a local CBC reporter was so drunk live on television that he asked an alderman, "What the fuck is your name?" Slap-happy days, but also brave days, certainly in the newspapers but especially in television, where there were no old pros, only new pros or pretend pros, and almost anything was possible.

Since I was working for television news (one of my first interviews was with a talking horse), I favoured the Celebrity Club.

My lady friend worked in radio and liked to drink draught beer so I drank beer in the early evening at the Neverclean and then ate supper and drank wine at the Celebrity Club – sometimes till eleven o'clock – when I would hope to take a taxi to catch the last show and a cognac at the only nightclub in town, the Barclay Hotel. I could afford all this – though I was in graduate school – because two years earlier, by phone, I had persuaded the news director of the Mutual Broadcasting System in the United States that – because they'd never had one – I should be their Canadian political correspondent. This meant that I made a weekly three-minute radio report on the state of my nation until someone in New York told the news director that Ottawa, not Toronto, was the capital of Canada. Wounded, as if I'd misled him, he asked if there was someone in Ottawa I thought might do the job and then he fired me.

I was sitting in the Neverclean telling this story to several radio people at the table, and after they had stopped laughing, a lean, delicately boned man said, "How would you like to talk about books on my morning radio program?"

I said, "Sure."

He said, "Good. Seven minutes. Talk about whatever books you want." His name was Terrence Gibbs, a soft-spoken man, who was really a classical music producer, a closet homosexual given to drinking binges and long bouts of weeping.

It is because of Terrence Gibbs that I became a literary journalist.

I say literary journalist because that is how Edmund Wilson described himself – a man of letters, of books, who got paid for writing about the world of politics and letters – and Wilson was the subject of my doctoral dissertation. Though I did complete my doctoral exams and did become a professor, teaching for thirty-seven years, and am now Professor Emeritus, I never did finish my dissertation. I was busy being a literary journalist.

When I told Wilson not too long before he died that I was never going to finish my work on his work, he said he forgave me. "Anyway," he said, "the best thing about academic writing is always the bibliography," and so I forgave myself.

He was a man who carried his portly weight well. He was Jeremy Brown, a senior editor at the Toronto *Telegram* and he took me to lunch at poolside at the Four Seasons on Jarvis Street. I had never been taken to lunch at poolside, not by someone who wanted to hire me, and certainly not by a senior editor for a very big and aggressive newspaper that had only a few years earlier been known as the *Pink Tely* because its front page was pink!

He asked me if I would like to be the Books editor of the paper. Looking back, I can see that there was only one question on the lunch table: Was I willing to be lucky. I took the job and I stayed lucky until four years and some months later when I found myself out on Rue Morgue Avenue. My luck had run out.

In between, it was a time.

I sat down and wrote the best words that I could write . . .

Not just at the *Telegram* – where two editors, Tom Hedley and then Ron Evans, let me loose – but on radio, too, and on television, travelling to wherever writers were and to wars that I could get to, and all the time teaching, a seminar evolving into an essay evolving into a talk, a talk evolving into a film, a film evolving into writing and then revising the writing, as if what I'd printed yesterday could, as Bobby Dylan had said, be *the reincarnation of Paul Revere's horse today . . .*

It was a time when I was trying to find out who I was as a writer and trying to do what Matthew Arnold had said a critic should do – "try to see the thing for what it is in and of itself" – because, if a writer did that he would not slide slothfully into "the ready acceptance of received opinion" – H. L. Mencken's definition of mediocrity.

Received opinion!

In 1970, I said in print and showed on television that the Palestinians *existed* and that was the beginning of the end of me in my home territory.

The *adelantado* got knee-capped.

By the end of 1971, I was out of work, except for the university, and I'd almost lost my place there.

Such is life.

I have said since that a journalist – especially a literary journalist – is only as good as his editors will allow him to be.

Somebody has to give him space.

I went without space for seven years.

There are two kinds of journalists. Those who do what they do and never look back, like the senior editor at the *Telegram* who had told me, "Get it as good as you can get it today, because it's tomorrow's fish wrap," and those who look back and revise and rewrite to beat the wrap. I am one of the latter.

It is curious: I have said – especially to my students, since I was always five minutes late – that punctuality is the virtue of the bored, yet, as a journalist I have always liked writing to deadlines – like the hangman's noose, a deadline concentrates the mind. But once the deadline has been met I've been only too willing to re-work lines, sharpen phrases – never changing the spirit or the point of the piece – but honing it. Honing it in the same way I would hone a story or a poem, because I've always thought a review – if written in a certain way – could be not only a story about another story but possibly a deft parable of its time (years later, traveling in Germany, I discovered that in the 20s several writers had referred to themselves as *feuilletonistes* – the *feuilleton* being a prose piece in the popular press that captured in a glimpse the temper of the times). In 1972 and 1973, deprived of deadlines, I revised several reviews and shortened a long piece about travelling across the country with Pierre Trudeau in 1968 (it had been published by Ron Evans as three full folio pages!) – bringing the work into *feuilletoniste* focus, into an almost Aristotelian fulfillment of a form that had been inherent in the beginning, the beginning being that page of Saturday morning newsprint.

I remember watching a televised Washington ceremony at which a little man who looked like an owl was given a special award by other Washington journalists. After the ceremony, Walter Cronkite loomed over the little man and said in his stentorian avuncular way, "If you ever get to New York, give me a call." (I could not help but think of Mae West.) The little man, who was I.F. (Izzy) Stone, looked mildly bothered, as if he had been unnecessarily distracted. He was his own man. He researched, he wrote, he edited, and he published *I. F. Stone's Weekly.* Other than Edmund Wilson, he was the journalist I admired most in America. He read everything that nobody else in Washington read, page after boring page of the Congressional Record. He knew what politicians had *actually* said. He knew when politicians lied, when they dissembled, and he said so. He had the facts. He was fearless.

I did not start a *Callaghan's Weekly* in Toronto. Instead, when my Dean at York University, Harry Crowe, asked if I'd like to edit and publish a literary quarterly, I said Yes. He said Good, he would bankroll the first year. I started *Exile.*

Since I was sure about everything, I had no idea what I was doing. A quarterly! I didn't know anything about quarterlies. But again, I was willing to be lucky.

In 1972, the first issue of *Exile* appeared. The only editorial in *Exile* read:

> There are many excellent reviews in which the writer of imaginative prose and poetry seems to become merely fodder for the dancing scholarly horse. The writer of the critique becomes more important than the writer of the poem, especially if the critic offers a new fund of useful scholarly information. But useful for what? It is the day of the information deluge. Who sorts it all out? The imaginative writer, who can rely only on his own eyes, his own heart and sensibility for his information, is, in a sense, in exile now. There ought to be a small haven somewhere for such exiles. In these pages the imaginative writer will not be led in by a scholarly praetorian guard. He will be on his own.

It was not my intention then – but years later I realized that when I started *Exile* I turned everything I had done at the *Telegram* inside out. At the *Telegram*, I had written as a critic about Jerzy Kosinski, Marie-Claire Blais, John Montague, Yehuda Amichai – but as I approached the first issue of *Exile*, as its editor, I asked those same writers for poetry and fiction *only*, telling them that there was going to be no critical writing in the book at all, there were going to be no book reviews at the back. No apologies. No explanations. The writer was going to be on his own, and the reader was on his own, too. Our motto, taken from the Québécois painter, Paul-Emile Borduas, was "Better a catastrophe than a false success."

In 1978, the lights began to flicker along Rue Morgue Avenue. On a Sunday evening in March, *The Hogg Poems and Drawings* were published and the drawings were exhibited on the walls of the middle room at the Isaacs Gallery on Yonge Street.

At the launch, confounding the canapé crowd, the front gallery was turned into a dance hall. With amplifiers stacked by the front window, the rhythm and blues band, led by Donnie Walsh and his blues-shouting brother, The Hock, was Downchild.

"I don't know what to think," the poet, Miriam Waddington, said, "because I can't hear myself think."

"Then get up and dance," the novelist, Timothy Findley, told her. And hugged his lover, William Whitehead.

Back in the summer of 1974, as I'd stood at the magazine rack in the International Bookstore on Yonge Street, a man had asked if he could speak to me. "I'd like you to know," he said, "that I am an Armenian from Palestine, from Jerusalem, and I know what speaking of the Palestinians has cost you, and some day I may be in a position to show you my appreciation."

In 1978 the phone rang.

"Remember me?"

I remembered him.

He said his name was Jerry Tutunjian and he'd become the editor of *Leisure Ways* magazine.

"Okay," he said, "what do you want to write about, where would you like to go?"

"How about Berlin," I said, "how about the pilgrimage route to Santiago de Compostela, how about glaciers . . . ?"

Before I could go anywhere for Tutunjian, John Macfarlane and Gary Ross at *Weekend*, the national magazine, asked me to go to central Africa. They wanted me to find Cardinal Léger in his leper camp in the Cameroon, and they wanted me to talk to the ghost of Albert Schweitzer in his hospital at Lamberene in Gabon.

They wanted me to shake hands with the leper.

Almost all the lights were back on along Rue Morgue Avenue.

And then Tom Hedley came back into my life in late 1977.

He had left the *Telegram* and gone to work as an associate editor at *Esquire.* He'd done brilliant work over ten years, but now he'd quit and he was back in town, biding on becoming a screenwriter. In the meantime, he took over as editor of the magazine, *Toronto Life.* He gave me a monthly column, and called it "Callaghan," saying, "Write about the city, whatever you want, and if it's reporting, OK, and if it's fiction, OK, let the reader figure it out."

We held our editorial meetings at Café des Copains, a cellar bar for jazz singers, or at Gimlets, an intimate little dive of ten tables and a postage-stamp stage for naked dancers, or the Dominion House, a bar on Bay Street close to the bus terminal that catered to transvestite bus drivers.

So, *I sat down and wrote the best words that I could write . . .*

Of the early "Callaghan" columns that appeared in *Toronto Life,* I sent two to the editor of *Punch,* the brilliant satirist, Allen Coren, who had somehow come to read my work. I called one column "The Black Queen" and the other "Crow Jane's Blues". He published both as his featured fiction of the month, and over the next six months he published six more of my "true" stories from *Toronto Life* as "fictional" stories in *Punch.* Then, at his invitation, I found myself seated at a long table in London as guest at a *Punch* lunch, where – plunked down between a young man who had porcelain skin and an elderly woman whose skin looked like cheesecloth – I watched Charles Laughton throw little bread balls at the *Punch* cartoonists. The young man, seeing my amused wonderment, said to me quietly, "Yes, I sometimes feel I'm guesting on the *Muppet Show* at these lunches."

A little more than a year before I collected those stories and published them as The *Black Queen Stories*, Marq de Villiers, an Afrikaner who had been the Moscow correspondent for the *Telegram* in the late 60s became the editor of *Toronto Life*. (Tom Hedley, taking the scene at Gimlets with him as a seed, had gone away to write the film, *Flashdance*.) de Villiers thought, as I did, that the life of Toronto as it appeared in *Toronto Life* could be as big as our imaginations wanted it to be. I wrote short fiction, I wrote poems from Leningrad, I wrote about everything – Ottawa political conventions, Munich and Dachau, the forgotten Baltic republics, the local politics of telemarketing and lotteries, Rome, the vandalizing of my home by drug addicts, the Orient Express, international horse racing – and one day in those years, in the early 80s, while reading Baudelaire, I realized that, yes, I had always been a scholar, and maybe a *feuilletoniste,* but perhaps I was also something of a *flaneur*, "a stroller, a loiterer, someone who ambles through a city without apparent purpose but is secretly attuned to the history of the place, and is in covert search of adventure, aesthetic or erotic."

I told this to a friend of mine, George Yemec – then the publisher of *Millions* magazine – and he said, "A *flaneur* is a skimmer, you're no skimmer." I didn't bother to say that Walter Benjamin had taken the *flaneur* very seriously (suggesting that between the voices one absorbed into oneself and one's own voice there was a silence – like the silence between notes – and it was in that silence that the *flaneur* stretched his legs). No, Yemec had made his point, and because he was a horse owner and more importantly a horse player, a man only too willing to be lucky, I said, as if we were talking about horse breeding: – How about seeing my blood lines as Edmund Wilson out of I. F. Stone by Petit Flaneur?

Maybe.

But then, maybe not.

A few years later I owned a race horse, a gift from Yemec on my 50th birthday. It was a Great Gladiator horse called Fox On The Prowl.

I liked that. Maybe I was a fox on the prowl. The thought-fox:

A body that is bold to come
Across clearings, an eye,
A widening deepening greenness,
Brilliantly, concentratedly,
Coming about its own business
Till, with a sudden sharp hot stink of fox
It enters the dark hole of the head.
The window is starless still; the clock ticks,
The page is printed.

The horse won four races before it was claimed. And then he won three more. And then he was put out to pasture.

Boomlay, boomlay throughout the 80s and early 90s, and then –

BOOM.

Everybody got claimed.

Allen Coren had left Punch.

Tutunjian lost his magazine.

Weekend had disappeared.

And de Villiers, God bless him, retired from editing to live by the sea, to write his own books.

I had published poetry, seven books of translations, two novels, and another book of short stories – *A Kiss Is Just a Kiss* – but once again, as a literary journalist, the lights had gone out on Rue Morgue Avenue.

And they've pretty much stayed out since.

Such is life.

❧

And so I wrote a memoir, *Barrelhouse Kings.*

And *Hogg, The Seven Last Words.*

But it was not until 2000, after I had written "True Stories," a story about story telling for Brunella Antomarini, the editor of a philosophical review in Rome, *il cannocchiale*, that I decided to gather my non-fiction together. As soon as I'd decided to do that the question on the table became – not whether I was willing to be lucky, but what was I going to do with all those pieces out there, those half-forgotten fillies and colts in the desert, stragglers on the prowl in need of a good herding. But what would a good herding be like? I had sometimes thought of my work as forty years of prowling, waiting for a shape to take hold, because I knew the shape could never be simple chronology. I had no interest in chronology. Instead, I had a hunch that there was a wholeness to the work – no matter the different times and lengths and forms – and, if brought together in no pre-ordained schematic way – there might be a music between notes in the work, even a melody to be found – first, in what would be volume one, and then two and three. Strict chronology, of course, would have been a simpler story, an easier edit, but less fun, less resonant, less the way I think my mind works, less like a blind man handicapping the horses. For years, when asked about my non-fiction, what I was going to do with it all, I've sloughed off the question, saying, "I'm fattenin' frogs for snakes." Well, the snake's about to be fed, the song is sung, the story's told.

B.C.

TRUE STORIES

In memory of Earlie Fires

I knew a man who was born in a peasant village in Galicia, close to the Polish border. By the time he was nineteen he had worked his way to Vladivostok and then to Siberia. "Up there," he said, "the snow got deep. Men stole food, and then one man killed another and the police locked the murderer in a cage with the corpse. The starving man went so crazy he ate his dead man before he died, too. The police left the cage in the forest. In the spring, the trees were in flower, birds built nests in the bones."

He came home to his village and worked as a stable hand. He thought he might join the army but then he saw a small poster, a handbill that said: COME TO SASKATCHEWAN. He told me: "Because I didn't know where it was, I went."

He sailed for Canada.

He worked on the prairies and for a while he lived with four other farm labourers in a one-room *boorday*, a sod hut, half underground.

"It was strange," he said, "like living together in your grave."

At the same time, a young Ukrainian girl arrived by boat in Montréal. In her home village an old priest had made her sister pregnant. She thought he was going to make her pregnant, too. She had come to Montréal to marry a shoemaker. It was an arranged marriage. The shoemaker wasn't there. He didn't show up. Someone took her from the docks and gave her a bag of sandwiches and put her on a train for Saskatchewan.

Five days alone by train, two thousand miles.

A girl who couldn't speak English.

The Galician was working there on a farm.

She went to work on the same farm.

He heard his boss sing:

Works like donkey,
looks like monkey,
must be hunky.

They came to Toronto, got married and had a daughter.

"We made a nest," he said.

He was a man of stamina, of stoic courage. He worked as a plumber. He pressed pants. He set pins in bowling alleys. He was a barber. He laid cobblestones between the city streetcar tracks.

He saved his money and bought a small house.

Then he got sick, a terrible arthritis in his spine. Doctors fused his vertebrae together to ease the pain.

He couldn't turn his head.

"It doesn't matter," he said, "I never look back."

Over the next forty years, in pain, he often could not work. He had to stay home, sitting upright in his chair, and he read books, novels in Russian ordered by surface mail from Moscow, a people's press, newsprint pages and cardboard covers.

He said he liked Tolstoy. He felt Tolstoy was talking music to him. He didn't like Solzhenitsyn. Solzhenitsyn was just talking, talking.

His wife kept a cat, and kept a canary in a cage. It made her smile, watching the cat watch the bird. She was amused by the steadfast stillness of the cat's yearning. She was pleased by the bird's chirping. She talked to the bird.

The daughter got married.

In the year his daughter gave him a grandson, two of his farm-labour friends from the old country who had lived with him in the sod hut in Saskatchewan died.

Their names were in the local Ukrainian newspaper.

His wife had cataracts on her eyes, so he read the death notices aloud to her.

She was strong but she could hardly see and didn't realize that she had left the canary cage door open. The bird flew around the house and then out the back door.

"A bird flying in the house," he said, "means death."

But he grew older and older.

He grew feeble and hardly slept.

A deeper pain had nested in his bones as he sat upright staring straight ahead.

"I know how to do a hundred things," he said, "but I don't know how to die."

Two weeks later, he died, though he still didn't know how to die, because he died in his sleep.

He had almost never talked about his life. He had never looked back. He certainly didn't know how to tell his story.

I have told his story, the story of how he will be remembered.

It is who he will be.

Is it who he was?

I don't know.

Details may be wrong, but what is worth knowing in the story is entirely true. If details are wrong then they are lies only in the way true lovers give each other the lie when they say: "I'll love you till the day I die." The more layered such lies, the more biting the truth.

Such is art.

Such was a man called Paul Rabchuk.

This is how I know him.

Now you know him, too.

What are the implications of this story?

That a story begins in memory and memory is not the end but the beginning of a story.

And what does this say about history? It says something as old as Aristotle: that history is an assemblage of facts, the bits and pieces of time past, with a tinge of the present, and little more.

A story, though, is a shaping of the facts, a molding act of the imagination.

And the imagination, said Jacques Maritain, approaches metaphysics; that is, it approaches first truths.

Where does the imagination begin?

In memory, with the story.

Let me put what I mean in another way, by saying something about one of the greatest stories ever told.

I was bred in the bone as a Catholic. I went to a parochial school, I studied the lives of the saints, I sang in the choir and learned to sing in Latin but did not learn what Latin meant, I learned the liturgy and what all the colours of the Mass vestments signified – from death to resurrection – but I did not read the Old and New Testaments.

Catholics did not read the Bible stories.

That's how all the Protestants like Luther and Calvin had got into trouble, by reading the Bible stories for themselves.

I did not get into trouble until late in life.

I sat down and read the Genesis story.

I didn't know what to expect so I read all the little chapters of the story as if it were the memoirs of the Jews.

And with the first chapter I knew something unexpected was afoot. I had always been told that the Great Beginning had begun with the light, and then there was the garden, and Adam and Eve and the first temptation, the apple, the snake, sin, shame, and the expulsion from Eden – and we were the children of the expelled, trying to shed sin and shame in this vale of tears so that we could go back over the garden wall, which is death, and get into the garden again.

It's a good story and Christians have stuck to it.

As in all good stories, however, there is another woman.

But there is an extraordinary twist to the Jewish story, because the other woman does not weasel her way in and break up the marriage. She was there first. She was there before Eve. And she wasn't born from Adam's rib, she wasn't bonded to him by the bone. She was her own woman, equal, and she looked around and said, "This place is for the birds," dismissing Adam, his God of light and lightning bolts, and the garden. She went over the wall and took the name Lilith.

Then the story starts all over again.

This time with the rib and Eve, and this time everything and everyone in the story is under control.

But where did that woman Lilith go? Who was she? Is she still out there, indifferent to all the patriarchal prating that goes on through all the stories in the Bible? Did she break out of the bondage of death forever?

The idea of breaking out of bondage, of passing over, led me to read the Exodus story.

Every year, Jews celebrate Passover, the coming out of Egypt.

They celebrate the story as a truth that lies at the core of their being Jews.

But what is the story?

People of a historical bent, who need to believe in facts before they can believe in belief itself, have had a hard time with this passing-over story.

Were the Jews really in Egypt? Where and when did the Red Sea part?

Where is the mountain where Moses talked to God?

What is manna? And was it a gift from God?

There are hundreds of Bible cops out there on the beat, saying, "Just the facts, ma'am, just the facts."

Such a man wrote a book called *The Bible as History*. It was a best-seller because he had lined up all the facts like little ducks and he had worked out all the answers, even for the mystery of manna.

Manna, he said, was the pure white, sweet-tasting excrement that certain desert insects left, and still leave, on foliage during the night.

That, he said, as if he had proven something triumphant and profound, something to bolster the faith, was what the wandering Israelites ate for breakfast – insect shit, sweet to the tongue, and full of protein, too.

He, like other fundamentalists and creationists, piled up literal facts to justify a literal reading of the story, insisting he could prove that Moses had actually crossed over in a certain year, that Moses and his several thousands of men, women, and children had actually marched around Sinai for forty years, that the sun had actually stood still and trumpets had actually blown down the walls around Jericho.

But wait a minute.

The Egyptians were extraordinary bookkeepers, and we know how to read all their hieroglyphic records. They kept track of every camel herder who crossed the Sinai desert. There is no mention of Moses or his army prepping for pitched battle around Jericho. As a matter of fact, the chosen people are singled out for mention only once in the whole mass of Egyptian records – a passing reference to the mountain town of Jerusalem.

And as I read this story for the first time I asked myself: "Forty years! How big is the Sinai?" The fact is, the Sinai is so small you can walk across it in four days. So what were they doing out there for forty years? Where were they hiding? Were they the greatest vanishing act in history? Was Moses some kind of *faux Bismarck*? Were they ever actually there?

In asking these questions, am I inviting a laughter that belittles the story?

Absolutely not. The story is intact in my imagination. It is intact in the imagination of the Jews.

But I am belittling the fundamentalists who insist that a story must be literally true in its factual details if its great truth is to be trusted.

Aristotle had their number.

Chronological detail, he said, is a low level of awareness. Telephone books have chronology.

But the imagination gives shape to the experience that is in-herent in the form of the story.

Like a bee, a story becomes itself.

Like a bee, a story gets in your bonnet.

It becomes what it is in your memory. The memory of passing out of bondage is central to the being of all Jews. They did not know who they were until they had got their story straight. Every year at Passover, by entering into memory they begin again. That's what Passover is, a story renovated through ritual from generation to generation, and the details may be historically true to past time or not, and borrowed from other past tribes or not, but who the Jews are *is*, and the way they discover who they are and affirm who they are does not end with a memory but begins in memory.

That's their great story as they remember it and they are sticking to it, to the truth in it, the coming out of bondage into a freedom. In my own memory, that is Paul Rabchuk's story. Coming out of the bondage of Russia into the open expanse of Saskatchewan, going there because he didn't know where there was.

Paul Rabchuk told me the story of his four friends, hard-working men who had promised each other in the dank light of a prairie *boorday* that they would be millionaires.

Years passed. Two of the men died as millionaires. Their children became chiropractors. Paul worked hard but he also stayed home a lot, week after week, locked in pain, staring straight ahead. He was well off but he was not rich.

He had nothing to do so he read books. Tolstoy. Turgenev. Dostoievski. Chekhov. Babel.

When he wasn't reading, he went for long walks in a great park that was across from his house, High Park.

Then his two living friends retired. Paul, because he was not a millionaire, read books and went for walks.

Months passed and he did not hear from his friends.

Paul said he felt very alone, and then he told me this story.

He got a phone call.

Leonid had tried to kill himself and Boris was on the verge of a nervous breakdown. They met in the park. Paul was astonished. His friends looked haggard and broken, like homeless men.

"How?" they asked.

"How what?"

"How are you so calm?"

He gave them Tolstoy's stories.

Over the months they sat on a long bench by Grenadier Pond in the south end of the park, where several swans swam in the water. They fed bread crusts to the swans.

Boris was reading Babel and Leonid was reading Dostoievski, even the letters.

They read for hours without stopping.

Leonid kissed Paul on the cheek.

"I owe you," he said. "You can punch me."

"Why would I punch you?" Paul asked.

"If you meet a stupid man," Boris said, "beat him. He will know the reason why."

They kept on talking, week after week, telling each other the stories they had read. "That was good, I tell you true."

Then one day Boris said, "I'll tell you a story. About my father and some other men who'd been arrested. By someone's command. And they made one man undress and he was missing a leg, so they took his crutch."

"How do you know this?"

"Because the mother of one of the men kept a whorehouse in Minsk and I used to go there."

"And they took his crutch?"

"And another man had lost an arm and they took his artificial limb."

"The bastards."

"And they told him they wouldn't feed him if he complained."

"Didn't someone have to sign for the arm?"

"My father. He signed, and he said to them, 'Somebody turns in a leg, another an arm, so I'll give you an eye.' And he gave them his porcelain right eye."

"Your father had a porcelain eye?"

"Even I couldn't tell till he told me, the eye was such a good match."

Paul thought maybe this was a true story and maybe it was made up or maybe it was borrowed, but he didn't want to say anything because he didn't want to offend his friend. Boris went on and said, "Father, standing naked, told them, 'Pretty soon you'll have all the body parts you need.' And they said, 'What is there you won't give up?' And he said, 'My soul, you can't have my soul.'"

"And your father told you that story?" Leonid asked.

"True."

"I think I read a story like that somewhere," Paul told him.

"Good," Boris said "If someone else told the same story, then it must be even more true."

They sat on the bench in silence, tossing bread to the swans who honked, waiting to be fed.

After Paul died and was cremated, I told my father his story. He was sitting facing me, and his eyes were alive like a child's because he was not only listening to the story but was beginning to see it in his own way. But what was his way, and how would he make it his own and yet keep it true to what I had told him, and true to what Paul had told me, and to what Boris had told Paul, so that someone hearing the story would say, "How true."

✻

To make any story like this into a true story demands a curious eye, a cold eye. Not ruthless, but a lens-eye unmoved by the impediment of emotion. The kind of eye that Morley had. He could look at me that way, and often did. And at my mother. That, of course, was the distance I always felt in him. The distance that allowed him to take our intimate private moments and put them in his stories, on the public page for his own purposes. He looked at himself that way. Unflinching. By temperament.

There is an astonishing scene in his story *A Passion in Rome*, astonishing to anyone who knew my mother, who suffered for years from a terrifically painful disease, *tic douloureux*, the most painful of all neurological afflictions, and it is a scene in which the lovers are in Rome in a rented flat over a shop and they have been through a night of sexual ecstasy, a night of cries and moans – the same kind of cries and moans that my mother made in her agonies – followed by a fierce wrangling and loud recrimination. In the morning, in the story, to mollify the old landlady the man tells his lover what to write in a note: "We are sure you were alarmed by the cry of pain you must have heard last night . . . I have a neuralgia of the face, an old disease. Perhaps you have heard of it. It is called *tic douloureux*. It strikes me suddenly. The pain, as doctors know, is unbearable. I am ashamed that I cry out . . ."

What, I wondered, did my mother think of that? Not only a little lie told by the characters, but her pain masked as sexual ecstasy. This was a world where the lens-eye of the writer, your husband, could steal your thoughts, your shame, your soul.

Then, in the year after I returned home from my honeymoon, I had a casual conversation with my father in which I told him about the first little fights I had had on the road with my new wife, Nina Rabchuk, Paul's daughter. Later, in Morley's story *A Fine and Private Place,* I read:

> He had her arm and felt her shoulder go up stiffly. Then he knew that she felt neglected and he trembled with resentment. Rome was the loveliest of all the cities, and here she was, wanting to be treated as the only really lovely thing in Rome. From then on, he was aware of other surprising little oppositions. He liked wandering at loose ends: unexpected ruins, restaurants, boutiques, tie shops and churches – they all delighted him. Then, if he suddenly wanted to cross the road, she argued: It wasn't where they had planned to cross. In Christ's name, what does it matter? And he was harsh with her, for there seemed to be a map in her head which only she knew and he couldn't know; if they didn't follow the secret map, everything would go to pieces.

I remember thinking, What a remarkable memory, what remarkable reporting of what I had said, but he knew and I knew – and perhaps Nina knew, too – that a private moment in my marriage had been seen through the lens of his eye and then laid bare on the page.

Yet I never said a word.

He stared at me. I stared at him.

It is dangerous to stare, to look upon your father, and even more dangerous to go into his tent, to plunge into his privacy, and see him in his aloneness, in all his dark nakedness.

I did.

I looked at him with my own curious eye – and it was at the worst of moments – when we both thought he was about to be told he had cancer – a curious eye unmoved by the impediment of emotion.

Morley sat down one day and read in my story, *The Way the Angel Spreads Her Wings*, about the afternoon we went together to Wellesley Hospital to see if he had cancer. The character in my novel is called Adam, and he goes with his father, who is called Web:

> . . . and as his father undressed in the cubicle in the hospital's emergency room he thought I don't want to see him stripped down, defenseless: years ago I wanted him dead but now I don't want him defenseless. His father stood barefoot on the grey marble floor, naked, talking about baseball as if nothing were the matter, as if they were in neutral space, all emotion neutered, and neither spoke of a silent un-seen tumor, nor said the dreaded word, cancer, the big C, but only stared at the yellow, purple, pink, sepia blood in rippled layers, a relief map under his translucent skin, all the places he'd been, the altitudes. But the doctor, a young man wearing steel-rimmed glasses, shrugged and smiled as Web sat up on the brown rubber sheet of the examining table, his slightly bowed legs, Adam thought, and his penis is so small, remembering when he was a child in the bathroom, his father standing over the toilet, his penis between two fingers, thick, so big, so heavy, and now it looked like his memory of his own childhood penis, small, hooded, shriveled by fear, his only sign of fear, and why am I looking at his penis? when it is actually his bony feet, the long bony yellow toes and toenails that appal me, the hard yellow nails and the thin shins and crinkled blue veins and the flesh hanging loose under his arms like a woman's, the little womanly tits with tufts of hair around the small nipples (why do men have nipples? what taunting sign of ineffectuality, lost powers, sign of the lost rib), and laughing lightly, Adam said, "Goddamn, you sure look like the resurrection of the dead to me."

Morley never said a word about that passage.

He never said whether it was accurate or false; he only said that the prose of the novel was very sensual, that it was not the way he wrote. No, not at all . . .

Yet in the years before his death, writer to writer, stealing from each other's lives, stealing and shaping little lies to tell big truths, we ended up yielding in a complete and silent trust our private moments to each other's storytelling devices and public scrutiny.

Perhaps that was a nakedness beyond facts, beyond a kiss, beyond sensuality. Beyond even trust, since it was neither asked for nor given.

Perhaps that was our passing over, our coming out of bondage into a love, the telling of lies that told a story that enhanced the truth of how it was with us.

il cannocchiale, 2000

PONCE IN PUERTO RICO

Ponce de León was a plunger, a man who had put his dream on the line and had called out, "Raise you five," a man who'd come clanking across the sea in an iron suit, a soldier who had scoured all the old scouting reports and maps of islands, tracing little zigzag lines with his long forefinger, zigzag rivers that he believed were lined with gold pebbles. He was a scoundrel but he was a scoundrel in love with the hills of his illusions. He'd gone off over an ocean that practical men of good sense and fear had insisted was flat. He'd gone off into the abyss of the unknown believing that the abyss is always filled with possibilities, that catastrophe is better by far than a false success.

Before he died, he'd been in Cuba and he'd found Bimini and he was part of the map-makers' news. Balboa was on a peak in Darién, de Soto was not yet dead at the Arkansas, Cortés was in Vera Cruz pretending he was a plumed serpent, and Pizarro was on the road to Machu Picchu. Ponce had surrounded himself with tattooed ladies, but even love in the afternoon had loomed up at last as too boring for him, boredom becoming a constant ache in the back of his brain, and so he had hauled anchor for the green hills one hundred and fifty leagues east, Boriquén, the port called Rico. Runners across the water had told him about gold and rivers where handfuls of gold pebbles lay in shallow water just for the taking, and within the week he had rowed in on the breakers on the north shore and announced that among conquistadors he was the *adelantado*, the front-runner. He'd also told the gawking Indians that he was a son of the sun, and he set up a sundial so that they would know at exactly what time they were going to die.

The Indians thought Ponce, with his flesh the colour of the ash of dead fires, was supernatural, but then a chief, a man called Brayoan, ambushed one of Ponce's scouts and held him head-first under the magic water. He drowned, and since that drowning seemed easy enough, the Indians killed six more men. But the white scouts kept coming in their leather and iron and the Indians concluded that they could only be coming back from the dead, resurrected, just as Ponce had said their magic lord had been resurrected, the lord they called Jesus. In two years Ponce had conquered the island. His men, carrying the true cross, had become rich; thirty-four years later, when Carlos V abolished slavery in the gold mines, some forty thousand Taínos were dead. They did not come back from the dead.

It happened that Ponce had a close friend, Don Cristobal de Sotomayor, who – as he was being hung up by the heels by the Indians on the road to San Juan – made a last request, and that request was that Ponce should look after his ward, a child countess back in Spain. Ponce, whose skin by this time had taken on the putty hue of coming old age, with a liverish blue under the eyes, was wealthy and respected, and tired. He sailed for home. But when he saw his sloe-eyed, sprightly, sharp-minded ward, who soon would come into one of the largest dowries in Spain, he first licked his dry lips and then he fell in love. He picked up a mirror of highly polished gold, winced, and wanted only one thing. He wanted his youth. Because cannibals had told him that there was a miraculous fountain of youth in the islands, he decided to gamble everything. Possibilities lurched in his mind; he packed up, smiling, full of hope, and set out to discover the front porch of the dead, Miami Beach.

In that year, 1521, the year Cortés took Tenochtitlan apart, Ponce saw Pascua Florida for the first time, a flower-covered land, and he went ashore with three hundred and seventy men, and soon he was rooting around in the rivers and streams for his youth. He let water from a phosphorous bay run down his outstretched arms, droplets of light. He called out the name of the child countess. Indians who wore their hair tufted and cut like acorn tops stood silently by on the banks of the rivers, some hunched forward inside stag skins, wagging their antlers, and then the stags attacked. They hacked the white men to pieces.

An arrow hit Ponce in the thigh, close to the femoral artery. The arrow splintered in the bone. Ponce, weakening from loss of blood, cried, "Jesus, I couldn't help myself, help me now." He waited for a little help and got none and, watching his blood spill away, he wept because he'd only wanted to be loved, to embrace life, to be the *adelantado.* He knew it was for the last time but anyway he called out, "Raise you five."

Now he stands at the centre of a square in old San Juan amidst dwarf trees and wrought-iron benches. He stands on a high stone pedestal, Ponce de León the plunger, in his iron suit with feathers in his hat. His one hand on his hip, the other is pointing off into the hills, his bottle green body is made out of discarded cannon melted down and at his throat he is dressed with a scorpion's tail, he is still invincible at ballroom dancing, and is eager to sup on alligator wine and a little serpent's fat, and learned in magic, he woos a woman . . .

Toronto Life, 1978

WHAT DARKNESS IS FOR

One discovers the light in darkness,
that is what darkness is for . . . What the light
reveals is danger, and what it demands is faith.

—James Baldwin

The Ogowé in Gabon is a river of swamps and pocket lagoons and a spongy shoreline. The water is yellow and filled with sandbars. Upriver, near the equator, there is an island called Lambaréné. Years ago, Arab runners used the crossing at Lambaréné to take slaves south to Cape Town and north to Tangiers.

From a pirogue in the late afternoon light the small hotel on Lambaréné Island seemed to wobble in the hillside of leaves and vines. It was very hot. An old man wearing a wool cap sat in a ditch of the road up to the hotel cradling a harp, a block of hollowed wood charred black and covered with iguana skin. There was a small white head carved on top, white to ward off evil spirits. The man plucked the strings as I went by up the hill to the hotel.

The lobby was unlit. It was all brown shadows. In the small empty barroom, a ceiling fan turned listlessly. The sun was beginning to set. I tried to remember Albert Schweitzer's face, his lank white hair, his thick nose, and the lines cut deeply into his face as if time were water. A walrus moustache hid his mouth, letting his eyes float free, like a half-truth. I had no idea of what half-truth there could be, nor any idea of what truth I could find here, what presence of an old man who had come out to West Africa to preach and to play a lead-lined pedal piano in the primeval night . . .

Later, I lay upstairs on a narrow cot-bed in a small room, a concrete floor and French doors to the windows, held closed by a chair propped under the handles. Sweltering in the humid heat, listening to the animal and bird ruckus in the trees, and reading in the lamplight from several of Schweitzer's books. Long, big-winged insects seeking the light came in through the loose casement and the doors, wobbling out of the shadows, landing on my bare skin.

Schweitzer, before the First War, had built a mission station on a rise farther along the shore, and he had put up several frame buildings. Then he'd had to go back to France, interned during the war. When he'd come to the river again in 1924 the buildings were in ruins, overrun by brush and eaten away by white ants and termites. He'd had to begin all over again, helping to cut timber and dig postholes while doctoring sick blacks who came downriver out of the bush. They'd called him the *oganga* – the fetish man – and to my surprise, lying on the narrow cot-bed, I discovered in one of his books that he had kept a fetish for himself, a charm against the night: "The most important objects in it," he wrote, "are two fragments of a human skull, of a longish oval shape and dyed with some sort of red colouring matter . . ." Magical bones, fear-bags of little bells and buffalo horns, small sacks of teeth – these were the fetishes to protect him from evil spirits. "He does not worship his fetish, but regards it as a little bit of property which cannot but be of service through its supernatural powers . . . and I myself am the possessor of a fetish."

It had begun to rain, water suddenly pouring off the corrugated roof. I closed my eyes, at ease with the sound of water, entering into an ease with Schweitzer as if I could believe a bond had been struck between us because I was holding my own fetish, a small carved amber-coloured antelope horn that fitted into my fist, the figure of a kneeling man, his chin in his hands, mouth open, a little zero, staring wide-eyed . . . a fetish that had been given to me by a woman a few years ago on the road to Zambesi. I went to sleep.

In the early morning a milky steam rose out of the earth, a steam that turned sour yellow in the first sunlight and lay like rags over the slow-swirling water. I stared through the shutters, waiting, listening to the rippling call of little birds and whistling parrots, brooding over Schweitzer. The bottled water I was drinking was tepid, a greasy weight on the tongue. There was a clammy feel to the air, but the sun, a blurred hazy ball suspended low in the sky, was clearing the brush, turning the river into a sepia glass, a flutter of mirrors. It was a light lacking something, a light filled with the dead weight of silence, a light lacking joy.

It surprised me, reading Schweitzer, that all his life he had sought to live in this light that lacked joy, and "only at quite rare moments" had he felt really glad to be alive. He had played Bach in all its exhilaration and felt only regret at the pain he had seen around him, and not only the pain of specific men "but that of the whole of creation."

The pain at the heart of creation was caused by evil in the heart, and no explanation for this evil in the heart ever satisfied him. He wrote that there was only one thing he could understand: "Each of us has to go his own way, as one who means to help bring about deliverance."

As the sun rose in the sky, the trance-like liquidity of things lifted, and across from Lambaréné Island I could see gently rolling hills, and the water suddenly became a soft slate blue and the leaves were glossy with light and there were clusters of red and pink flowers. The joylessness was gone. There was a strange porcelain sheen in the air.

I left the hotel. At the foot of the mud road from the hotel to the river there were pirogues pulled up on shore, canoes hollowed out of grey and coloured logs. Two leper boatmen, one wearing an old bowler hat, were sitting on their haunches. The sun was still low but it was getting hot. There were tan-shaded sandbanks in the water and deadwood driven by the undercurrents. The forest came down to the shore, tentacled mahogany, palms, breadfruit and tall okoumés with their pearl-grey bark and wing-like roots above the ground, and papyrus groves and reeds.

Going along a shoreline just like this, Schweitzer, staring moodily at the luxurious rot and growth, had suddenly formulated his famous phrase "reverence for life," words that had touched people all over the world. He had been sitting in a pirogue brooding on the wound within himself, the paradox at his core: his deeply felt sense of inevitable decay and death, and his just as deeply felt conviction that life must be affirmed and that such affirmation reflected the undeniable will to live that was in all men, in all of nature. And then it struck him; there, along the shore, life was leaping up out of the rot and collapse, reaching out of roots in death toward the light. He sat in the canoe confronted by the forest purging itself so that it might live, and he decided that acceptance of this process and reverence for that reach toward light and life must lead to a compassion for all those trapped in pain. This powerful feeling of pity, he thought, would not only allow a man to purify himself but lead him to succour the helpless, to atone for the rot at the heart of life. He had discovered a rationale not only for the human condition but for an almost absurd assertion of life's dignity in the midst of misery and dying.

I saw, about a mile from Lambaréné Island, a cleared space on the shore, a sand beach under tall palm trees, and along the gentle slope, long, narrow sheds with peaked roofs of corrugated iron. They were raised on piles to let the rainwater run downhill freely, and built from east to west so that the sun would not beat on the roof directly, except at noon. They were, I discovered, tribal wards; men and women were sprawled in the doorways. There was an open cooking pit, a pharmacy with cramped consultation rooms, locked cells for mental patients, staff sleeping quarters, and on the crest of the hill a central cool, tree-shaded clearing, the little staff graveyard of plain crosses: Schweitzer, Mrs. Schweitzer, Nurse Kottmann . . . and stairs up to a long porch, his rooms.

There were two rooms and they were small. Wooden crossbars and screens were on the windows, a graceful bedstead was draped in white mosquito netting, and white wall shelves and boxes held some of his books and papers. There were two small tables covered with white cloth, one of them his work desk. Magnifying glasses, yellowed letters, his spectacles and watch were laid out on the desk, and there was a kerosene lamp with a tin shade.

I don't know why, but the whiteness of the room made me wonder how tall a man he had been, how close he had come to the sky. I had no idea. I remembered only his rounded shoulders in a white short-sleeved shirt, the black bow tie, his sunken chest sloping out into a paunch. The blacks had nicknamed him Misopo – Big Abdomen.

His old piano stood in the next room, the varnish peeled and the ivory nearly all gone from the keys. I sat down on the bench and tapped a few notes from the music sheets open on the stand, feeling a sudden melancholy in the cool little room. Despite the books, the mosquito net and the piano, I felt no presence of the man but only shadows, as if his real presence could never be touched, even in his own rooms where he had slept and written his journals.

As I tapped the warped keys, the piano totally out of tune, my sense of him as a shadow in the folds of white cloth seemed appropriate. After all, he had explained that his feeling for the presence of Jesus in his own life had been only that of a shadow in a blurred landscape, and the more I thought about this, the more I realized that his approach to Jesus lay at the very heart of both his dark pessimism and his dogged determination to affirm life.

Before coming to the Ogowé as a medicine man and missionary, he had written about Jesus, Jesus the man, the historical

Jesus. His life as a man, he said, had come down to us only in garbled reports, the Gospels, and the Gospels were full of gaps, and those reports had been distorted even more by theological finger-work.

Nonetheless, as far as he was concerned, the life as told contained a remarkable story: a child Jew who had heard a voice tell him he was the Son of God, a child who knew that in this life of attrition, pain, and suffering he was destined to be the man who would tie his life and death into the actual moment when cosmic catastrophe would signal final judgement and deliverance . . . deliverance from evil and the dark night, a deliverance he would bring to pass through moral renovation, good work among the downcast.

Schweitzer knew that this was a vision and an ethic so deep and so naive that most men would never have accepted it. But Jesus did. In his messianic consciousness, so obsessed with pain, affliction, disease, and persecution, Jesus had seen that his miracles were a prefiguration of the kingdom of deliverance to come. Through atonement, his voluntary sacrifice, his chosen death, he would save those who believed in him.

The only trouble, as Schweitzer looked back into this story, was that the cosmic collapse did not come after Calvary. Jesus had deluded himself. There had been no deliverance, and affliction remained everywhere. But for Schweitzer one profound truth had emerged, a truth perceived by St. Paul: there was the promise of redemption through atonement. In this, our terrible vale of suffering, the life of Jesus could be emulated, for between Calvary and the promise of the Second Coming a man could lead a life of sacrifice, and such sacrifice might help bring to pass the final liberating event: reverence for life would renovate the future. There would be deliverance. Death would die, and there would at last be the light of joy.

Sitting at the piano, I stopped tapping out the notes on the open page. I realized, surrounded by his whiteness, that none of this light, none of the light that could suddenly put a sheen over the river, could be found anywhere in Schweitzer's writings. He saw only mist and gloom and monotony along the shoreline. How extraordinary, I thought, that a man could live for years in this light, keeping a journal, and never write about it, almost as if he refused to see it.

I opened his journals and walked back and forth beside his bed, reading. In his mind's eye, the river country was all "clumps of palms and palm trees . . . the rotting stems of dead giants . . . So it goes on hour by hour. Each new corner, each new bend is like the last. Always the same forest and the same yellow water . . . monotonous repetition. You shut your eyes for an hour, and when you open them you see exactly what you saw before."

His only relief from joylessness and misery, his only sensual moments, came in the dead of night when, free from daylight monotony, he moved upstream along the river banks where the "wood and water are flooded with an Easter full-moon." In that pale light he felt something close to a thrill, a release, in that he almost refused to believe "so much misery and terror" could exist, could inhabit moonlight.

The fact is, he was afraid of the sun, afraid of sunstroke. He always shied away from the strong, bright light, requiring any white guests who came to see him to wear topis or hats and carry umbrellas as if, in the nature of things, the white man was an alien in the equatorial sun and in need of a blue umbrella. In sunlight, he knew – no matter how hard he tried – that he was not of the place, though, ironically, he had built his mission home on the ruins of N'Kombe's village, N'Kombe being the black Sun King.

How misleading the lightness and ease of his rooms suddenly felt, the almost courtly fall of white mosquito netting around his small bed, the light breeze . . . misleading because he had lived here "in a state of perpetual anxiety," enduring not only "the entire absence of discipline in our savages" but "their absolute inability to understand that anything can be valuable."

His struggle went on day after day, a monotonous "trial of patience and nerves as severe as anyone could imagine" because "many of them are, indeed, men who have become human animals, not merely savages, but creatures who . . . have sunk even below the level of savages. They do not even feel any gratitude for what we do for them . . . I daresay we should have fewer difficulties with our savages if we could occasionally sit round the fire with them and show ourselves to them as men . . . but there is no time for that."

It was not just a matter of time. He was a man full of distrust. All doors around him were locked, and he kept the keys. And his distrust went deeper than doors because there was a fundamental contradiction at the core of his being. He had come into the bush to minister to the blacks, and yet he kept white and black patients in separate wards and he never allowed blacks at his table, not even his black medical assistants. He said that the black "is a child, and with children nothing can be done without the use of authority" and, having become the Big Abdomen on the Ogowé, he explained that it was only "right for the black to suffer, recover, or die in his natural surroundings," and so he let the families of sick men crowd into the hospital wards with their animals, where they shared cooking pots and used open cess-trenches with the infected and got sick. And when a Benjabi man refused to stop sharing a cooking pot with a dysentery patient and said he would rather be with his brother and die than not see him, Schweitzer threw up his hands and said, "It is useless to preach carefulness to the patients . . . Homesickness is with them stronger than fear of death," but at the same time, out of reverence for life, it was he who forbade the killing of vermin, even an ant. Indeed, he sometimes set out a little sugar to feed the ants, out of that reverence for life.

I got up and went out and stood on the porch facing the clearing, struck by the contradictions in the man, the melancholy, the determination to seek the light while so afraid of the sun. The staff dining room and the storage house lay in front of me; in the road was a woman who had just squatted and given birth in the brush. Close by were the laundry and the temporary operating room. I realized that nowhere among these forty buildings had this Christian missionary built a chapel. The only crosses stood over the dead.

A woman driving a Jeep called out, wanting to know whether I'd like to see a gorilla. "Yes, we have a baby gorilla, very amusing; it laughs just like a human, like a man." I got in the Jeep and she drove to another house with chairs and a table outside under a thatched palm roof. A man, his wife, and a middle-aged nurse, a lean woman with grey eyes, were talking and playing with a small gorilla about three feet high. It bolted and bounded around me, clutched my leg, reached for my arm, took hold and tried to gnaw my fingers.

I held it high in the air by the hands and spun around as if dancing with a dwarf, and then he swung his legs around my waist, lips drawn back in a cheerless smile, and I held him under the armpits and began to tickle him and he began to giggle, a broken tenor laughter just like a playful man; then he wrenched free and leapt away, circling behind a chair, peering warily at me. They put him in his cage under the house stairs and then I went walking down toward the river with the nurse.

There was an energetic ease about her, a stillness in her eyes, and yet she was open, calling out to the black women and men, and they called back, laughing, throwing open their arms, pleased to see her. We stood for a while by a newly built pediatric ward with women in a row on benches, babies in their arms or between their feet. Slowly, a little shy about herself but surprisingly trusting, she began to tell me how two or three years before Schweitzer died she had come to the mission on a bicycle, penniless and tattered. Schweitzer, she said, had had a good sardonic sense of humour, and he had looked up and called out to her, "Dr. Livingstone, I presume."

"And to this day," she said, "I'm called Livingstone, except I prefer Living Stone, the secret in the stone . . ."

"But on a bike, where in the world did you come from?" I asked.

"A long way. Dakar."

"Dakar?"

"Yes. I bicycled down the coast, all the way. A thousand miles."

She had been a woman of about forty-five, she said, the daughter of an English naval commander who'd once told her, "Don't be afraid of danger; if you walk into it, it will dissolve." She had been twice married and had two grown children. She and her second husband had taken a vow to serve God, and she had had visions at the ages of nine and thirty-seven, the same vision, and in Matthew she had read, "He that loveth father or mother more than me is not worthy of me," and so she had left her family and gone to London, living on oranges and honey, not even drinking water. She stayed on this diet for three years: "For a very special reason. Through it I was able to lose the stigmata of womanhood, if you know what I mean by that. And I succeeded, so that my travels and service to God are easier to carry out."

She was a fairly tall woman of five foot seven, her flesh tight on the bone, and she had gone to Paris where she had worked among poor Vietnamese refugees, and when she got her call from God to go to the Ogowé, the refugees had bought her a bicycle and friends had bought her a boat ticket to Dakar, and she had gone from Dakar to Abidjan on the Ivory Coast.

She had had no money, her clothes were on her back, she had lived on food given to her by villagers and she had bicycled out of Abidjan and down rough roads through scrub, swamp, bush, jungle, and plains, unafraid of the tribes though some were cannibals. When she had come to Cameroon, the consul had tried to stop her because revolution had broken out in the countryside. But she had bicycled on. "I never could understand it, they were shooting everywhere into the forest from the roads and it was as if I wasn't there; they didn't even look at me." We were walking near the shore along a path close to the cement pier and the pirogues, and in the strong sunlight she was bemused.

"But put yourself in their place," I protested. "One of those soldiers scared to death in the middle of all that machine gunning and he looks up and over the hill you come, a white woman on a bicycle. I'd pretend you weren't there, too. Otherwise, I'd think I was crazy."

"Yes, yes, I suppose that might be true," she said, and hurried along the path that took a crescent shape through long grass under tall trees, separating us from the cluster of hospital wards, and she took my hand. "Do you want to come into the Village Lumière?" At the end of the path on one of the highest hills there were short rows of small one-room white houses and a little village square. "I named it, you know. Village of Light, and it is, it's full of light." She went ahead, all eagerness, filled with a guileless pleasure. She broke into a trot as a tall black man stepped out into the path to meet her. They clasped hands and embraced, and she kissed him on the cheek. She went on into the village, calling out, waving, and men and women began hobbling toward her as I followed behind. It was a village of lepers.

Two women were at the communal water tap filling buckets. Their ankles were bandaged. They heard the laughter and turned, and one woman's cheek was pinched by creeping leprosy of the eye, but when she saw the nurse standing sockless in her white sneakers, reaching out to kiss hobbled mothers, she threw her arms up and let out a low, moaning cry and hurried to her. They draped their arms around each other, beaming. There was more laughter.

The nurse went down the narrow alleys between the block houses, hunching up in the shadows in front of an old grey-headed man wrapped in a frayed brown blanket, and she touched his cheek with an intimacy that was entirely open. He crossed his stump arm over hers and rested his head against her hand. Her eyes were wide open and there seemed to be some fixed locus of effortless enthusiasm in her, a constant touching and cradling while she rewrapped loose bandages, squatting in the dark doorways, fondling watery-eyed children, and the shackling aloneness of leprosy was broken. As we walked slowly out of the village she said, "I am so lucky; they give me so much, they fill me with joy."

"But you give to them," I said, surprised that she should see it that way. "You open yourself up to them, you come to them . . ."

"Perhaps," she said, "but I'm the lucky one. I come away filled with the joy they give me. I called the village the Village of Light and, did you see, we cleared away all the trees, how filled with sunlight the hill is?"

She had hold of my forearm. "You see," she said, "it's a disease I love; it's alive. I hate tuberculosis. Dead, it's a dead thing, but this is alive; you can surround it with love, with your mind."

"Unless . . ."

"Unless nothing."

Up ahead in the long grass there was a little cemetery, a dark place under tall palm trees. There were very old Muslim stones carved in crescents and strange fetishes suspended on sticks. She stopped and stepped off the path into the cool place, saying, "I'm absolutely sure they'll discover the cure. It'll be in the mind; the disease comes from the mind, I'm sure, some unbearable stress. The Africans are so spiritually alive in a way we know nothing about, and the stress . . ."

The light in the graveyard was soft on her grey sandy hair. Her arms were straight and stiff, her fists closed in her smock pockets, and she was still smiling. Her even teeth seemed whiter. She seemed coiled with energy, caught up by an absorption in herself so intense, so filled with delight, that she seemed open, vulnerable, and able, paradoxically, to absorb all around her, to welcome life as if life, decaying or not, could only increase her delight. She seemed one of those rare creatures who are determined to detach themselves from their own shadows, free themselves from the fear of mortality. Though she had come all this way on her bicycle to be with Schweitzer, she was in search of an entirely different deliverance, a deliverance not deferred by distrust but made real through an openness, an embrace. "This is where I want to be buried," she said. "You're sewn into four palm leaves and the hole is very shallow; that's why those mounds are there, and in four days you're gone. The ants get right in and clean you out."

In a little while we were back among the long, narrow buildings painted white, ducking under washing with all the colours of life hung on lines between the shanty wards with their bunk beds, and there were communal cooking pits and the old Schweitzer bell still hung in its scaffolding. We went into two small rooms off the pharmacy, the old doctor's consultation quarters . . . open shelves of jars and bottles, a long checkered table with a flat pillow, a small blackboard, and a loosely hung curtain; and then, Schweitzer's operating room . . . plank cupboards, a simple A-frame stool, a steel operating table, and a big overhead light, like a dead moon, the only electrical light he had allowed on the grounds, and I said to the nurse, "You know what's surprising, no one here talks about him. It's almost like he's passed and been forgotten . . . pushed aside."

"He was a great man," she said.

"Yes, but what about him? How did you find him?"

"At the end – well, he wouldn't change. But he had a good sense of humour. He liked his little jokes. He always called me Livingstone, and sometimes when I was working with one of the natives he would say to me, 'Livingstone, don't pay any attention to that monkey.' He always called them monkeys. I didn't like it but he meant it in a friendly way."

"But wasn't he the only one who washed in clean water, purified? What did the others do?"

"Oh, well, I've never needed drugs," she said. "I've never taken any drugs, not even malaria pills, not to this day." We were walking in the narrow alleys of the wards again. "Anyway, we've no idea at all about him; all the books tell nothing," she said. "The mystery of him is lost, but I'm sure he was a great man."

In the doorway of one of the sheds a blind old man sat cross-legged. She let out a little cry and hugged the old man, then stepped back, and he felt for her in the air, his hands waving like flippers in water. She said, "He's one of Schweitzer's workers, the last one alive. He's blind now, blind." The old man, his head tilted, smiled. His dead eyes had the lustre of mercury. She held his hand in hers. He settled back into his dark corner.

Farther along the alley, where a man was weaving a sleeping mat from thin papyrus strips, there were wooden lattice bars on the doors of cells. Inside on the dirt floors and litters were solitary men who were the mental patients Schweitzer had written about almost helplessly, men and women bound hand and foot and dragged out of the bush by their families, suffering maniacal disturbances too deep and too dark for his drugs, and he had taken them and put them in these strong cells; otherwise they would have been thrown screaming into the river, or been poisoned, because they were dangerously demented.

It was stifling in the cells, closed off from the light and unbearable on the hottest humid days, and such confinement would certainly cripple an already cocked mind. The nurse moved slowly from cell to cell, peering in and talking quietly, and she unbolted one of the doors although the weaver warned her that the young man inside was violent.

He was about twenty-two and naked except for trousers sheared off at the thighs. There was a bowl of uneaten mealy-mealy beside him. He was very black and thick through the shoulders and he stared out into the light, a shrouded gleam in his eyes, the whites grey-brown. In the darkness, each dart of his eyes was a warning of an impending lunge out into the light, where he might throttle life, hug it to death.

The nurse lifted the bowl and said that he should eat something. He didn't move. He stared at her, kneading his knuckles. She moved within arms' reach and quietly said, "Yes, yes . . ." They stood that way, silent, staring, and he began to laugh a little, a playful clucking at the back of his throat, and then he turned away as if wary of the sound of his own laughter. She closed the door and the young man lay back down in his darkness.

"We don't understand the powers of the minds of these people," she said, walking slowly toward a clearing, "their purity and their power. I've been in the forest with them, you'll believe this if you've ever had a vision . . . I've seen an old man – they initiated me, you see, they have such a feeling for trees – he concentrated so hard for so long that the tree bent down toward him . . ."

I could see the river ahead and the pirogues drawn up on the shore as we went down the sloping path. She suddenly said, sternly, "You know my name but you mustn't use it. I'm no longer that person, not the person who had my name."

"What do you mean?"

"I no longer have a name."

"But then who are you?"

"I expect someday I'll move right out of my body, I am so filled with an energy, a joy all the time, I hear it like music inside me, like the sound of bubbling water. No, no, you must not imprison me with my old name."

We stood in the late afternoon light on the sandy shore close to the cement pier and the pirogues, a leper boatman waiting for me. Suddenly she said, "Would you like a mask? I'll give you a mask." She turned and loped back up the hill path, disappearing between the buildings.

I sat down to wait, brooding about this fierce joy of hers and the swell of happiness she had aroused in the leper village, and I thought how little Schweitzer had talked about joy. He had spoken of the attractiveness of life only in asides about the shadowed calm of his graveyard, or the *obbligato* rustle of palms at night, and of course he had found a joy in music, but it was a music that lifted him out of what he called the dark prose monotony of the primeval forest. That was how he described it, his prose labours, and I remembered reading the night before in the bug-ridden hotel room his only attempt at a metaphor. It was a hymn to hard work:

A day with these people moves on like a symphony. Lento: They take very grumpily the axes and the bush-knives that I distribute to them on landing. In snail-tempo the procession goes to the spot where bush and tree are to be cut down. At last everyone is in his place. With great caution the first blows are struck.

Moderato: Axes and bush-knives move in extremely moderate time, which the conductor tries in vain to quicken. The midday break puts an end to the tedious movement.

Adagio: With much trouble I have brought the people back to the work place in the stifling forest. Not a breath of wind is stirring. One hears from time to time the strokes of an axe.

Scherzo: A few jokes, to which in my despair I tune myself up, are successful. The mental atmosphere gets livelier, merry words fly here and there, and a few begin to sing. It is now getting a little cooler, too. A tiny gust of wind steals up from the river into the thick undergrowth.

Finale: All are jolly now. The wicked forest, on account of which they have to stand here instead of sitting comfortably in the hospital, shall have a bad time of it. Wild imprecations are hurled at it. Howling and yelling they attack it, axes and bush-knives vie with each other in battering it. But no bird must fly up, no squirrel show itself, no question must be asked, no command given. With the very slightest distraction the spell would be broken. Then the axes and knives would come to rest, everybody would begin talking about what had happened or what they had heard, and there would be no getting them again into train for work.

> Happily, no distraction comes. The music gets louder and faster. If this finale lasts even a good half-hour the day has not been wasted. And it continues till I shout "Amani! Amani!" (Enough! Enough!), and put an end to work for the day.

The nurse came back down the hill. She was carrying a big white-faced mask with long, loose straw hair and a straw beard. The eyes were lopsided holes gouged out of the wood and there was a pug nose and a pursed mouth. "It was here when Schweitzer was here and I'm the only one who was with him, so I can give it to you."

"The white face," I said.

"To ward off evil and to remember why I'm here."

"How shall I call you?"

"Living Stone. That's all. Make sure you sit still in the pirogue," she said. "The water is dangerous." She kissed me on both cheeks and lightly on the mouth, still a sensuously alive woman. The boatman helped me into the dugout, his leper hand streaked pink by the wound in his dark flesh. We pulled out into the river, clouds coming with the falling sun. There would be more night-rain. When I looked back she was not there, no one was on the high cement pier; gone, but I kept looking for her until I passed around the headland.

Weekend, 1979

COUNTRY STOMPS

Muscular young black men wearing calfskin aprons, angora goatskin leggings, and tin ankle rattles entered the field in a double line, an *ihele.* One of the leaders leapt into the air, twirled, dropped down, and started a soft stomp in half-time. Two rows of dancers stood with legs astride. Like long-legged birds. Then they stomped, too.

The stomps, the drum rhythms, were explicit, they were relentless. A charted stomping pattern with no rests was laid down as each song began and it was repeated again and again and again, with all variations by the "master drummer" imposed on the particular pattern.

The rhythm might be a pattern of (3+3+2), (3+2+3), (2+2+3+2+3), (3+2+3+2+2), etc. No two drums played in unison, no two drum rhythms coincided exactly with the rhythms of the singers, and any two men drumming the same pattern always staggered their entry, playing ♩ ♩ as:

And then they produced two different stomping rhythms, 2 against 3:

The relentless rhythmic patterns, this strenuous gaiety, had the feel of syncopation, even a jazz feel, a feel that was increased by polyphonic overlays, but there was absolutely no improvisation of any kind. There was no place for individual scat dancing. Each drummer, each dancer, was engaged in an act of strict synchronization, strict metronomic accuracy, strict conservative communal accommodation.

1979

A GLASS OF WATER FREELY GIVEN

So geographers in Afric-maps
With savage pictures fill their gaps;
And o'er uninhabitable downs
Place elephants for want of towns.

—Jonathan Swift

In the coastal city of Douala on the road to the local cemetery a black boy rattled a silver tambourine as he walked ahead of a small white man who was carrying a blue umbrella to shade himself from the sun. There was a hole in the umbrella and the man was staring at the sky through the hole.

The boy shook the tambourine. Pariah dogs scattered to the side of the road and disappeared through a fence. The boy then wore the tambourine like a crown. At the gate to the cemetery the man said, "Life is like milk. Milk with a drop of lemon."

He and the boy disappeared into the tall grass of the dead. The blue umbrella with the hole in it bobbed above the tall grass. Then it stood still above the grass. The grass wore the umbrella like a hat. Then the grass took off its hat. The umbrella, too, disappeared.

A map of the old empire lay under glass on the front desk of the hotel. Three green oranges sat on the map. They sat in the southeast corner of Cameroon. I pocketed one of the oranges.

I was going northeast to Yaoundé with my driver, Abdullah, who sprinkled the hood of his car with water, blessing the motor. As we drove along one of the old roads I kept thinking of David Livingstone, who had wandered through the jungle trying to find the five springs of the Nile, certain that they flowed like the five wounds of Christ, a sick man dependent on the slavers he loathed, wearing a seaman's cap, making his last trek through the bush in a pair of too-tight French patent leather shoes, deranged, sapped, deflated, and, worst of all, close to breaking faith with himself.

Outside Douala, a diesel engine shunted an empty flatcar onto the railway bridge over the greasy brown water of Sanaga River. On the shore, two naked men lathered each other with soap, rubbing the lather into their shoulder muscles. They were watched by a woman who wore a drum major's shako. She was standing in the doorway of their house holding their pail of water. Blue smoke leaked out from under the eaves of the corrugated roof of the house.

Behind the men, beyond the Sanaga, the road was pitted with holes, and then there was only a mud road corded and crimped by rainwater. There were big logging trucks on the road, enormous tree trunks chained together on flatbeds, the lime-yellow sap running out of the black hearts of the trunks. The immensity of the forest made the road through the jungle to Yaoundé seem like a scar half-healed in the wall of vegetation, a webbing of branches, leaves, boughs, vines, and towering trees. I could see only a wall of ennui, a tangled weight of green. There were gaps in the wall, paths and trails, but they only went deeper into what was endlessly the same, and even from a high place, a knoll by the side of the road, the immensity increased. There was no perspective. Nowhere was everywhere.

With a flutter of panic, I realized my whole sense of myself was rooted in perspective. We speak of a person's point of view, his angle on things, relationships that point to possibilities or conclusions; but in the jungle there are no possibilities because there is no perspective. There is exuberant growth or there is the machete and a cleared space. And everywhere there is sickness – sleeping sickness, dysentery, boils, whitlows, polio, empyema, blackwater fever, malaria, phagedenic foot ulcers, beriberi, leprosy, and pariah dogs circling, sniffing, mewling, and mounting their lean bitches.

A few days earlier I had been in a pirogue, a long dugout canoe, slowly crossing the Ogowé, a wide sepia river of sandbars and eddies, crocodiles and hippopotami and snakes swimming in the water. On one shore, at the end of a path up a gentle sloping hill, was a leper village: a squared space on the crest of the hill with houses and alleyways down the other slope, houses with one room, the doorways and stoops filled with squatting or stretched-out lepers, suddenly smiling, pulling themselves up.

I remember thinking, Along these rivers you end up touching something deep inside yourself. Leprosy has always filled men with fear; the slow corruption of the body, not secretive and sudden like cancer, but a continuous public prefiguration of death itself; a dry yet glistening white and yellow wound attacking all the softest parts, the fingers, the toes, the disgusting disfigurement as the fingers come off, a hand, a foot; and still the living man or woman hobbles out into the sun, alive with disease, outcast. Always the leper has been outcast, cut adrift with his living rot, cordoned off, as if he reminded others too terribly of the wound that no one ever wants to touch: the possibility of a death so solitary that even the gods might shun you.

In that leper village, a man draped in a worn grey shawl had come toward me. His hooded eyes were wide open and his hand was out, the hand one man extends to another, the thumb, forefinger, and little finger gone, the creamy white scar in the black flesh where his thumb had been, a stub hand, almost a club, and there in the still, hot silence of the afternoon there was no choice. He was inviting me to acknowledge, to share in, his manhood. To refuse was to recognize only his rot, his corruption, his death; better to cut and run than withdraw from the proffered hand. And yet, as his two hard fingers went into the palm of my hand, I felt a shudder of recognition. There was a bond, with him, with myself; I had not turned away from him or my own fear and loathing. But also there was welling up in me an inevitability as pressing as those two fingers: the leper's kiss, death, deeply felt. I wanted to weep for myself, for him; but he was smiling, his eyes filled with laughter, some enormous satisfaction that seemed so simple, so open; an embrace of life.

And later that night, listening to the wild calling and screeching in the jungle, from birds and creatures that could find the coolness to sing and fill the air with noise only in the night, I had been filled with dread and wonder as I read what Paul-Émile, Cardinal Léger of Québec had once said: "I met a thousand lepers, and from the abyss of their misery they gave me a terrible lesson: our gifts can succor them, but we would be fortunate if they allowed us one morsel of their serenity, their joy. You must live with the leper to understand suffering. God is present in his fevered face."

Now and then on the road to Yaoundé we had to slow to a crawl to cross small bridges that were only loose planks laid side by side. At one bridge, a butcher working over a stone slab table set up on oil drums was wringing the necks of chickens, chopping off their feet, tossing them into a bucket. A radio blared martial music. After we had got up the grade, I looked back to make sure that the butcher was not an apparition, but the road had disappeared around a bend, the road that had become my inroad to the life of a man, Cardinal Léger, who in 1968 had dramatically put aside his red robes, a man who'd been brought up in a modest two-storey brick home and a general store in St. Anicet, a small village not far from Valleyfield, Québec.

He had been an altar boy, and his maternal grandmother, a religious, even mystical woman, had urged him to imitate the local priests, and saying Mass had become his favorite game. At the age of twelve he had gone into the Seminary of Saint Thérèse, but in his second year he had fallen sick. He had tried working as a mechanic, an electrician, a butcher, but one Christmas morning in 1923, after receiving Communion during midnight Mass and while meditating alone in the choir loft, he had heard a voice: "You will become a priest." It was, he says, the decisive call in his life: "I've never been sick since." Meditating myself on the sickness I had already seen, driving farther into the foothills of the jungle mountains with the afternoon sky a lemon yellow over the tree line, I knew he was now a man in his mid-seventies, tired and worn down; and perhaps old age was now his sickness, life leaking out of his bones.

The city of Yaoundé, spread over gullies and the slopes of hills, was a pastoral mountain town, the plastered one-storey shanties all tinted by red dust, so that it seemed a locale of ochre and sienna and russet light, a gentle place.

In the narrow, twisting streets, there were tiny shops and shacks, and people dressed in slacks and sneakers, rubber sandals and galabiyas. The women, tall and burnt sienna like the earth, were beautiful, their hair hanging in beaded curtains of braids around their heads, or gathered into rococo crowns. The streets were friendly with hand-clapping, hand-clasping men and women who moved slowly, exchanging four ritual kisses in storefront beer parlours and pinball joints. There was an albino wearing Elton John glasses, a big man with the limp little legs of a six-year-old who went by in a box on wheels, and in the market stalls, a man with his head shaved except for a pillar-like tuft of top hair who sat primly behind a sewing machine surrounded by high-stacked crates of empty beer and water bottles. Blood from butcher stalls seeped along the shallow gutters toward a row of women sitting on their haunches under black umbrellas, one smoking a pipe the size of her thumb.

On the concrete steps of the hospital a fleshy man was sprawled, his head bobbing, his eyes staring, mouth open, soundless, a dark zero. His thick hands fumbled with a robe that hardly covered his thighs, and just below his knees his skin was encrusted, greyish, wrinkled like animal hide, and the calves were swollen down into enormous ankle joints; there were no ankles, only huge pink-bottomed hooves, the toes like bulbs, the toenails black, a big man weighted down by his bigger elephant feet.

As dusk fell, a huge electric cross came on, pinholes of light in the dark green hillside. It was suddenly overcast, a pearl-grey sky with slashes of translucent white. Dogs tucked their tails and took cover. Black unravelling thunderheads moved through the valleys, decapitating the hills and obliterating the cross of big light bulbs, and in their wake came a solid sheet of pewter cloud cover and a downpour so heavy the city began to disappear in mist and rain; and then it was gone, as if it had never been there.

In the morning, on the way out of Yaoundé to N'Simalen, the mission where Léger lives, we again passed the concrete steps of the hospital. The man with the elephant hooves was still there, sprawled, his head half lifted, his mouth still open, the zero of silence, and as we got out into the bush again, passing women who were bent over and scoop-hoeing tubers out of the ground in front of their huts, I asked Abdullah, an ebony-black Muslim from a desert village near Lake Chad, what he thought, if anything, about the cardinal, and with a shrug, shifting gears, he said, "He is a god."

We turned off the road near a way station, a stopping place for trucks and buses, and there was a sign staked by the side of the road that said CAFÉ, but there was no café. There was a winding dirt track through high brush and then a cleared space, a low white building with a long porch walkway, and, on a slight rise, a big church built of bricks.

He was standing in the doorway of his small office, the doorway an oblong of darkness, the outside walls plastered white. He was wearing a freshly washed white but worn soutane, frayed at the throat, too short at the ankles. He seemed shy and yet there was something studied about his reserve, his long, deliberate silences as I stood before him. He held the bridge of his nose between his thumb and forefinger and he kept his eyes closed as he said, "Yes, I must talk with you. I don't want to but I must. You have come a long way. Charity is the first virtue." He looked tired and drawn, with a bristle of white whiskers on his cheeks. His eyes seemed settled back in their hollows, almost hidden when closed under the shag of grey eyebrows.

He entered his office, whose windows are covered with rococo wrought-iron burglar bars painted white, and as he sat down in his corner chair, with his eyes closed, he said, "You are in front of an old priest, and that is all I am now, an old priest, and I think, at this time in my life, what is most important is to think about my fidelity. Fidelity," he said, unlinking his hands and then locking the fingers again, "is for me the essence of virtue, keeping my eyes on what God asked of me." He sat back in the chair, back in the shadows. I could not see his eyes.

"There comes the time when you have to compare what you decided to do with what you actually did. These are my reflections at the end of my life, because I have to realize that this is the end of my life; my health is not good." His eyes were still closed. His hands rested in his lap, like two people together a long time. He sat silently, as if alone, and yet all too aware of my being there, a presence that caused him a certain weariness. There in the sparseness of his small office – a desk at which he writes his letters, two chairs, and a bookshelf – his every gesture reflected his sense of being watched and watching himself, the exercise compounding the tiredness he already felt. He turned back his cuff and checked his watch, a man who had shed most of the rituals of self-importance; and yet one of his workers had told me he needed careful handling: he needed calm, a lack of outside impositions, a time for prayer, and time for talk with himself. "And what I feel," he said, "is that in my seventy-five years I never failed in my fidelity. What I am, the gifts given to me by the Lord, were always at the disposition of the Lord, and so if I become sick, I will accept my sickness, and it will be the end."

Earlier in the morning I had been at the mission dispensary, a grey board-and-batten building under spreading trees with waiting women seated on the box-like veranda. A white nursing sister, eyes alive with girlish laughter, hurried into the maternity ward, a room of six or seven camp cots. Young mothers were nursing in the occluded light. In the far corner, where a mother was buried under heavy blankets because it was a damp day, the sister reached into the conical tent of white netting and lifted out a tiny child, the head smaller than her hand, and she held it aloft and said, "See, only fifteen minutes old – look, life – isn't it wonderful?"

And now the cardinal, at his desk, moving his thumbs back and forth like wigwags, his eyes still closed, began to talk about his vocation, and how his life had been a succession of miracles: a sickly boy, he had entered the Grand Seminary in 1925, making his novitiate with the Sulpicians at Issy-les-Moulineaux outside Paris, and then he had been chosen to establish a mission at Fukuoka in Japan. "That was," he says, "a shock, a military regime, and it was not so easy for me," working there through the pre-war years; then he was sent back as pastor to his native parish in Québec, where he worked for seven years through the war.

"After that, another miracle," he said, opening his eyes but still not looking at me, staring at a point of meditation inside his own memories.

"At the end of the war I was sent to Rome, and Italy was really the Third World; it was practically impossible for us to find the necessary food to live. I discovered what misery is. In Canada we don't know what it is. Even in Japan I hadn't seen such misery. So I began to help the Pope, who was at that time Pius XII, especially in finding food and drugs, and the Pope was very grateful, and he loved me. That's the word I can use. He was a timid man and shy, but I tried in every way to help him and I was open with him, and I think that's why he loved me so much. It's a great memory in my life, that I was loved by a pope who was a saint." He opened his hands and took hold of his knees. "I can say our relations were not only friendly, but like a father with his son. I was his very beloved son."

He closed his eyes again and eased back into the shadows. He said that "in a certain way" it was this relationship with Pius that explained why, in 1950, he had been made the Archbishop of Montréal, "where I was a stranger, and the situation wasn't good, it was another kind of Third World . . ." It seemed, listening to this old priest, that he had begun in sickness and he had sought or was destined to seek sickness and the suppurating wound all over the world. "At no time was Christ more human than when nailed to the cross with the five wounds bleeding, the stigmata, the marks of his passion."

The pursuit of wounds, the pursuit of pain, if only as a prayerful witness, is a way a man can prove he is alive, because pain is a living presence; it inhabits the nerve ends, the spirit, it makes a man cry out passionately or so saps him of his fibre that his cry becomes a silent, dark zero. But the paradox, the possibility that the priest carries inside himself in his imitation of Christ, is the transcendence of this pain, not only through the alleviation of poverty, but through love, charity, a conviction that joy can live in the midst of pain, the conviction that, as Léger the priest put it, "The glass of water freely given is still the most convincing proof for the existence of God, who is present in the fevered face of the poor man."

"But back then in Montréal," he said, "I was a stranger, and the question was, How could I reach my people, be a presence in their lives; so an old bishop told me I must speak on the radio. That's how I began to recite the rosary every night at seven o'clock. To be always present every night at seven o'clock for seventeen years means you believe what you're thinking. That is what I said to you about fidelity."

The picture of the cardinal telling his beads, telling his way around the prayer circle of the five decades, the five wounds, for seventeen dogged years, made me recall an overcast afternoon when I stood on the edge of the gigantic open mine pit at Asbestos, a town on the south shore of Québec; the deep walls of the pit were a silverfish color, the color of insinuating illness; it was the mine where – at the end of the forties – a revolt among the workers of Québec, underpaid and ill fed, had begun, men with no worker's protection, men with asbestos in their lungs, their blood. The town had been built on the rim of the asbestos wound; it was as if the mine were alive, an ever-widening leprosy; gouging and stripping machines had cut down and cut back layers of the earth, gnawing at the town's rim, the streets, the frame homes and small hotels, the chapels and altars and baptismal fonts – they all went down under the sledgehammer so that the mine could spread outward, eating away at the innards of the life it had fostered, killing the miners it had kept alive; this was a suppurating social and spiritual wound that the cardinal was appointed to heal; he had tried to cleanse the wound by saying the rosary.

We sat in N'Simalen in his office, lost in silence; not a sound, not a cicada, not a bird, no wind; only a stillness and his voice, the husky, considered words of a not inconsiderable or inconsiderate man, a man who had played his devotional – if not a socially active and approving – part in the resurgence of a city, Montréal, and in the resurgence of his people, their collective and private selves. In 1963, as if he found the progressive theology and the social radicalism of the Quiet Revolution – the removal of religious instruction from school curriculums, the ridicule of sterile religious vocations in Montréal and Québec City – too unsettling, he'd grown restless and he travelled thousands of miles in and out of nineteen countries – through villages of the orphaned, the sick and hungry, the lepers. He saw misery as he had never found it before, and he believed that he had found a religious fervour among the maimed: the presence of a joy in the midst of pain.

"Then," he said, "there was the synod of the bishops in 1967 and that's where the shock came, with bishops coming from

Africa and Asia, countries where there is misery, and I myself in Montréal, a rich city; so I said to myself, in my conscience, 'You are speaking of the miseries of the Third World but you don't know anything about it. You are speaking to people who don't understand what changing the world means, because that is the great scandal . . .'"

For the first time he looked at me with his dark eyes, not accusingly, but as if a sin of omission, of unawareness, was something he could share. "It will be the great scandal of the history of our century," he said, "that six hundred million people are eating well and living luxuriously and that three billion starve, and every year millions of children are dying of hunger, and so I said then, 'I am too old to change that. The only thing I can do which makes sense is to be present.' That's all I could do, not speak, not write, not say to other people that they should do what I do, but simply be in the midst of them."

It was hard to know what "in the midst" meant to him, or means at all; perhaps, in my own case, I am and was a curious kind of carrier of diseases, neither a witness for the prosecution, nor for the defense, but a man of disinterested yet intense curiosity – someone who had gone the previous day, for example, to be "in the midst" so that I could say what I had seen of a small village near the mission, a cleared space of plastered blockhouses facing each other and a sheltered wall with long benches against it, the doors and windows closed, and there had been no sound. And then, as if a silent signal had been given, the doors opened and staves and poles like antennae reached out into the light. Stumps of arms, feet in cloth bags, old men and nursing mother lepers, heads down, poling themselves forward as if the air were water, saying nothing. It struck me: almost every day that I had been in the bush there had been these apparitional moments – the blue umbrella, the man with the elephant hooves, the drum majorette by the river, the smile of the leper clasping my hand – and now it was as if the dead had risen, except that they all sat down on benches against a wall, a seated lineup, some crossing their withered legs, pulling pieces of coloured cloth across their throats, putting a forearm stump under a chin, posing, wanting to be seen, a head tilted with haughtiness, vitality. In their midst, my presence had been all that was demanded: someone to excite and elicit an assertion of themselves.

The plight of these lepers, I said to the cardinal as I told him what I had seen, seemed appalling. He fluttered his fingers. "No, no, the lepers are not the worst; they have their families, they can do a little work. It is the handicapped children who are vulnerable; they are in an awful situation." Though he had lived briefly at the Nyansong leprosarium, the cardinal told me that the government authorities, as soon as he had come, had asked him to invest his energies elsewhere; *actum ne agas* – do not do what is already done, because, in fact, he had come to Cameroon too late to be of decisive use to the lepers . . . another priest, unknown outside the jungle, had done the essential organizing, and even though – to the outside world and for fundraising purposes – the cardinal had become Léger Among the Lepers, he was, as soon as he had arrived, a man adrift, a presence without a place (much as he had felt himself to be in Montréal) . . . but who, it must be said, soon applied himself elsewhere, applied himself to the accomplishment that is now closest to his heart – an accomplishment that is far more significant than any work he might have done among the lepers – fourteen functional buildings on a shantytown hill on the outskirts of Yaoundé, his Centre for the Rehabilitation of the Handicapped. Children are brought into occupational and physiotherapy rooms and prosthetic workshops; they are in wheelchairs or on small rolling beds, or they crank and hobble on mechanical legs or crutches in and out of classrooms, children polio-struck or born with a withered arm or no colon, reptile children dragging themselves through the dust.

I remember going by pirogue far back into one of the villages in the forest, family clearings linked by sunless trails through the dense overgrowth. I saw a boy of about seventeen, a sculpted head, skin taunt on the bone, and a muscled torso down to his hips. He sat on the ground with flopping thin legs like hoses under him, and as his family led me along a trail to another clearing deeper in the darkness to drink palm wine from the communal cup, I looked back, and in the gloom of filtered afternoon light, half-heaving, half-swinging on his hands down the trail, a wild gaiety in his eyes, laughing, like a deranged crippled spider, the boy came along after us, legs flailing over roots, through long grass, beaming, a kind of crazed serenity in his eyes.

"Yes, yes, this serenity," the cardinal said, waving his hand at the door. "Oh, we have a dispensary and there is an old woman there, a widow. She entered two or three weeks ago to die. She is still living, the old lady. For an African," and now for the first time he began to talk eagerly, "life is, I should say, the only reality. They don't believe in death. Death's not natural for them. That's why they can accept so much pain, to live. There is in them a biological joy that we don't have. Death is a great tragedy for them because life is the reality. But through faith you can help them keep the dead more present, and they are present. You see, they bury their people in mounds near the house. There is no cemetery here in the bush. They are living with their dead; it is a spirituality, still talking with their dead."

"But will their spirituality survive, survive us, our material ideals?"

"Well, that's the question."

"Wouldn't it be a tragedy if, in trying to help people so destitute, we robbed them of their sense of life, their capacity for joy in the midst of pain?"

"That's why," he said, settling back into the shadows again, "I pray. I have more time to pray and I understand more and more because being weaker and weaker I understand that if there is not the mightiness of God, we cannot do much. I can help: I built a large handicapped centre, and now I take a little sugar to my novices, and I can pray for myself and others, and that's the great joy of my life. So just tell people you met an old priest. I am a priest who is happy to be old and still a priest. You met a man who could have been the archbishop of a large diocese for ten more years, but I think my presence here is more eloquent, and I think the only light is the light given to us by God. That's faith. I find that that faith is my fidelity . . ."

In the night the old widow in the dispensary died. By morning she was laid out, wrapped in white except for her face and her hands, with a rosary strung through her black bony fingers. She was laid in a pine box in the centre of the church, and women, their bodies wrapped in all the colourful patterns of life, sat around her, silent for a moment, and then they took up the soft chanting of the litany for the dead, the call and answer. And there was a bird in the house, swooping low and then up into the loft, and in the distance I could hear the laughter of children playing on the far field near the mission classrooms.

As I walked up from the church, feeling the rising heat, one of the young doctors who had been working all morning in the nursery with a newborn child invited me into the staff dining room to have lunch. "Great," I said, "my driver won't be here for nearly two hours. My driver thinks the old priest is a god." Ahead I saw the old priest in his white soutane, standing in that oblong of dark, the doorway of his office, looking disconsolate, as if he had been impinged upon. He was carrying a furled umbrella under his arm. The doctor asked me to wait by the stairs – he wanted to warn the cook to set an extra place – and he went into the refectory, joined by the old priest. I waited, and waited for what seemed a long time. There were several dogs sitting at the edge of the bush. They looked as if they were waiting, too. Then the doctor came out to the stairs, grim, his neck flushed.

"He says you cannot come to lunch."

"I can't?"

"He wants to be alone."

"Alone?"

"Yes."

He handed me a plastic bottle of water.

"I am sorry. There is nothing I can do. He's like that. You cannot come in."

"The glass of water freely given . . ."

He was about to ask me what I meant but then he shrugged. He was late.

The sun was high. It was very hot. It was getting hotter. I sat down on the stairs to wait, the bottle of water between my feet. A pariah dog, seeming to cower close to the ground, came up to my knee and stared at me and then skittered on his way when he saw that I had no food. In an hour, with lunch over, the old priest came out of the refectory, still carrying his furled umbrella. He tucked the umbrella under his arm, regarded me for a moment, said nothing, and disappeared into his room to sleep.

Weekend, 1979

SHEARING

He had been awake all night, unable to sleep, and when he told her that a man has to have sleep, she told him about sheep, white and black sheep on either side of the border. She told him how black sheep crossed to be with white sheep and turned white and how white sheep crossed to be with black sheep and turned black. But one day God took away the border, pulling it like a rope through the long grass and all the sheep turned grey as they chased the rope to the end of the world and disappeared into nowhere and that is how God, who has to keep an open eye on things if He is going to be God, stays awake, by counting sheep.

God is still counting sheep because the sheep keep coming.

Hogg, 2001

DAVID ANNESLEY

David Annesley was tall, bony and sandy-haired. He had a long face, wide-open yearning eyes, and slightly crooked teeth that gave a crooked gaiety to his shy laughter. It was the shy laughter of a man watching carefully, a country man's wariness. He was from the country, the town of Strabane in County Tyrone, the second son of Ulster protestants. His father had hired Catholics as scrub labour and he had been hard on them, but David was not hard, and had no prejudice, no religion. He'd left his home, footloose, and he'd had his fancy, but he was by no means free. He'd always wanted to draw but the Belfast College of Art had turned him away. In 1963, he came to Canada and worked as postman, delivery boy and draftsman. He was a desultory worker, hating the nine-to-five life. He began drawing heads, hoping to get published somewhere and get out of the grind.

He walked into my office at the old Toronto *Telegram*. It was February of 1968. I was the Literary Editor, writing a long book review or a personal piece every Saturday. There were other reviews by other writers. The book section had its own character and needed distinctive drawings. David said he'd sold one drawing for eight dollars but it had never been published. He had a small portfolio. The drawings were a mish-mash of cartoon heads, but there was something I liked about his line, and about him, a sheepish lackadaisical laughter that belied his eagerness. Within a few weeks, he was on regular salary.

He soon found his style, his own line, an elegant cleanness sometimes fractured and frenetic. He fascinated me. Week after week, he drew the heads of writers and politicians and yet seemed to have little or no interest in their ideas. There was only once that he asked about a writer's moral world. It was François Mauriac, and he was working from a grainy, dull photograph. I told him Mauriac made me think of a driven stake in the heart. "I know about that," he said, and drew Mauriac with a head hewn down to a point, but such talk was uncommon. By and large, he kept a distance between himself and the play of ideas. He almost never drew from life and seldom saw his subjects. If faces, as he drew them, had a character, it was because he tried to find the essential structure of the bones. He was interested in line. He had no moral and satirical axe to grind, no political point to make. He thought cross-hatching was clutter. One day, when I showed him a book of drawings by Matisse, he said full of excitement, "They're like water." It was a way of saying something about himself: he wanted to look at a face with as little clutter between his eye and the object as possible, and for him, emotion was clutter, muddled waters. With few exceptions, emotional involvement in his drawings led to confusion and cartoons.

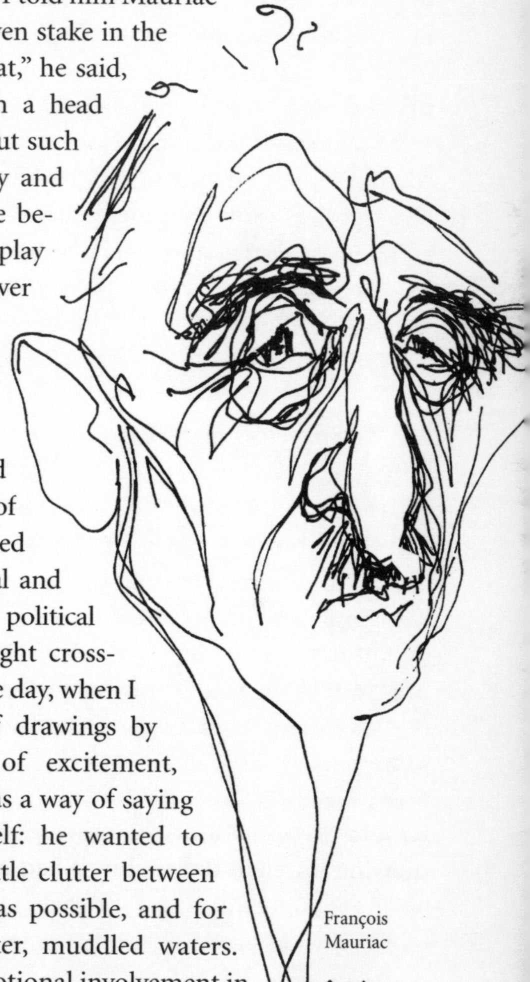

François Mauriac

I thought this was why, until the years close to his death, he could not draw women. He could draw ugly and older women like George Eliot or Golda

Meir, but the rest he rendered as blank-faced starlets, cartoons devoid of personality and presence. We talked only a little about women, and he was a great womanizer, but he seemed burdened by a fear and sometimes a contempt for them. All this was blurred by a boyish awkwardness. When we talked, it was usually in my office at the newspaper, which was in the library, an office partitioned off by shoulder-high, pebble-glass walls. I kept cognac in a drawer, and there was always rowdy music from a portable record-player: Otis Spann, Junior Wells and Muddy Waters. Very few reporters came into the library. There was a glossy photograph of a naked, big-bosomed girl taped to the glass wall over the typewriter. We were talking about the face of James T. Farrell.

"You know her?" he said suddenly, eagerly.

"Yes," I said.

"Her nipples are too big, they're no good." He blushed, "But I love big breasts."

He was a loner who found women difficult and was difficult with women. It was not until he was divorced after an early and almost immediately unhappy marriage that he began to work well with colour, and his drawings of women's faces – like that of Joyce Carol Oates – took on an energy and life. But his drawings of the naked body remained trite.

The confusion between us was more understandable, easier to explain. It came out of our working nights together. There was a big white-topped table on the other side of my pebble-glass wall. Sitting at the typewriter, drifting through my own stalled thoughts, I could see his shadow hunched like a big-boned bird, and sometimes he would get up and circle and shuffle, upset and fed-up because he couldn't capture a likeness, and one night, the first time he tried to draw Philip Roth, he cursed and handed me his drawing. It was three in the morning.

"It won't do," I said.

"I can't do any better."

"You must."

"I won't."
"You must."
"I will, and fuck you."
"You're right."
"About what?"
"Do it again."
"No."
"You must."

A certain closeness grew between us, and every year he tried a drawing of me, wanting to give me a gift. But the drawings never looked like me. His line was full of uncertainty, and at last, blushing, he tore them up and said, "I can't draw anyone like you knowing you like I do."

On one occasion, however, his angry confusion gave him a very good drawing. It followed a mid-afternoon lunch I'd had with the visiting Irish poet, John Montague, who'd been brought up as a Catholic in Ulster. We were in the office having a drink and listening to music. The door opened. David, with his crooked boyish smile, stepped in. Montague cocked his head and cried playfully, "I smell a Prot." David turned red, stammered, and then stood silently and furiously staring at the floor. Montague, a

John Montague

man of mischievous wit, needled and stitched his countryman. There was no animosity on Montague's part; only the prickliness of the place they came from. David fumed, and later we all went to supper. He was not up to the verbal play, and afterwards, he stormed and stomped.

"I won't draw him. I can't," he insisted.

"You must."

"I won't."

But he did, and brought in the drawing, flushed with satisfaction. He'd given Montague a pursed mouth, a chicken neck and empty eyes. It was unkind and cruel, and yet the twisted lines told a truth.

His talent, his ability to take hold of a face's truth, got him into trouble among men who were not so good humoured as Montague. He'd done, for example, a wonderful whimsical Marshall McLuhan, a face appropriate to puns and metaphysical probes. To David's delight and surprise, he got a call from McLuhan, asking him to come around to the Centre and David, always pressed for money, hoped for a sale. But for some reason he did not take the drawing along, and when McLuhan asked for it, he said, No . . . he had not brought it. McLuhan told him he was lucky, that he hated it, and he'd hoped to tear it up in his face. David was shown out of the famous office with the Cambridge oar on the wall, chastened and bewildered. He was still short of money that week because he existed on what he was paid at the *Telegram.* That was only fifty dollars, which the senior editors regularly tried to cut back to thirty-five, and when, in my last year with the paper, I gave him seventy-five, a senior editor said to me, somewhat prophetically, "Here's your hat, what's your hurry." Too often, David had to depend on such men.

It was partly this problem of money, but I think it was more David's nature that he settled where he did, in an abandoned brick school house outside the country town of Beaverton. He was, after all, a country man who liked to work with his hands, and he was expert at castrating pigs. He did a lot of carpentry, digging and haying, and he began to try sculpture. There was a lovely river a short walk from the house. He felt calmed beside

Marshall McLuhan

the river and, for a man so tied to the whims of editors, it was strange that he had no telephone. In the winter, with drifting snow closing the roads, he was often shut in and untroubled by it. Obviously, he was self-sufficient and took satisfaction at being alone with himself so many days on end.

But there were times, such as the night I wrote about Auden or the night John Steinbeck died, when someone had to be phoned who drove around to him in the dark and then he drove down to the early morning city.

These were our closest working moments, separated by the pebble-glass wall, shadows of each other as we tried to get hold of the right line, the right word. He showed me his drawing, I read my piece aloud, and then took them down to the composing room.

He was suspicious of that room because some of the men and women were quite peculiar, one woman sometimes so drunk she wore her dress backwards and there was a man who refused to set deadline type unless he was fed free Chinese food. But more unsettling was the fact that someone was stealing his originals. It was a constant problem for him, not only at the *Telegram*, but later when he sold some drawings to the *Globe and Mail*. He told me they had treated him shabbily and lost several originals and when he tried to charge them, they told him to get lost. He did not work for the *Globe and Mail* again.

He did well enough, however, locally and internationally, appearing in many magazines, among them the *New York Times*, the *Atlantic*, the *National Review, The New Yorker*, and *Saturday Night*. He was more and more excited by working with color, and sometime before he died, he made a leap in self-esteem. He stopped signing his drawings. He was at last convinced that his line in itself was his signature. He was in his stride, ready to make new discoveries, but he died young, drowning in the Gulf of Mexico at the age of thirty-three. He was buried on a cold rainy day in February of 1977 in a country graveyard.

David Annesley
self portrait

The Annesley Drawings, 1980

W.H. AUDEN: WHERE THE DECENT OUTNUMBER THE SWINE

He was much taller than I had expected, heavier, and long-armed, and there were pouches under his eyes and intricate web-lines on his brow. His voice was low, a singsong, broken in rhythms set to some inner machine, clicking away, and between poems he appealed to his wristwatch, nearsighted, his lips moving, as if counting down the seconds allowed for breathing space.

At a verbal gaffe he hurled back his arms and head in laughter, except there was no sound from him – only the wide gape of his mouth, as in one of Goya's screaming women, except there was no sound and he was laughing, slapping his thighs with his long arms.

He read one of his poems about his house outside Vienna, a house once owned by a great Austrian poet who committed suicide. His tone was one of sadness, methodical, a nostalgia for dogs and gardens and banisters and chairs and a light that once was and friends lost and friends alive in memory, kept alive in his curious knocking rhythms that clicked off the years, the rooms, in time clocked,

> *Time that is intolerant*
> *Of the brave and innocent*

And indifferent in a week
To a beautiful physique . . .

Still, there was a certain gaiety about him, his love of puzzles and word tricks and an urbanity of wit that would please a Pope, whether he was in a London coffeehouse or the Vatican. A good deal of this, of course, was merely cute, made up of little drawing-room jokes:

Joseph Hayden
  Never read Dryden;
John Dryden
  Never heard Hayden.

It was the sadness, not the leap of the imagination into the unknown, but the sadness surrounding the bric-a-brac of life, the tables, the chairs, the friends he once had, flattened to the scale, whether sordid or elegant, of the room and then another room that touched me about Auden, and then the playing out of precise emotions in those rooms where his men and women never seemed larger than they were but only alone, alone:

> Alone we choose, alone we are responsible. So many people try to forget their aloneness, and break their hearts and heads against it . . .

And then they die, to be remembered by Auden in one of his slanted versions of an elegiac distich:

I wish you hadn't
caught that cold, but the dead we
miss are easier
to talk to . . . anyway,
when playing cards or drinking
or pulling faces are out of the

question, what else is there
to do but talk to the voices
of conscience they have become?

Still there was also a certain sharpness in him, a sharp distilling of words into the stiletto of aphorism:

A dead man
Who never caused others to die
Seldom rates a statue.

In semi-literate countries
Demagogues pay
Court to teen-agers.

A coldness, and something astringent about these aphorisms, the grand sweep of men's emotions and motives diminished to a sharp saying, to a deft touch of scorn, and surely this came out of a distrustful view of the world, this wanting to reduce men to a witty phrase. But then, this was not altogether true of Auden. Among the great maxim-makers –

Those to whom evil is done
Do evil in return

– he was also a man touched in his severity by pity:

When we do evil,
We and our victims
Are equally bewildered.

It seemed, for Auden, to be a question – in rhythmically rhymed quatrains – of perspective. An evil world of evil men: men bewildered in a bewildering world: pitiable, and perhaps not beyond redemption:

O look, look in the mirror,
O look in your distress;
Life remains a blessing
Although you cannot bless.

There is a dreadful, touching sense of apartness in those lines. Whatever is going on is going on no matter the distress of the face in the mirror, no matter the goodwill, no matter the hatred. (Auden said: "By all means let a poet, if he wants to, write *engagé* poems, protesting against this or that political evil or social injustice. But let him remember this: The only person who will benefit from them is himself; they will enhance his literary reputation among those who feel as he does. The evil or injustice, however, will remain exactly what it would have been if he had kept his mouth shut.")

Evil or injustice or indifference, or even that cold, impersonal blessing, these have no ending; but love and the reaching for the sun, these have an ending, the human cry soon forgotten:

. . . Icarus for instance: how everything turns away
Quite leisurely from the disaster; the ploughman may
Have heard the splash, the forsaken cry,
But for him it was not an important failure; the sun shone
As it had to on the white legs disappearing into the green
Water, and the expensive delicate ship that must have seen
Something amazing, a boy falling out of the sky,
Had somewhere to get to and sailed calmly on.

But then, this cruel sense of calm indifference was not the whole of Auden (he said: "We are not commanded [or forbidden] to love our mates, our children, our friends, our country, because such affections come naturally to us and are good in themselves, although we may corrupt them. We are commanded to love our neighbour because our 'natural' attitude toward the 'other' is one of either indifference or hostility").

O stand, stand at the window
As the tears scald and start;
You shall love your crooked neighbour
With all your crooked heart.

It was a command, not from an evangelical preacher, but from, perhaps, a worldly cardinal poised in his high-back chair who understood the order of such things – that Man is fallen and fallen low into bestiality, lying down with and even in love with his pigs, but at the edge of gloom, he did not slip. He knew – if he did not deeply feel – that God had become Man and had died for Man, and Auden observed this redemptive truth from his own ironic perspective, of course. He said:

> Just as we were all, potentially, in Adam when he fell, so we were all, potentially, in Jerusalem on that first Good Friday . . . It seems to me worthwhile asking ourselves who we should have been and what we should have been doing. None of us, I'm certain, will imagine himself as one of the disciples, cowering in an agony of spiritual despair and physical terror. Very few of us are big wheels enough to see ourselves as Pilate, or good churchmen enough to see ourselves as a member of the Sanhedrin. In my most optimistic mood I see myself as a Hellenized Jew from Alexandria visiting an intellectual friend. We are walking along, engaged in philosophical argument. Our path takes us past the base of Golgotha. Looking up, we see an all too familiar sight – three crosses surrounded by a jeering crowd. Frowning with prim distaste, I say, "It's disgusting the way the mob enjoys such things. Why can't the authorities execute criminals humanely and in private by giving them hemlock to drink, as they did with Socrates?" Then, averting my eyes from the disagreeable spectacle, I resume our fascinating discussion about the nature of the True, the Good, and the Beautiful.

The irony, the unrelenting irony, leavened only by pity, by a certain urbane wit, by a willed love out of the crookedness of the heart. Christ, Icarus, they cry, they fall, and men are either eating or opening a window or just walking dully along, running their course, and as everything runs its course, so may everything be distilled to the stiletto of aphorism:

The decent, probably,
Outnumber the swine,
But few can inherit
The genes, or procure
Both the money and time,
To join the civilized.

As he read a last poem in memory of Mozart, I thought of his mouth, gaping wide in laughter, black, silent, and how Mauriac used to say that he always wished to write with the lightness of Mozart, but when he took up his pen the dark angels bore in upon him. Auden's angels have always been a little grey about the wings for me, but they have been angels nonetheless. That was Auden's genius, his surpassing of chic and attitudes, the way he refused to let go, or perhaps more accurately, had allowed himself to be borne forward by his grey angels, imposing his own order, his own constant voice, his wit, his laughter, in the rooms and hallways and all the sordid lanes and still gardens – and perhaps he was consoled knowing that

Altogether elsewhere, vast
Herds of reindeer move across
Miles and miles of golden moss,
Silently and very fast.

The Telegram, 1971-72

DIN DON DIN

There was an old man called Rosie who had eyes like swamp water. He stood night after night outside the Imperial Theatre and sold long-stemmed red roses from a seeding box. He was so shabbily dressed the theatre manager asked the police to make him move away from under the marquee. He stared impassively at the police and they went away.

Then, late one night just before closing time, Rosie caught my eye. "Ding dong ding . . ." he whispered in a child's singsong as the yellow and white lights from the theatre marquee rippled across his face. I looked hard into his eyes, trying to recall where I had heard that *ding dong ding*. Then I remembered an early morning a few years ago in a faraway cathedral town, when I had gone to Mass to hear Mahler's *First Symphony* for the dead, and during the funeral march I'd heard a little tune between the requiem notes, the composer's joke, a nursery rhyme . . .

sonnez les matines, sonnez les matines,
din don din, din don din . . .

After the requiem Mass I went down the town road from the cathedral to a fenced-off place called Dachau, the concentration camp, and for the first time I walked those killing grounds. I got up into one of the box beds. I stood outside the little brick house with the ovens in it and, on the edge of tears, sang out loud to myself, *Sonnez les matines, sonnez les matines, din don din, din don din* . . . until a stout woman, walking arm-in-arm with her frail old father, who was carrying red roses, looked at me and said scornfully, "You ought to be arrested."

2001

GOYA

Call me Goya!
Shock troops made shell-holes
of my eyes, a stricken field.

Call me grief.

Call me the blow-horn
of the snow-clad cities of '41.

Call me hunger.

Call me the gullet
of a garotted woman's body tolling
above the bald square.

Call me Goya!

Grapes
of wrath, enemy ashes strewn through the indelible
sky, stars ringing like hammered nails, O...

Call me Goya.

• Translated from the Russian of Andrei Voznesensky

1974

IN THE EYE OF THE DUNG BEETLE

SCENE: *Circular walls with a recess upstage centre. A large, very sparsely furnished room. To the right, going upstage from the proscenium, three doors. Then a window with a stool in front of it; then another door. In the centre of the back wall of the recess, a large double door, and two other doors facing each other and bracketing the main door: these last two doors, or at least one of them, are almost hidden from the audience. To the left, going upstage from the proscenium, there are three doors, a window with a stool in front of it, opposite the window on the right, then a blackboard and a dais. Empty chairs. A gas lamp hangs from the ceiling. The curtain rises. Half-light. The* OLD MAN *is up on the stool, leaning out the window on the left. The* OLD WOMAN *lights the gas lamp. Green light. She goes over to the* OLD MAN *and takes him by the sleeve.*

Ionesco said the subject of his play *The Chairs* is "the chairs themselves; that is to say, the absence of people, the absence of God, the absence of matter, the unreality of the world, metaphysical emptiness.

"The theme of the play is *nobodiness*."

Not luckless men, unknowing men, insects, mice, and apes, not viciousness and avidity, cowardice, gluttony, and the pettiness of men – not a dog – but nobodiness.

In Samuel Beckett's *Happy Days,* nothing happens, nothing moves – nothing sprouts or grows, until the sudden appearance of an emmet. It crosses over the woman who is buried in sand up to her neck – carrying what appears to be an egg – and the emmet provokes her husband, who has been hiding behind the sand, to exclaim, "Formication." There is always laughter at *formication.* Some hear it as *fornication.* Some think formication is Beckett's sniggering pun on *fourmi* and fornication, that the joke is about sex, procreation, even biological continuance. It is not. Beckett is always exact. Formication *is* formication – to be overrun by ants, by swarms of vermin.

In Kafka's *The Metamorphosis*, the dutiful clerk Gregor Samsa wakes up in his bed. He is vermin, a parasite, a dung beetle. In a passage left out of *The Trial,* Kafka wrote: "It is really remarkable that when you wake up in the morning you nearly always find everything in exactly the same place as the evening before . . . that's why the moment of waking up is the riskiest moment of the day." Gregor Samsa has become a dung beetle. This is the great trick of the story: he does not cease to be human. With insane ease he accepts his carapace. He still thinks of himself as a man, he loves music, he yearns for his sister, and, most important, he is still capable of shame. His refusal to become a bug in his head – even as he examines his twitching legs – is what makes his plight poignant and appalling. It is not a story about nobodiness.

During the Hitler war millions of people woke up and found that they were vermin. *Ungeziefer.* Each Jew – "*fand er sich in seinem Bett zu Ungeheuren Ungeziefer verwandelt.*"[1] It had been

[1] found himself transformed in his bed into a monstrous vermin.

decided, clear as crystal, in the night. They woke up and everything was the same and everything was out of place: Jews were parasites. To be exterminated. Old and loving and sensible neighbours looked at them and said they saw dung beetles. Vermin. Like Gregor Samsa, the cornered Jews held on to being human till the end. They refused to give up hope, to give up shame, and their maddening refusal to be anything other than compliantly optimistic is what makes the death that came in the morning to towns and ghettos across Europe so appalling and so poignant.

Moshe was the beadle of such a town in Hungary. It was called Sighet. He had seen the Gestapo at work. He had seen soldiers lead each and every Jew "up to the hole to present his neck." Moshe the Beadle warned his brethren that they were about to be killed like bugs, but they refused to believe that they had "actually become beetles. A wind of calmness and reassurance blew through houses. The traders were doing good business, the students lived buried in their books, and the children played in the streets."

This is Elie Wiesel's story; it is called *Night.*

This was in 1943! It was maddening. These Jews refused to recognize a fact for a fact. They were crazy. But wait a minute. Wait a minute. How crazy can you be? The Jews were crazy enough to believe that they were still human, but millions of their fellow citizens were crazier still, crazy enough to believe that overnight their neighbours had become bugs.

The good burghers agreed to exterminate the bugs, the Jews.

> *This way for the gas, ladies and gentlemen.*
>
> It is the camp law . . . The heap grows. Suitcases, bundles, blankets, coats, handbags that open as they fall,

spilling coins, gold, watches; mountains of bread pile up at the exits, heaps of marmalade, jams, masses of meat, sausages; sugar spills on the gravel. Trucks, loaded with people, start up with a deafening roar and drive off amidst the wailing and screaming of the women separated from their children, and the stupefied silence of the men left behind . . . The train has been emptied . . . We the cleaners climb inside. In the corners amid human excrement and abandoned wristwatches lie squashed, trampled infants, naked little monsters with enormous heads and bloated bellies. We carry them out like chickens, holding several in each hand . . . The morbid procession streams on and on – trucks growl like mad dogs. I shut my eyes tight, but I can still see corpses dragged from the train, trampled infants, cripples piled on top of the dead, wave after wave . . . freight cars roll in, the heaps of clothing, suitcases and bundles grow, people climb out, look at the sun, take a few breaths, beg for water, get into the trucks, drive away. And again freight cars roll in, again people . . . The scenes become confused in my mind – I am not sure if all of this is actually happening, or if I am dreaming.

The angel Gavriel appears in town at the foot of Elie Wiesel's mountain, a town crowded with ghosts. Posters announce the Good News: "By the grace of God, the town is at last *Judenrein*: rid of the Jewish poison, of the Jewish plague, of the Jewish vermin." The angel speaks to the last Jew left alive, a child, whose name – appropriately enough for a bug – is Gregor.

– Are you listening?
– Yes, I am listening.
– You won't forget?
– No, I won't forget.

> – You mustn't forget laughter either. Do you know what laughter is? I'll tell you. It's God's mistake. When God made man in order to bend him to his wishes he carelessly gave him the gift of laughter. Little did he know that later the earthworm would use it as a weapon of vengeance. When he found out, there was nothing he could do, it was too late to take back the gift. And yet he tried his best. He drove man out of paradise, invented an infinite variety of sins and punishments, and made him conscious of his own nobodiness, all in order to prevent him from laughing. But, as I say, it was too late.

Flaubert said that a laughing man is stronger than a suffering man.

Beckett said: "The laugh that now is mirthless once was hollow, the laugh that once was hollow once was bitter. And the laugh that once was bitter? . . . The bitter, the hollow and – Haw! Haw! – the mirthless. The bitter laugh laughs at that which is not good, it is the ethical laugh. Not good! Not true! Well, well. But the mirthless laugh is the dianoetic laugh, down the snout – Haw! – so. It is the laugh of laughs, the *risus purus,* the laugh laughing at the laugh, the beholding, the saluting of the highest joke, in a word the laugh that laughs – silence please – at that which is unhappy."

As Gregor hears the dianoetic *Haw*, he opens his eyes. It is morning; he is alive. He is a beetle, he is a scarab. A scarab is the sun. Gregor Samsa is a dung beetle made in the image of the sun god. As a god lying on his back wagging his feelers he asks Rilke's question: *Was war wirklich in Alle?* (What was real in the world?)

And so in the camp one of the cleaners asked, "What's new with you?"

"Not much. Just gassed up a Czech transport."

"That I know. I mean personally?"

"Personally? What sort of personally is there for me? The oven, the barracks, back to the oven . . . Have I got anybody around here? Well, if you really want to know what personally – we've figured out a new way to burn people. Want to hear about it?"

I indicated polite interest.

"Well then, you take four little kids with plenty of hair on their heads, then tie the heads together and light the hair. The rest burns by itself and in no time at all the whole business is gemacht."

He burst out laughing . . .

Paul Celan:

your golden hair Margarete
your ashen hair Shulamith we dig a grave in the breezes –
then as
smoke you will rise into air
then a grave you will have in the clouds

So amidst death-house laughter, amidst formication, Ionesco's Old Man and Old Woman end as they began, in *nobodiness.*

Long live the Emperor!

(Confetti and streamers thrown in the direction of the Emperor, then on the immobile and impassive Orator, and on the empty chairs.)

Long live the Emperor!

(The OLD WOMAN *and* OLD MAN *at the same moment throw themselves out the windows, shouting* "Long Live the Emperor." *Sudden silence; no more fireworks; we hear an* "Ah" *from both sides of the stage, the sea-green noises of bodies falling into the water. The light coming through the main door and the windows has disappeared; there remains only a weak light as at the beginning of the play; the darkened windows remain wide open, their curtains floating on the wind.)*

ORATOR *(has remained immobile and impassive during the scene of the double suicide, and now, after several moments, he decides to speak. He faces the rows of empty chairs; he makes the invisible crowd understand that he is deaf and dumb; he makes the signs of a deaf-mute; desperate efforts to make himself understood; then he coughs, groans, utters the guttural sounds of a mute)* He, mme, mm, mm. Ju, gou, hou, hou. Heu, heu, gu gou, gueue.

(Helpless, he lets his arms fall down alongside his body; suddenly, his face lights up, he has an idea, he turns toward the blackboard, he takes a piece of chalk out of his pocket, and writes, in large capitals: ANGELFOOD

then:

NNAA NNM NWNWNW V

He turns towards the invisible crowd on the stage, and points with his finger to what he's written on the blackboard.)

ORATOR: Mmm, Mmm, Gueue, Gou, Gu. Mmm, Mmm, Mmm, Mmm.

(Then, not satisfied, with abrupt gestures he wipes out the chalk letters, and replaces them with others, among which we can make out, still in large capitals:

? ADIEU ? DIEU ? P?

Again, the Orator turns around to face the crowd; he smiles, questions, with an air of hoping that he's been understood, of having said something; he indicates to the empty chairs what he's just written. He remains immobile for a few seconds, rather satisfied and a little solemn; but then, faced with the absence of the hoped for reaction, little by little his smile disappears, his face darkens; he waits another moment; suddenly he bows petulantly, brusquely, descends from the dais; he goes toward the main door upstage centre, gliding like a ghost; before exiting through this door, he bows ceremoniously again to the rows of empty chairs, to the invisible Emperor. The stage remains empty with only the chairs, the dais, the floor covered with streamers and confetti. The main door is wide open onto darkness. We hear for the first time the human noises of the invisible crowd; these are bursts of laughter, murmurs, shh's, ironical coughs; weak at the beginning, these noises grow louder, then, again, progressively they become weaker. All this should last long enough for the audience – the real and visible audience – to leave with this ending firmly impressed on its mind. The curtain falls very slowly.)

1983

THE AXEMAN COMETH: NIKITA KHRUSHCHEV

Just as King Midas turned everything to gold,
Stalin turned everything to mediocrity. If Stalin
was everything, did it not mean that other men
were nothing.

—ALEXANDER SOLZHENITSYN

Nikita Sergeyevich Khrushchev was born in 1894. He was a *narodnik*, a Ukrainian of squat peasant stock. He had shining piggish eyes, a dull menace behind the shine. And a wide mouth, chicken teeth. As a youngster he worked as a metal-fitter in the mines. One year after the 1917 Revolution, he joined the Bolshevik Party. Semi-literate, he shied away from doctrinal debates and survived the infighting among the intelligentsia, and then he not only survived the purges of the thirties, but as chairman of the Ukrainian Party committee he oversaw and administered deportations and the death squads; he tracked down and entrapped small businessmen, small farmers, fascists, freethinkers, fellow Trotskyites, and nationalists. He had thousands shot or imprisoned in the Siberian gulag, and thousands – hardly more than boys – were sent, untrained and ill-equipped, to the front-line trenches of World War II to die helplessly and stupidly fighting German armoured columns. He said they died "heroic" deaths. Then he went to Moscow, where some treated him like a clown who pretended to be a spiv; others treated him like a spiv who pretended to be a clown. He kept Stalin guessing until Stalin died in 1953. More secret – for all his affable bluster – than the secret police, he outmanoeuvred the murderous Lavrenty Beria. Eventually he emerged as leader of the Communist Party and then, in 1956, speaking to a closed session of the Twentieth Party Congress, he astonished the Praesidium and the International Party by denouncing Stalin's "personality cult," his "despotic character." Up to his own elbows in blood, he denounced the killings. The deportations. The "heroic deaths." He kept a straight face. He was engaged in a brilliant stroke: he not only distanced himself from twenty-five years of malevolence, turpitude, and bungling, but by saddling Stalin with the ostensible failures of two decades, he purged the Party of Stalin and restored a purity of ideological purpose to Communism as a movement. The speech rattled every Stalinist in the world. Poland's dictator, Boleslaw Bierut, died of a heart attack, there were countless suicides, and it especially rattled the Hungarian Communist Party. The Hungarians revolted. It seemed that the revolt might succeed. Khrushchev sent Soviet divisions to Budapest and the revolt was crushed. He went to New York. He pounded his shoe on a desk at the United Nations, and then in 1962 he brought Moscow and Washington nose to nose with nuclear war over Soviet missiles in Castro's Cuba. He bullied and barnstormed and held on to power until 1964. He was deposed. He wasn't killed, banished, or imprisoned. With *besstidstvo*, brass, he has written his memoirs, or, as he has put it, he has written down what he remembers.

I cannot say that this text, as translated, is Khrushchev remembering. But those who know the man, those who've been down among the onion domes, like Edward Crankshaw and Harrison E. Salisbury, say it is his voice, give or take a paragraph, and they are Kremlinologists of consequence. Salisbury, writing in *New York*, has best described the text's character:

> We are dealing here with a corpus which began as an inchoate jumble of rambling family-taped conversations. These raw notes (often confused and inaccurate) have

> been censored, patched, excised, potted, twisted, distorted and strained through a variety of editings which probably began with Khrushchev himself and his immediate entourage, including son-in-law and ex-*Izvestia* editor, Aleksei Adzhubel. Other fingers in the pie almost certainly belonged to a Politburo member or two, and one or more factions of the Soviet police establishment which finally seems to have authorized the chameleon-like police literary agent, Victor Louis, to carry the manuscript to the West.

With such antecedents, only Kremlinologists dare quibble over whether a KGB clause has been inserted into the Khrushchev commentary. But of the hacks, thugs, and apparatchiks who held power around Stalin, and of Khrushchev himself, a good deal can be learned and said. The bulk of the man – and I don't mean his girth – is here in the text: he was a manic cutthroat; he was coarse, brazen, tactless, and erratic; he was self-promoting and irascible. Bewildered by economic theory, he was beguiled by his own disastrous five-year economic plans; duplicitous, he knew how to play the dupe; he applied principles as only a man who has no principles can; and, lacking subtlety, he could be sardonic: "Death," he said, "is the only cure for the hunchback."

Describing the early days of the Revolution, he is openly boastful about killing or breaking men on behalf of the Party: "We justified what was happening in a lumberjack's terms: when you chop down a forest, the chips fly." Out in the forest were bureaucrats, the bourgeois, toadies and buffoons. They stood haplessly and witlessly in each other's shadow. They stood in the way: "We had to catch up with the capitalists. Sometimes achieving this goal required sacrificing moral principles."

Principles were sacrificed by men like Yezhov – the director of Stalin's secret police – and Khrushchev's mentor, Lazar Kaganovich: "He was a man who got things done. If the Central

Committee put an axe in his hands, he would chop up a storm; unfortunately he often chopped down the healthy trees along with the rotten ones. But the chips really flew – you couldn't take that away from him . . . He was as stubborn as he was devoted."

These political thugs, handy with an axe, shared a stubborn ideological devotion to the Party. They were militant. They were the chosen. They were triumphal as they surveyed a field of stumps. They were the Communist elect, just as Calvinism has its elect – predestined by history, predestined by God – cousins of the spirit. Saints or Party members – purging themselves of the damned and dispossessed, the poverty-stricken or the politically stricken, beyond the pale of the Council of Predikants, beyond the pale of the Party. "The Communist Party of the Western Ukraine was filled with unstable and even subversive elements, and all the personnel we could get our hands on were eliminated as provocateurs, turncoats, and agents . . ." Grace, the grace of the gift of life, arbitrary in its justification, was in the hidden eye of the beholder, the eye in the sky, the Father of all the Russias: Stalin, whose genius, according to Khrushchev, lay in his capacity to be – through his secret police – "all-seeing." No one was safe, no one could stay hidden. Party members, whether lilies in the field of stumps or sinners, kept their eyes open for "evidence" of their salvation, reduced to a strange furtive lethargy, silent, wary, looking, looking every day, every hour, penitent, spiteful, submissive, and scared shitless. Even the condemned, the imprisoned, the *zeks* in the Siberian freeze, in all innocence, accepted their fate – accepted their destiny in the dialectical imperative of history – and asked Stalin for forgiveness: Stalin, the redemptive force in their lives, the redemptive force of the Revolution; Stalin, who could do no wrong, who sat down and broke bread with those – the terrified – who loved him, and Khrushchev was first among them. He actually describes himself as Stalin's devoted apostle.

But then, as if it were part of the supper's conversation over vodkas, Khrushchev's personal litany of death and disappearance begins:

> – Comrade Redens. He was Stalin's brother-in-law, a Pole by nationality. He was a good comrade and had been a member of the Party since 1914. Stalin had him shot.
>
> – He [Tabakov] was one of my staunchest supporters in the academy, a politically sophisticated comrade and a Communist of the highest order. He was shot.
>
> – He [Kharkov] was a good man and a good Communist, devoted to the General Line of the Party, to the Central Committee, and to Stalin. But he, too, perished at Stalin's hand.

On it goes, insane in its contradictions.

Khrushchev had not only committed acts of great cruelty himself, but he had accommodated himself to Stalin's bottom-feeding brutality; he had not foreseen that Stalin would kill the innermost members of the Party, the party of the faithful. By 1937 he, too, was caught in what he calls "the meat-mincer." No one could breathe easy. "His was a sort of inborn brutishness . . . All of us around Stalin were temporary people . . . the moment he stopped trusting you, Stalin would start to scrutinize you until his cup of distrust overflowed. Then it would be your turn to follow those who were no longer among the living."

Khrushchev heard "fear tremble in a dry laugh," he watched as "tumbleweed ran riot like a hunchback clown cavorting." He did what he was told:

> A proposal from Stalin was a God-given command, and you don't haggle about what God tells you to do – you just offer thanks and obey . . . I remember once Stalin made me dance the Gopak before some top Party officials. I had to squat down on my haunches and kick out my heels, which frankly wasn't very easy for me. But I did it and I tried to keep a pleasant expression on my

> face. I later told Anastas Mikoyan: When Stalin says dance, a wise man dances.

But, he says, the dancing master was also a frightened, lonely man, foolish and sometimes confused in his needs: "He was coarse and abusive with everyone. I often experienced his rudeness myself. But Stalin liked me. If he hadn't liked me or if he had felt the slightest suspicion toward me, he could have gotten rid of me anytime he pleased." Khrushchev was on tenterhooks, especially since Stalin had been stunned into ineptitude by Hitler's blitzing advances. Khrushchev says that Stalin completely cross-wired the war effort through witless miscalculations, terrible misreadings of what was going on that sent him spiralling deeper and deeper inside himself, becoming hopelessly paranoid, until he made all others at his supper table taste every dish of his food. These others fawned, they tasted, they danced and kept watch, and danced and listened to the metronome of history tick as time stood still. They knew the struggle to stay alive would really begin when Stalin died.

The Party faithful gathered at the deathbed:

> No sooner had Stalin fallen ill than Beria started going around spewing hatred against him and mocking him. It was simply unbearable to listen to Beria. But, interestingly enough, as soon as Stalin showed signs of consciousness on his face and made us think that he might recover, Beria threw himself on his knees, seized Stalin's hand, and started kissing it . . . As soon as Stalin died, Beria was radiant. He was regenerated and rejuvenated. To put it crudely, he had a housewarming over Stalin's corpse before it was even put in the coffin. Beria was sure that the moment he had long been waiting for had finally arrived. There was no power on earth that could hold him back now. Nothing could get in his way.

Khrushchev the *narodnik*, the canny peasant, got in his way, pleading for party stability. Bright-eyed, he manoeuvred; full of menace, he manipulated, until one day Beria opened his own piglet eyes and found himself under arrest, and then one day he closed his eyes. He, too, was shot. Khrushchev stood grinning. He was not Father of all the Russias, but he was certainly in charge.

This is a tale of murder, decline, and decay. Just as the Saints in the stern and unforgiving theocracy of Salem bred descendants who sought evidence of their election as nickel-plated lawyers, accountants, brokers, factory barons, boiler-room and backroom hacks, so too the Party of the ruthless Lenin (Gorky said his words had an "amazing simplicity" – they had "the cold glitter of steel shavings") declined into political bosses who were slug-like in their outright brutality and stupidity, gutter fighters, bureaucrats who wielded power but left behind only a snail's trail of military incompetence and industrial pollution – a system that is not only murderous but has fostered ennui, boredom, stasis. A dialectic that is directionless. Power in the vacuum that it abhors.

What can one say of Khrushchev's rudderless prose, his anecdotes of political squabbles and betrayals, his gossipy truths and incoherent half-truths – set against a backdrop of millions of dead – anecdotes passed through so many soiled hands? Solzhenitsyn was right: Stalin turned everything to mediocrity.

The Telegram, 1971-73

MERMAID: A TRUE STORY

Earlie Fires woke up hearing the ocean. He closed his eyes as if he were still asleep and listened because he was nowhere near an ocean. He had been born in a concentration camp and he had survived the camp and made a life for himself selling insurance and now he was sixty years old and having never been to an ocean he was in bed with a woman who thought she was old because she was thirty-eight and he thought she was young because she was thirty-eight. It was her bed, the pillows were of soft down.

"Do you hear the ocean?" he asked. He had never slept all night in anyone else's bed.

She opened an eye. Her left eye. It was a pale ice blue, it was a blue clock, he thought.

He couldn't remember her having blue eyes.

"Yes," she said. "I love swimming in the ocean."

"You do?"

"Yes."

Earlie was worried that if she opened her other eye it would be blue, too.

"I was sure you had brown eyes," he said.

"Because I'm a mermaid," she said. "All mermaids have brown eyes."

She laughed. Her teeth were very white and the tip of her tongue between her teeth was pink. She drew his head down to her belly, between her thighs. He took a deep breath.

Earlie could smell the ocean.

He tasted the ocean.

"Only great men have ever slept with a mermaid," she said and opened her other eye.

It was blue.

"You're no mermaid," he said.

"Welcome to the real world," she said.

"No, no," he said.

He was still strong, lean and muscular. He made a fist and showed her the inside of his forearm, a tattoo.

It was a mermaid.

"You've got a mermaid tattoo on your arm," she said.

"No, look very hard, he said, and he drew her head down to his arm.

She said his skin smelled like smoke, she had smelled it all night. He said, "No, just look, look hard."

She looked and at last she said, "Numbers. There's numbers inside the mermaid."

Earlie said, "Yes, they disappeared in my little mermaid."

"Why'd you do that?" she asked as she lay back in her soft bed.

She looked almost unbearably young to him.

"Because I am alive and she is now my real world. She has brown eyes and those others who gave me the numbers are dead and they had blue eyes," and he leaned over her and lightly kissed her eyes closed and said, "Now we make love again."

2004

THE MASTER AND MARGARITA

I would like to call them by name,
But the list was taken away and I can't remember.

Mikhail Bulgakov began work on *The Master and Margarita* in 1928 or 1929, the year that Stalin took power in the Soviet Union. Those were the years of the Terror, the corrective ideological purges and an induced famine in Ukraine; the NKVD – the secret police – led by an alcoholic dwarf, Nikolai Yezhov – who arrested "the enemies of the people" in the night; and the show trials, the millions of peasants who were railroaded into the army to die in anti-tank ditches or into the Gulag forced-labour camps. Cowed writers knuckled under. A few survived uncompromised. Gorky was compromised. Sholokhov was compromised. But Mikhail Bulgakov was not.

Forced into isolation, Bulgakov wrote – before he died a natural death in 1940 – thirty-five plays (only eleven texts have survived), a life of Molière, *A Theatrical Novel* (based on his Moscow work with Stanislavsky), *Heart of a Dog*, and his masterpiece, *The Master and Margarita.* The text of this novel, altered by Soviet censors, was published in Moscow in 1966. The paragraphs cut and pared by the censors are hallucinatory scenes of sex, scenes of money speculation and police procedure, but (nothing ever makes sense in the Soviet Union) not the damning statement about political cowardice that is repeated throughout the novel: "Cowardice is the most terrible of the vices."

Layered like an onion – every totalitarian state has the nature of an onion – the story opens with two Soviet men of letters sitting on a bench in Patriarchs' Ponds in Moscow. Berlioz, editor of a fat literary journal and chairman of the Moscow literary association Massolit, has been arguing about the identity of the historical Jesus with a minor poet, Ivan Pongrev, who writes under an assumed name, an assumed identity, "Homeless." Berlioz, a hard-headed dialectical materialist, is insisting that Jesus was only a mythical figure, and as he castigates Homeless for having inexplicably created a Jesus who is all too alive upon the page, all too real, he realizes that the sweltering air around their bench has thickened,

> and a transparent citizen of the strangest appearance has woven himself out of it. A peaked jockey's cap on his little head, a short checkered jacket also made of air . . . A citizen seven feet tall, but narrow in the shoulders, unbelievably thin, and, kindly note, with a jeering physiognomy . . . His grey beret was cocked rakishly over one ear; under his arm he carried a stick with a black knob shaped like a poodle's head. He looked to be a little over forty. Mouth somehow twisted. Clean-shaven. Dark-haired. Right eye black, left – for some reason – green. Dark eyebrows, but one higher than the other. In short, a foreigner . . . "May I sit down?" the foreigner asked politely, and the friends somehow involuntarily moved apart; the foreigner adroitly sat down between them and at once entered into the conversation:
>
> "Unless I heard wrong, you were pleased to say that Jesus never existed?" the foreigner asked, turning his green left eye to Berlioz.
>
> "No, you did not hear wrong," Berlioz replied courteously, "that is precisely what I was saying."
>
> "Ah, how interesting!" exclaimed the foreigner . . .
>
> "Forgive my importunity," the foreigner says, "but as I understand, along with everything else, you also do not

believe in God?" He made frightened eyes and added: "I swear I won't tell anyone!"

"No, we don't believe in God," Berlioz replied, smiling slightly at the foreign tourist's fright, "but we can speak of it quite freely."

The foreigner sat back on the bench and asked, with a slight shriek of curiosity:

"You are – atheists?!"

"Yes, we're atheists," Berlioz smilingly replied, and Homeless thought, getting angry: "Latched on to us, the foreign goose!" . . .

"But allow me to ask you," the foreign visitor said after some anxious reflection, "what, then, about the proofs of God's existence, of which, as is known, there are exactly five?"

"Alas!" Berlioz said with regret. "Not one of those proofs is worth anything, and mankind shelved them long ago. You must agree that in the realm of reason there can be no proof of God's existence."

"Yes, too bad!" the stranger agreed, his eye flashing, and went on: "But here is a question that is troubling me: if there is no God, then, one may ask, who governs human life and, in general, the whole order of things on earth?"

"Man governs it himself," Homeless angrily hastened to reply to this admittedly none-too-clear question.

"Pardon me," the stranger responded gently, 'but in order to govern, one needs after all, to have a precise plan for a certain, at least somewhat decent, length of time. Allow me to ask you, then, how can man govern, if he is not only deprived of the opportunity of making a plan for at least some ridiculously short period – well, say, a thousand years – but cannot even vouch for his own tomorrow?"

Mr. Berlioz, certain of who he is and certain of his place, confident of his tomorrows, and upset that this foreigner should actually feel free to casually forecast how he, Berlioz, is going to die, steps alertly away from the bench and the Ponds. Fulfilling the foreigner's prophecy, he promptly slips in the street on spilled sunflower seed oil, falls under a streetcar driven by a woman, and is decapitated. The moment has the feel of hallucination. The bewildered and frightened Homeless, realizing that he is in the presence of a terrifying power, goes to the police and tells them his story about a foreigner who has not only appeared out of nowhere in Moscow but who says that he actually spoke to Pilate at the trial of Jesus. (A menacing note: The scene is a fantastic inversion of the normal state of Soviet terror: men did not appear out of nowhere in Moscow, they disappeared into nowhere.) Homeless – of the assumed name – is put in a home for those assumed to be mentally disturbed.

The satanic foreigner, the supposed figment of Homeless's imagination, has appeared in Moscow because powerful Party editors and censors have refused to publish a novel written by a nameless man – a man known only as The Master. This novel is about Pontius Pilate and – set in historical time – it deals with the actual staged examination of Jesus, his actual condemnation, and, since that dark day of the Crucifixion on Skull Hill, Pilate's state of perpetual remorse in purgatory – "24,000 moons in penance for one moon long ago." Satan, to set the trial record straight, to give it – and therefore the Master – an authenticity, says, "Jesus did exist, you know," and as someone who was there, as a bona fide witness to the actual trial, he has come on special assignment to help the Master – who has imagined being at the trial – to free himself from a bout of deep manic depression, depression brought on by his failure to get his novel published – a depression increased by the fact that officials have burned his manuscript papers (the nameless Master, stripped of his identity, resides in the clinic that is now a home to Homeless).

Satan and his fantastic cohorts (a huge gun-wielding cat plays the Fool in his royal Luciferian retinue) turn metropolitan Moscow into an extended lunatic asylum. Wearing the slouch pants and patched coat of a trickster flim-flam devil and operating under his own assumed name – Professor Woland – his purpose, oddly enough for a devil but appropriate to a society in which everything is inverted, is ruthlessly moral. His illusionary tricks – clothing vanishes off the bodies of vain ladies, heads are stolen from corpses, banknotes transform into champagne labels, frauds confess their crimes, mindless managers go mad, bureaucrats are unable to stop singing "The Song of the Volga Boatmen" in full chorus, and lechers turn into pigs – are not cheap thrills intended to belittle a Faustian Master but are pranks meant to expose the horrid greed, sloth, stupidity, and brutishness of Moscow and its citizens. This is hilarious, but it is hilarity edged in black, as everything in Stalin's Moscow is edged in requiem black.

Obviously, Satan's intention is to create situations that will refocus – in a fresh analogical light – the trials, the purges, the ministerial sleaze, the police incompetence, the betrayal of psychiatry, the repression, and the idiocy of the apparatchiks who constructed economic five-year plans. But at another level, Bulgakov is urging a point about individual political responsibility. Pilate, suffering from an endless headache brought on by his cowardice, suffering because of his expedient refusal to save himself and Jesus from a show trial and a brutal legalism, is a warning to each and every citizen of the Soviet Union. When the state lapses into callous manipulation of the law, when the state maintains preferment and power, and when authority crushes the individual, the citizen must respond, and the writer – who has been given a gift, the ability to shape actual experience, not only to shape the fantasies of other men but to tell their stories – must not submit to orthodoxy, must not submit to censors, to the received and conventional wisdom. Rather, the writer must assert his apocryphal and, if necessary, apocalyptic, point of view; he must be prepared not just to insist, whatever the cost, that there was a historical Jesus – a man who had a real identity – but to insist also that there is a "Jesus" – a unique and sacred light – in each man and woman, and that each citizen, each carrier of the light, must be spared wrongful characterization, wrongful arrest, wrongful trial, and wrongful imprisonment – ultimately, spared a loss of personal identity. (It is one of the ironies of the book that a well-meaning witness to Jesus' trial – who turns out to be one of the actual gospellers – hears most of what Jesus has to say with a slanted ear, and in telling Jesus' story he keeps turning Jesus into someone who is admittedly interesting – even compelling – but someone Jesus was not; meaning that a true story is not always reportage, but – as in a novel like the Master's – it is reportage shaped by the imagination into a lie – a lie like the Gospels – that tells a great truth – a truth that *is* and *is not* historical.) The Comrades who are the custodians of Party authority, of law and order and ideology, are certain that they know who the enemy is when they see him and – among Satan's retinue – a huge cat carrying a gun and having his own free and footloose way is someone to be arrested:

> At about four o'clock one warm afternoon a large squad of plainclothesmen climbed from three cars stopped a short distance from No. 302A Sadovaya Street in Moscow. They converged on apartment No. 50 and as they threw the door open, the leader of the squad drew from under his overcoat a black Mauser.
>
> Fanning through all the rooms, they found no one – but they had heard piano music and singing. On the dining room table were the remnants of a meal, and then, in the drawing room, they found a huge black cat perched on the mantelpiece beside a crystal jug. They hurled a net at the cat but caught only the jug. The cat screamed, "Missed . . . I challenge you to a duel." And the cat jumped into a chandelier while whipping out a Browning automatic.
>
> "Stepladder!" came the cry from the policemen.

> The cat swung over the police like a pendulum and both sides fired round after round. The faces of the policemen showed total bewilderment. The cat had suffered not a scratch. They had pumped volleys at its head, stomach, breast and back, but the cat just sat there, blowing nonchalantly into the muzzle of its Browning, and finally it said, "I completely fail to understand the reason for this rough treatment . . ."
>
> Suddenly, at the sound of low rumbling voices from another room, the huge cat threw kerosene on the floor. There was a great flame, and amid desperate cries, the cat went out the window and faded into the westering sunlight. Three other dark figures, apparently men, and one naked woman, floated out of the windows of the apartment house on Sadovaya Street. And so, Satan and his retinue departed from Moscow.

As Satan turns out the lights on his act, the Master (Pilate and the Master – one trapped in depression, the other trapped in penance – are two sides of a mirror, indicative of the stasis at the heart of Soviet society) is freed from his ongoing depression by a special agent: his mistress, Margarita. She has not sold her soul but has struck a bargain with the departing Satan. She undergoes an underground ordeal in Hell – she presides as the black queen at a magnificent dress ball (one of the curious aspects of Bulgakov's work is the intense sensuality he gives to many scenes – it is a sensuality that never becomes sexuality). She survives her trial. She has demonstrated loyalty and courage rather than cowardice, that "most terrible of the vices." She joins the Master, and Satan restores the Master's burned manuscript. He says pointedly, and as an alert to state censors, "Manuscripts don't burn." The couple travel to a world of eternal peace. Satan and his band, their work done, leave behind a bewildered police force. Official Moscow, true to its nature (and true to how the story began), denies the magical by rationalizing each fantastic event. We end by realizing how perverse diligent citizens are – willing to give their loyalty to brutal force in all its mediocrity – while, when confronted with a visionary novelist, they not only agree that he must be put away among the Homeless, but when confronted with a good man of electrical presence, Jesus, they must kill him and then make him into a god. The novel ends with hundreds of Moscow citizens – informers by temperament and by force of habit – turning hordes of tiny black cats in to the police, one more Stalinist ritual of deadening stupidity.

The Telegram, 1968-69

LETTER FROM MARINA G.: LENINGRAD, 1979

I am happy to tell you that I now live alone in my own one room flat. There is a little alcove in the room and in the alcove there is a two-burner stove and a sink with a swan's neck for the water and a long narrow window to the room more like a slot than a window that looks out over a narrow canal and a stone foot bridge from the old old times and a short road that runs to one side of the canal.

The canal road is a dead-end, though the canal itself runs under an old military embankment, going out to the sea. I have never seen any boat travel the canal out to the sea. And because the road is a dead-end not so many people walk alongside the canal water or on the sidewalk, and no one skates the short stretch that freezes over in the winter. I like this very much. Crowds upset me. I feel, if there are crowds there will be plain-clothes police in the crowds, secret police who are able because they are the police to touch me, to breathe against me, my neck. I have committed no crime, never, but I know that not knowing what you have done does not matter. My mother and father did not know what they had done but they disappeared.

One morning, I found a French fashion magazine on the seat of a chair where I sit always in a café on Nevsky Prospekt. I could not imagine in my mind where this magazine on the chair had come from or who was the person who left it on the chair. I slid it into my cloth bag and took it back to my room and I am turning the pages over and over, pages of skinny women in dresses and suits that I could not myself imagine wearing. But for a reason I do not understand, since automobiles are of no interest to me, it was the photograph of a long limousine, black, that I kept turning back to, a black limousine that seemed to float on sand dunes that ended nowhere, dunes that were white as white summer clouds. I felt light-headed, dizzy, staring at the black-smoked windows, especially one that seemed to be reflecting the moon in the night sky – but since it was a bright blue sky above the dunes – the moon had to be the sun, or maybe a bare light bulb, an interrogation light bulb that was shining in my eyes. I scissored the page from the magazine and suddenly I felt I was going to fall asleep on my feet so I tacked the limousine to my door and went to bed, to sleep, and did not dream.

In the morning, I came out of the apartment courtyard, I stopped and stood very still. There was a long black limousine parked on the canal road. I went cold like ice, I was sure I was in danger, it was exactly the limousine that I had taken from the French magazine and tacked to my door. I could see the limousine had the same black-smoked windows. I believed someone wearing a double-breasted suit was sitting in the back seat watching me. I believe the men who sit in the back seats of long black cars, they are the ones who wear double-breasted suits.

I leaned forward a little and stared into the smoked window. There was no moon or sun. I was staring at myself in the dark glass. I had the sick feeling that the limousine was a black period, a stop, about to be put to my life. I brought my face close to the glass, sure I was nose to nose with someone's face inside, and to my complete surprise, I heard myself say, "Me. Yes, it's me." As soon as I spoke the limousine moved forward, moving away from me, down to the dead-end where it stopped, the motor still running because I could see the exhaust, sitting with its back to me, giving me a chance to run away down the road.

I am not a fool. I stepped back from the curb to the wall. The limousine, after several minutes, backed down the road, coming to a halt, again in front of me. I was not only being watched, I was sure I was going to be taken off the street to disappear. I fled into the courtyard, to the stairs, and into my room. I stood in the centre of the room, shaking, and I went close up to the window, and stood in the cover of the window curtain to see if the black limousine was still there. It was there. The motor had been turned off. I did not know why I had said, "Yes, it's me." Furious at myself, I snatched the black limousine and the sand dunes and the blue sky from the door. I crumpled them into a ball and tossed the ball in the waste basket under the sink and then I went to that little window where I pulled the curtain away and drew the window open and leaned my shoulder and head into the open window. There was no limousine. It had disappeared. The concierge to the apartment house, who admits he is always a little drunk, was standing at the curb. I tried to keep calm. I called, "Where did the black limousine go?" and the concierge, looking at me as if I was someone who had lost her mind, said, "Limousine? There's been no one, no limousine all morning. Only the street sweepers."

1979

A LITTLE B-BALL WITH RABBIT: JOHN UPDIKE

John Updike's bony head was too large for his slender shoulders, his hooked nose was a blade at the bridge and broad at the nostrils, his mouth pursed, chin receding. He was wearing a beige turtleneck sweater and, under the sweater, a checkered flannel shirt open at the neck, rolled at the cuffs. He was grinning, a feckless boyish laugh, shrewd eyes, as he cradled his head in the crook of his long right arm, fingers dangling, scratching the nape of his neck while he talked about his town.

"Oh, you can't call this Updike territory. Ipswich is a very old town, founded in 1633 by Governor Winthrop's eldest son, who came up here with twelve men in a boat, essentially to make a plantation for the harvesting of salt-hay. The hay was just standing there and all you had to do was get the horses out, shoe them up in wooden discs, and cut the hay. But the town has petered out since the beginning of the 1700s and has been more or less static – I resist the word stagnant – ever since."

We were walking in the afternoon stillness of the town, fallen autumn elm leaves on the lawns, walking toward his home, a thirteen-room saltbox house gleaming white in the sun, the door and wooden stoop nearly hidden by a high hydrangea. A pink plastic ball lay at the base of the bush. Updike darted up from the road and grabbed the ball, calling out, "I hear you used to play basketball." He pivoted and set the ball close to his chest, the old white man's one-hand push-shot – Rabbit shooting hoops – peering off into the trees as if there were faces scouting him in the leaves. Taking one short step he lobbed a shot spinning up into the sun. I caught the ball and yelled, "Two, a big two points," and fired the ball back to him. "One free throw," I called. "You were fouled." Updike palmed the pink plastic, set himself at the foul line to the left of the stoop, then bounced the ball, taking his time, a deep breath. His head bobbed. But as he bounced the ball it hit rough turf or a stone and angled off, and away. "Oh, what the hell," Updike mumbled and threw his arms wide, laughing. We went inside.

Updike lurched backward into the corner of a deeply cushioned chesterfield and sat with his left ankle crossed over his right knee, his half-off loafer dangling from his toes. The afternoon light streamed into the room through the ceiling-high 1680 windows, tincturing the huge brick fireplace, which was some twelve feet wide and made to take cross-sawn tree trunks in the coastal wintertime. What looked like an old single-ball rifle was fastened to the brick, but I don't know anything about rifles. Opposite the fireplace and close to one window, a grand piano littered and stacked with music sheets and books, the books all written by ladies. I didn't know anything about the ladies either. Several had three names, sounded Bloomsbury.

"My wife was from Cambridge. We'd known Ipswich briefly on our two-day honeymoon – you know I courted her by falling downstairs in the Fogg Museum – I wasn't sure I was going to stick here, but stick I have." Updike suddenly got up and fetched an apple from the kitchen and he tossed it recklessly high, catching it against his chest, and then, after biting out a chunk, he waved the white wound in the apple at the window, saying, "Across the street is an enormous elm. The elm blight has somehow coincided with my stay here and I've watched apprehensively to see if the tree would be the next to go; it has survived so far, but when it dies, I don't quite know what Ipswich will . . . do for me at the . . . it's a very precious tree."

His eyes were narrow but not sinister, crinkled at the corners but not with age, and crescent lines of mirth bracketed his mouth. He squinted, recalling past moments.

"I go for walks around here quite a lot . . . The wonder of the area is the marshes: tawny flat stretches of unusable land. It's so nice in this country to see land that can't be used for something. And up behind me, going up Spring Street, there's a sort of woods where I used to walk with the children, but, unlike Khrushchev's grandchildren, they don't seem to enjoy walks in the woods very much. And if you walk up the street a way, you can go through a cemetery. I always find that cemeteries are one of the most cheerful places in any town. The dead make a very amicable community, and you can walk and observe the old angels on the slate tombstones."

Strange that the softly laughing and still young Updike spoke with such feeling for forlorn places, with nostalgia for a decay and decrepitude he'd never known, and a stillness. He and his wife had apparently always been in the Ipswich social whirl: each played the recorder in a group that met on alternate Wednesday evenings; he sat on the Democratic committee; both participated in a formal year-round Sunday athletic program that went from volleyball to touch football to skiing to basketball and back to volleyball; he attended prayer service regularly at the Congregational Church, the local needle point in the sky. But, he said dryly, he had felt in himself and in those around him a failure of nerve, a sense of doubt, a deep doubt about the worth of any activity, and so I asked him if all his movements, frenetic or formal, were leaps out of a despond, like poor Luther leaping off his toilet crying salvation by Grace and Grace alone.

"You know, my first novel, *The Poorhouse Fair* . . . I was in New York working for *The New Yorker* and I was trying to write a six-hundred-page novel, and it was clear the novel was not publishable, and I went home to Pennsylvania. I saw that the poorhouse that had been up the street from us was being torn down for a housing development. In some ways the vacant shell cried out for a memorial. I was full at that period, I guess, of a sense of decay, of the loss of my grandfather's generation."

"Do you really feel," I asked, "that our generation is one of decay, that the values of our grandfathers were more solid, were better?"

"I think every generation is a generation of decay. I think that history, like geology, is nothing but decay, though there are eruptions in human history, volcanic movements."

"Why do writers like yourself take this attitude, that our society, our middle class is decaying at the core, as if our predecessors had something strong and true? . . . Seems to me that's a dream that only we can afford to impose on our ancestors."

"Of course, but I felt in *The Poorhouse Fair* that a certain kind of America was vanishing, the kind of America whose relics are being peddled as antiques, old weather vanes and whatnot. Christianity had shaped the lives of these people in a way that it has ceased to do."

"Well, this shank hour, this vanishing of values, with your Harry Angstrom in *Rabbit, Run* – he strikes me as a kind of latter-day Huck Finn, setting off down the suburban road, escaping to the wilderness . . . only once he's out there, he sees the countryside's been filled in; it's dumpster country; no matter how far he goes, there's no escape from his world of beer commercials and toilet cleansers and ladies with cheesecloth skin and varicose veins."

"That was meant to be a kind of angelic flight," he said, laughing, sounding playfully wounded. Suddenly Updike's long, thin legs shot straight out. He banged his shoes together, examined the glossy brown leather, and then said, "There was a great deal of talk then about beatniks, and *Rabbit, Run* is my B novel. At one point I had the idea of writing an alphabet of novels, and certainly the B – Rabbit plays basketball, and the two Bs in Rabbit and beatniks and so on . . . just as *The Centaur* is my C novel, very clearly. Anyway, *Rabbit, Run*, it was some sort of examination of the morality of becoming a saint. He's running toward something."

"He's running from everybody he's left broken and bunged up behind him; that's nice work if you can get it."

"You're so mean to the poor man, who was really only trying to do what's right."

"But Rabbit is a dreadful moral sentimentalist. He drowns in pools of self-pity and pools of grandiose optimism and self-congratulation."

"I must say," Updike said, lifting his chin, not indignantly, but like an imp, "that Harry Angstrom and I think almost exactly alike, so that I too am caught . . ."

"You're a sentimentalist?"

"Caught in self-pity."

Updike erupted in laughter. The lines from his nostrils down around his mouth gave a sudden oval shape to his laughter, an egg breaking across the middle. He went on, soft-spoken, precise: "Yes, the only thing in which Harry and I differ is that he was a good athlete. I was never a good athlete, and it was very satisfying to project all my anxieties into him."

"You know, it just struck me, the most prevalent criticism of your work is that your characters don't have much to say about anything, and here you're talking about morality, death, saints. What about a critic like Norman Podhoretz?"

"I did feel that in Podhoretz's case there was a kind of hysteria, a real inattention to my novel. He thought the father in *The Centaur* actually committed suicide. What novel was he reading? Podhoretz is representative – and not one of the more humane or sensitive ones – representative of a kind of New York – centred criticism which is very unaware of the country as a whole. This is terrible, this Manhattan inability to take seriously any set of assumptions which differ from theirs. I'm an inlander. I'm probably some sort of throwback, a kind of hick. I've read some theology. I take Christianity, as a set of ideas, seriously. All these things go against the grain of a criticism which in its own mind has passed beyond this. Somehow the *New York Review of Books*, although you have all those different writers, it all comes out the same, the same slightly oatmealy chip on the shoulder, a kind of writing that's not very life-enhancing."

Updike had linked his hands behind his head, and he wagged his arms back and forth slowly, so that his arms were like wings, angular and pointed, struggling to lift his beaked head up and out of the chair.

"I was talking with LeRoi Jones," I said – and Updike looked warily at me – "about your work, and he said he thought it stood for everything that was sterile, vacant, and horrible in the white middle class."

"I don't know to what extent Mr. Jones meant I partook of the sterility and vacancy, but that's about the noise I'd expect from him and not a terribly ponderable statement. Anyway, you write about what you have to write about, and I certainly suppose I deal with the middle class. I think it's the class where things have happened in this country, and I think it still is the centre, by and large."

Updike put on his loafers and suggested we go outside. I followed into his yard behind the big house. There was another pink ball on the ground and he picked it up and idly aimed at the house wall, let fly, and walked on, not looking back as the ball thumped hollowly against the wood and fell dead on the grass.

"Why is there," I asked, "not only in your work, but it seems since *Huckleberry Finn*, this American concentration on the boy, the adolescent reaction to life?"

Updike stared down at a spot near his feet. He turned his toes inward, rubbed the back of his hand across his eyes, and then, while answering, tugged at his forelock.

"The simplest reason is that a writer is cut off from his fellow men – the men who put on their grey suits, get into trains, and go off and do something. The writer did, however, share boyhood with these men. Do you have a clear idea of what the adult world is, and where it lies? I'm not certain I do."

"Are we always to be adolescents in North America?"

"The word adolescent, like the word sentimental, are words that purely have a sting to them."

"Adolescents . . ."

"They are tedious. There's no denying it. But there's something hackneyed and unpleasant about the idea of growing up . . . of coming to maturity. I bristle inside at the word. It may be that the whole concept of adulthood, of maturity, is a little like nineteenth-century ether – that is, something that people assume must be there, although it's invisible. It's possible that the adult is merely an adolescent gone to seed."

I laughed loudly as we stood at the front of the house, and my eye followed a tall, ramrod-straight woman striding along the road. She had a walk peculiar to many American white women – her hips had no swing and her legs snapped forward with the military precision that seems to fascinate American men, the sexlessness of the drum majorette, the sexlessness of the kick-line of long-stemmed ladies shoulder to shoulder moving like a machine, the sexlessness of square dancing, and just as I turned to say, "Have you ever wondered . . ." he shot by, pedalling furiously on a junior-size bicycle. His thin legs jutted out at ridiculous angles, like a whirring insect, and before I could call, he was gone around the corner, leaving me slack-jawed for several minutes. He must have sidestepped away while I was thinking, found the bike, and taken off. Then he was back around the corner, pedalling much slower, head down, looking a little sheepish. He let the bike ride out from under him and it crumpled to a riderless stop as he returned from his moment of angelic flight and we walked on, picking up the conversation as if there'd been no pause in the clock:

"What I really think," he said, "is that the great challenge in this day and age is to develop a positive feeling about growing up. I once discussed this with somebody who said that all experience is corruption, and I think, if the term moral challenge isn't too offensive – and it is somewhat offensive, eh? – that it is a challenge to develop a positive theory of adulthood, to break out of this sense of lost innocence that we have, lost intensity."

We were standing in the shadow of the tall steeple of the Congregational Church on the South Green, a large white neo-Gothic wood building, the black clock halfway up the tower at ten to two. It was three in the afternoon. "God's out of whack," I said. He gave me his impish little smile and pointed to the steeple top, where there appeared to be an ancient hammered cock turning in the wind, but said nothing until he let his arm drop and asked, "Do you remember crossing the old bridge as you came into Ipswich? It was at that bridge in the late sixteenth century that the selectmen of the town met the invading witching committee and told them that in Ipswich we take care of our own witches." I had come across the bridge in the morning, a gravel ocean road, stiff brown grass in the ditch. Milkweed pods. A pearl light along the waterline. Strange light, as if oil had been laid on lead, a dead sheen. Seagulls, an amber bead of light in their bill-hooks. You could feel witching in the air, if you wanted to. Anyway, it seemed that Updike, passing under the shadow of God, naturally had to consider witches, committees, cocks that might crow, and the casting out of devils.

He pointed down the road to South Main Street and the Dolphin Restaurant – STEAKS AND SEAFOOD – and he explained – like a good town businessman – that he rented an office over the Dolphin, and that office was where he did his writing. We stood and stared down the street at the Dolphin and then turned back toward his house, and he mused, his forefinger caressing the curve under his lower lip, "My . . . initial ambition, you know, was to be a cartoonist for Walt Disney, and at about the age of thirteen, *The New Yorker* began to come into the house and I wanted to be a cartoonist for it. That somehow deteriorated into . . . settling for anywhere getting into *The New Yorker* and I became sideways a light verse writer, and then a prose writer, and now I've turned to the novel . . . it's a hideous word, novel, but, you know . . ."

"You don't mean that writing . . . ?"

He took me firmly by the arm and whispered, "I'm haunted by the idea that maybe I've failed, that maybe I am in the wrong profession."

I stepped back, but then bent forward, reaching for a cloak, as if I were Groucho Marx, who had a moustache to twirl in disbelief. "You mean, that you should be working for Walt Disney?"

"That perhaps I should be . . . in Disneyland, perhaps . . . yes . . . yes."

Updike strode ahead. "At play. I should be at play." I followed, keeping my eye on all the ground cover to see if there was a pink ball lying about under a bush that I could throw to him, or a bicycle I could offer him, and perhaps a Texaco road map so that he could strike off into a wilderness.

CBC's *Show On Shows; The Telegram,* 1964-68

COUPLES: PLOUGHING THROUGH ACRES OF PUDENDA

Who knows what lurks in the hearts of self-absorbed small-town couples as they creep in and out of each other's beds, furtive, self-abusive, determined, in spite of their humiliations and their ennui, to be free, flexible, and decent? "Pity the poor bore," John Updike once wrote. "He stands among us as a creature formidable and familiar yet in essence unknowable."

This pitiable bore is a man who has no religion yet he sits attentively in the Congregational Church. He is listening to the organist, a mauve-haired spinster from Lacetown, as she rummages through a Bach prelude, and then he rises to sing Hymn 195: "All Hail the Power." He knows he is powerless. He knows he is on the downhill run to death. He has his puzzlements but no second thoughts. He plays parlour games like Ghosts and when he thinks he's losing one of these games he says a little rehearsed prayer, but the real language of his prayers is *put* and *call.* This bore has found his security in a town called Tarbox, where "there are two kinds of jerks, upper middle-class jerks and lower middle-class jerks. The upper went to college." These jerks are swappers. They swap lies. They swap wives. A lot. They fuck. They think sex. They think fuck. They think fuck is love and are afraid of love without fuck: "Jesus Christ . . . People hate love. It threatens them. It's like tooth decay, it smells and it hurts . . . People are the only thing people have left since God packed up. By people, I mean sex, fucking . . ."

Over one hundred feet in the air, on the Tarbox church spire there is a gilded weathercock from colonial times. The cock has an English penny eye. Children believe the penny is the eye of God. God has a cock's-eye view. Updike sees like that, too. He is like Grandma Moses. He writes from the top down: "First the sky, then the mountains, then the hills, then the houses, then the cattle, and then the people." The cock sees the red head of Piet Hanema (*me, a man, amen ah*). He sees that Piet is a latecomer, a man who is much like his boring neighbours, scurrying from bedpost to pew to bedpost to pew, saying a prayer as he plows through acres of local pudenda, a man of his time coupling among the eternal rocks.

But Piet Hanema is a little more. He is a puzzle, even to himself. His neighbours are not a puzzle. They are only tweaked by dread. He suffers from a deep, abiding dread, and he tries to overcome this dread by boffing several women at once and, even better, by talking to them about sex in a sacramental language. He talks the talk and walks the walk of transubstantiation. He speaks of his body as a holy wafer. Cunnilingus and copulation actualize the *esse* of his spiritual need. He knows that the closer he gets to his need the more likely he is to be punished. This is Calvinism on its hind legs, sacramental sex coupled with inevitable arbitrary punishment: "We'll all be punished no matter how it goes. That's a rule of life, people are punished. They are punished for being good, they are punished for being bad. A man in our office been taking vitamin pills all his life, dropped dead in the elevator two weeks ago. He was surrounded by healthy drunks. People are even punished for doing nothing. Nuns get cancer of the uterus because they don't screw . . ."

Piet Hanema has a job. He is a joiner, a carpenter who thinks he is cast in the image of his God, his God who has "roofed the world." This roofer, who is utterly free and – in his play with predestination – utterly capricious, calls some sinners to His bosom and casts other sinners out, and He calls this Salvation by Faith Alone. Piet is as arbitrary as his God. He calls some to his bed and casts others out. His orgasm is soul-saving, it calms him; he feels in his bones "a crisisless osmosis, an ebbing of light . . ."

Seen in this ebbing of the light, he is an adulterer, a coward, an accomplice to abortion, a clown, a businessman blunted by drink; he is fucked and re-fucked, sucked and re-sucked. His soulmates are ditzy broads, close-to-the-vest stockbrokers, merchants, dentists, and scientists. He takes on all comers, his lovers who live in contemporary colonial homes where tradition is a trend. Kierkegaard would be their house philosopher if only they could tear themselves away from television. If disappointed in the bed or by the TV, they turn to self-congratulatory depression. When they go out they don't go far. The mall is their modern state of mind. Huge parking lots give them a sense of democratic freedom. Their democratic political representatives are important only as pieces put into play in their puerile games of Ghosts: the murder of President Kennedy does not lead them to mourn; they want to know only whether he was a leftist, or young enough to sleep with.

Such men and women (to paraphrase Saul Bellow) mouth all the radical doctrines, right or left, doctrines they keep in abundance at their finger tips; they are conservatives who have no roots, doers who make nothing, witnesses who have no faith, careless cheats who live out their days demanding loyalty, passionately dedicated only to the dry machinations of couple swapping. Piet Hanema – the best among them – as the seeker, the joiner, takes Communion at the crotch:

> Lazily she fellated him while he combed her lovely hair. Oh and lovely also her coral cunt, coral into burgundy, with its pansy-shaped M, or W, of fur: kissing her here, as she unfolded from gateway into chamber, from chamber into universe, was a blind pleasure tasting of infinity until, he biting her, she clawed his back and came . . . Mouths, it came to Piet, are noble. We set our genitals

> meeting down below like peasants, but when the mouth condescends, mind and body marry. To eat another is sacred. *I love thee, Elizabeth, thy petalled rankness, thy priceless casket of nothing lined with slippery buds . . .* beneath the hanging clangor of bells.

Slippery buds, the casket, the bells, the sacred clangor: this is the bathos of spiritualized sex.

Updike is our Crashaw of the parking lots:

> *Blessed Be the Paps Which Thou Hast Sucked*
>
> *Suppose he had been Tabled at thy Teates,*
> *Thy hunger feeles not what he eates:*
> *Hee'l have his Teat e're long (a bloody one)*
> *The Mother then must suck the Son.*

Shunts, bunts, and stunts unknown to common cunts. Lawrence Durrell once said that D.H. Lawrence had only one important idea in his life and that idea was the good fuck, but then Lawrence, he said, screwed that up because "he tried to build the Taj Mahal around fuck." Updike, more of a Methodist, has erected only a colonial church in cunnilingus country.

That country is Tarbox, where men and women have little to say, even to themselves – so they do little more than suck, fuck, and cheat. This breeds boredom. Beyond that boredom, beyond cheating, beyond Piet's dong and the dong of the bell, there's little more to do. *Bong,* no matter how baroque the prose. *Bong.* There is nowhere for Updike to go, not beyond sadness and a kind of sweet, cherry Coke remorse, not with these people. Jerks are jerks. How much story can there be in men and women licking each other off? Lots of pages of lathered prose, but how much story? So, without a story, without an ending that was inevitable in its beginning, "The supernatural must proclaim itself," *deus ex machina:*

A thunderstorm rolls over the town.
Lightning strikes the steeple.

Piet's friend, a dentist, a man who has found the truth in mouthwash, says, "Stop fighting it, Piet baby. We're losers. To live is to lose." He passes a sheet of paper over. "Here it is. Here is your wonderful world." His written list reads:

Baby's fingernails
woman (zzzz)
Bach
Euch.
stars (xxx)
capac.
for self-decep.

XXX. BIG STORM, BIBLICAL STORM.

The cock sees a crack-up and clanging of the elements.

"The Congregational Church is burning. God's own lightning had struck it. The icy rain intensified . . ." Fire and water, water and fire: this is Updike's deluge, this – in Tarbox, of all places – is the local Massachusetts county apocalypse, and the all-seeing eye will be consumed in its own fire.

But as the penny drops, even the blinded see.

Updike's couples stand in the rain on Divinity Street, Prudence Street, Temperance Street. They stare in disbelief as the rain and fire persist as one, they are bewildered as they watch nature make war on herself: it is as if a conflict in God's heart has been bared for them to see. Piet – lacking real conflict in his own heart – is full of gratitude at having been "shown something beyond him, beyond all blaming."

At last the gutted church walls are all that stand. Piet, with nowhere to go and yet still light of heart, has tea with a neighbour woman and, by gum, he gets himself between her sheets and gets himself laid, glad that when the woman comes quickly it is "with grateful cries" – cries and whispers in a bedroom that was, apparently, like many in Tarbox on that apocalyptic night, a bedroom reeking of "wet char and acidulous smoke." Acidulous smoke!

The penny has dropped.

The bedded woman in her orgasmic moment tells Piet that she has "her hopes for god and immortality," but then she comes back to earth and ebbs off into remembrance of fucks past, a friendly couple that she used to swap sex with in the old days, and she says of that neighbourly couple, "Frankly, she was kind of fun, but he was a bore."

Grandma Moses calls it a day.

The Telegram, 1968-72

MARIE-CLAIRE BLAIS

I drove up the Provincetown Road and then into a pinewoods, the branches heavy from October rains. Marie-Claire Blais came out of her cottage, striding forward, wearing a long black skirt and heavy black sweaters, her smile eager but fleeting.

She was small and attractive, round-faced, with a high forehead and a narrowing chin, a pallor that was white but not pasty. There was a bluish porcelain tinge to her skin. Her hands and feet were small, her breasts full. Her direct look had the innocence of sincerity, but a sincerity full of ardour. Black eyebrows. Bangs. The coastal wind blew her hair back.

We sat under an apple tree, the apples unpicked, hanging like little blackening bells or fallen into the long grass, and we talked. All her gestures were graceful, not childlike, but with a modesty that invited protection, a modesty that was seductive as she told me, "After all, each man is born to pain, to sorrow. Each child has something consumptive in his soul." Silly though it was, I felt I should be protecting her from her sorrows, but of course what I had to protect her from was the intrusion of the film-camera eye coming at her from over my shoulder and my need to put an overbearing comforting arm around her. "It does not mean that the child does not laugh," she said, "but it is a loneliness . . ." She laughed. She had a good, open laugh. Aware of the dampness seeping into our bones, we stood up, our shoes clogged in rotted fruit, and walked through the woods. She seemed like such a little girl, her black hair blowing freely in the wind, murmuring quietly when the wet branches wiped across her face. We separated to go around a dwarf pine, and she said:

"This place is good for me. It is very lonely and peaceful. I like the loneliness . . . My time is for walking and reading and thinking."

We circled around a line of white birch trees – white against the black sky. I could hardly see her pallid face for hair. The line of white in the sky widened. We were heading back toward the cottage, but then decided to drive down to the ocean, to one of the high hollows in the dunes. Going through the scrub grass and along the top of the dune we could hear the waves, the surge, and then there they were: the waves, split ends of white on cold grey crests, collapsing, sprawling, thinning on the sand. We looked down the dune. "We are born evil, yes, and with fears, and you feel dependent upon your fears; you cannot escape, particularly in childhood. It is a kind of sickness, the dependence upon your fears." She touched my arm and said, "You have your tragic view of life. I can always see that in your face." I was about to laugh and let her know that a Mayan woman had told me the fish in my fingertips had teeth and needed to feed on tenderness, but I realized I had been assimilated into her view of things, her sense of *angoisse,* which she accepted so cheerfully that she smiled, entirely at ease. She pulled her coat up around her neck, the bright scarf at her throat the only sign of colour on her body.

We ran down the dune toward the ocean, holding hands, half-loping, half-falling forward, and then we walked slowly along the line of spent waves, sidestepping in the sand when a wave rolled close to our feet. "Always it comes, the ocean, with such power, such determination, and then it comes to nothing," she said. Seagulls were criss-crossing, the sky was the milk white that's more usual just before dawn, and then suddenly the sky began to close, to lower, darkening.

We took a winding path back up to the top and turned and looked out over the water. "You know," I said, "I hate to tell you this, but there are moments when what you are writing makes me feel . . . like the worst sin is to be born."

"It is a part of my feeling for life, though I feel the good part, too. Besides, I think my poems are young and gay. I feel they are. Maybe they are not for you. But when I write them, there is a gaiety."

Later, at her cottage:

"You seem completely isolated. In this weather, it seems desolate." I was worried, which was a twist on how it usually is with her; she's always fretting about whether I have been drinking too much, eating enough, gambling too heavily, or whether I am frayed by the conflicts of love – she who eats less than a bird, drinks straight gin, gambles on anything with number combinations or legs, and succumbs to love with joy . . .

"Yes, desolate . . . but I am not completely by myself," she said. "I have friends close by; this place is good for me. It is very lonely and peaceful. I think I will live in this country. I feel free, and that is good. I am more objective, more than I would be in the city. I would not like to go back there, because I have found this freedom here in the country. But then . . . that is how it is now . . . it will not be possible all my life. I will go to Québec again, I think, eventually . . . But now, when I return from time to time I am sad and not very hopeful. They are involved and very serious about their problems. They are passionate and there are some who like violence, who need it, but I try to understand though I do not approve of violence. There is confusion, they are not happy, they feel humiliated. Perhaps they sometimes fight against themselves. Anyway, emotions always change and give you the enemy to love again . . . but still, we are born with fears; we cannot escape, particularly in childhood."

"Escape?"

"From fear – *la peur* – it is not rational at all. It is a kind of sickness, the dependence upon your fears. Mind you, children have very peaceful moments, a sweet and completely peaceful state. Life can be very fresh as well as frightening. I never deny that there is beauty in life. Other writers will speak often about it and I will speak more about it when I want. But up to now in my novels I have been interested in the problems – *le problème du mal* – good and evil."

Mary Meigs appeared. She was a painter, a lean, handsome woman who had a natural elegance, but it was a naturalness so undercut by shyness that she seemed at a loss, embarrassed. She ducked her head. There was something resolute about her in the firmness of her mouth, but also something wary, vulnerable. We shook hands and she gave us two glasses of cranberry juice, which we drank, and then Meigs disappeared. Blais seemed thoughtful, as if she wanted to explain more of herself:

"I always change. I feel that I am always being born again, destroyed again. It is never all positive or negative. I like to live, I like to feel new and fresh. This sadness is not always there."

"When'll you write about people who did not destroy each other?"

"I make progress," she answered with a laugh. "There is a difference these days, a difference. I am not so tragic. Now there is a sense of humour . . . it is a difference that will come . . . soon . . ."

CBC's *Show On Shows; The Tamarack Review;*
The Telegram, 1964-65-68

BLACK LIGHT

It is true that I tell stories, but I am also a translator. I don't think of myself as a translator but the three poets I know personally, the poets I've translated at length – men from Paris, Beograd, and Riga – tell me I am. They say that I've sung inside their skins. It's strange hearing a man tell you that you are in his skin. They say they hear themselves in my voice. What can I tell you? Maybe they are right. How would I know? I only speak a little French and don't speak Serbian or Latvian at all.

Once, in Paris, I took part in a translation workshop. There were poets from many countries. We translated poems into French. We talked about the elasticity of words. We talked about that silent music that lies between the lines of good poetry. We agreed you can't translate the music if you can't hear it, and too many translators not only have a tin ear, they are tone deaf.

"What's a tin ear?" a translator from Paris asked.

"Everything sounds like canned music."

"Canned?"

So I said, "And what's worse, even if they can hear, it's like how people clap hands to the blues. White people clap on the 2-4 and black people clap on the 1-3, and that's why you don't hardly ever get a good drummer in a European jazz band, because they're always keeping the beat somewhere between the 1-3 and the 2-4."

"But surely," a man from Paris said, "etymology is where we must begin. Without etymology . . ."

"Nope," I said, "if you're going to translate someone like John Berryman, you've got to hear the syncopation, and his syncopation comes because the breath breaks are the silences of an alcoholic who's come up short for air, and then once you get that, you have to accept the thing that's really impossible to get in translation, and that's the intonation."

"But surely the intonation is right there in the meaning of the words."

"Nope. You take just about the most famous words in American public life – in Lincoln talking at Gettysburg, when he said, 'Government of the people, by the people, for the people' – and most folks put the stress on the prepositions, on the *of*, the *by*, the *for*, which makes it all an action by the government, but try reading that with the stress, the beat, on *the people*: 'Government of *the people*, by *the people*, for *the people*,' and it's not only an ideological difference, it's like the difference between the 2-4 and the 1-3. It's like there's music in a major key and music in a minor key.

"Berryman's a poet who sings in a minor key; he dances on the black notes. And the perfect music to play behind him is Irving Berlin, who composed all his songs in F-sharp – he composed and played only on the black notes."

That meeting in Paris did not end well. Or perhaps it ended as it had to end, in silence, a silence that had no music. The men and women who were the serious translators, who had their etymologies in order, got tired of listening to poets talk about silent music. They wanted to get down to matters like post-modernism, the influence of Lévi-Strauss, structuralism, Derrida, feminine endings applied to masculine words as a feminist political tactic within translation strategies, Foucault, etc. etc. My mind went blank. Other poets slumped in their chairs. We smiled a lot. The grammarians smiled. They were having a good time, they'd got into stride. Words flew, but "Joy within me dallied with distress." I began to daydream of old poets, the boys who had been to Mount Abora and back, and how anyone who'd ever seen one of the old poets would cry

> *. . . Beware! Beware!*
> *His flashing eyes, his floating hair!*
> *Weave a circle round him thrice,*
> *And close your eyes with holy dread,*
> *For he on honeydew hath fed,*
> *And drunk the milk of Paradise.*

The grammarians, the theoreticians, the etymologists, the guys who really knew something about language, they were pleased. They had measured "twice five miles of fertile ground" where "Alph, the sacred river, ran." They'd put everything in perspective. When they were done, one said, "I know a very good restaurant just behind the Sulpice Church. Cooking from Lyon: tripe, wonderful marrow on toast."

I love marrow on toast with rough sea salt, but I declined. Actually, I was brooding on Keats and he wasn't given to tripe. He was given to Shakespeare.

There's a puzzling thing about Shakespeare. He's no Norman Mailer. Everybody knows Mailer in the same way that everybody knows Hamlet, Macbeth, Lear. But nobody knows Shakespeare. He must have had an ego. He could not have created those characters without knowing how good he was. Yet he is not there. He disappeared into Hamlet and Lear and all the others. This fascinated Keats. Shakespeare was everywhere and nowhere.

Shakespeare, to get hold of the full, though elusive, concreteness of reality, had negated his own ego . . . he had submerged his self-centred consciousness of his own identity in order to become something bigger, the world around him. Keats called this negative capability. Shakespeare had negative capability in spades. He became negative space. He was the first black-light performer in history.

This is what the translator has to be, too, a black-light man, seldom appearing as more than a pair of white hands working in the dark. There's a freedom that comes with working in the dark, "a freedom," as Sartre said, "that resolutely puts itself into a state of passivity to obtain a certain transcendent effect by this sacrifice . . ." And what happens? After the translator has created what the poet has disclosed, both are compromised by their generosity.

As I've said, I know some French. I don't really regard myself as a translator, although I have eight and a half collections behind me (the half was a collaboration in compromise with my old friend Ray Ellenwood). So the real question is, What led me to translate a poet from a language I know nothing about whatsoever? – which I happen to have done with three books.

I'm happy to explain what is involved, to describe the mystery of the experience.

The fine, and singular, French poet Robert Marteau, for some strange reason unknown to man or beast, decided to translate a book of my poems called *The Hogg Poems.*

After we met he gave me a book called *Atlante,* one of his collections. It's a series of four- and five-line poems, very hermetic, and I decided because Robert was translating my work – and he is a brilliant translator – that I'd take a crack at it. I'd never translated before. I did about thirty of these little poems and realized I was in over my head, but decided to keep going out of tenacity. Michel Deguy, the French poet, laughed and told me, "Ha! You have picked the most difficult of all our poets." The book, when I was finished, received good reviews in the learned journals, which amused me enormously because I knew I was skating on thin ice. Then, a few years later, when I was living in Paris completing *The Black Queen Stories*, a collection of Marteau's work came out in English in the United States. He had given me another book of his, the *Traité*, which I found really remarkable. I read the translations in the U.S. collection and wrote to Robert telling him I thought it was unbearable that these beautiful poems were so haltingly translated. I set to work, and within a year I finished this book, which was again well received, to my amusement.

Then, the next year, life got very strange because I discovered that Marteau had translated a book by a Serbian poet, Miodrag Pavlović. I was back living in Toronto. Pavlović, the founder of modern Yugoslavian poetry, one of the most important Serbian poets, had appeared in Polish, French, German, Turkish, and Spanish. He was on a reading tour and he phoned and came around for supper. I found out that the English versions of his poems that he was reading were awful, were inept. He gave me a rough English version of *Singing at the Whirlpool* to work with. These poems are Pavlović's search for human experience in the culture of Lepenski Vir (the whirlpool), a neolithic site discovered in the valley of the Danube. Dating from 6000 BC, the remains of solid buildings and foundations, sacrificial hearths, and stone sculptures indicate that people had lived in a productive fishing and hunting community or, more accurately, a congregational meeting place, like Jericho or Çatal Hüyük. The great Danubian whirlpools provided ideal fishing conditions for these folk. Their stone carvings, featuring highly articulated faces, are the first monumental stone sculptures in the world, sculptures that, like early Eskimo carvings, appear to let the lines of the face emerge out of the animus of the limestone. The people, with their cult of the head, had a deep sense of human dignity. Pavlović had imagined a poet of that community and he had sung in his name. Now I was going to sing in that whirlpool poet's name, taking a gift of tongue from Pavlović. Bizarre. But I'd got a sense of the rhythm (I'd once studied Russian and so could get the Cyrillic sound), and I checked with Pavlović and all seemed to be fine when the book was published, but I could not know for sure because I still don't have any Serbian.

I thought I was done. Then I got a packet from Paris. Marteau had sent me his Gallimard edition of *Pavlović: La voix sous la pierre.* I understood. Since he had not told me what to do, I knew what he expected me to do. For two years, using Marteau's French version of the Serbian – trusting his version because Marteau is a fastidious man whose feel for the word is sacred, each word a seed – I worked on Pavlović's poems. Then I met with Pavlović in Beograd. He is a linguist, adept at English. We made a few changes. We walked late at night through the dinge-lighting of Beograd streets, following men wielding great leaping hoses, men sweeping the streets clean with long brooms made of willow branches. I did more work. Finally I said, "Okay, here it is." Pavlović was beamish. "Beautiful," he said. "Just right. You are me."

"Well," I said, "the guy we've really got to thank and bless is Marteau. After all, I don't know any Serbian, so I trusted his French completely."

"Ah," Pavlović said, smiling, "but Marteau, he doesn't know any Serbian either."

All I can say about translation is what the old whirlpool poet said to me as he spoke through the dreams of the poet Pavlović – what the old poet said about how the body and the soul are compromised by their generosity as they become one:

Body and Soul	*Тело и Дух*
A stone	*Камен*
seminates itself	*оплођуое себе*
surmounted	*с леђа*
by its shadow	*помоћу сенке*

il cannochiale, 1994

THE BUTLER'S BOOT AND THE KITCHEN SINK

Not so long ago the important dramatists in England were Terence Rattigan, James Bridie and Agatha Christie, Graham Greene, Christopher Fry, and T. S. Eliot. Of an evening in London's West End, a well-heeled audience would applaud when Maurice Evans or Bea Lillie or David Niven came to grips with a dyspeptic wife who had dyed her hair or a sister who had fled to Paris to find love beyond the pale of the parsonage.

On a weightier level, Eliot and Greene gave the West End religion. But, as dramatist John Arden has said, "I have no sympathy with T. S. Eliot's attempts to make verse sound like Noel Coward comedy . . . You get them in there and make them think they are listening to a comedy, and then you insert religion. I find this distasteful . . . It's a way of deceiving the audience." Actually, rather than Coward, *The Cocktail Party* plays like ecclesiastical Kipling.

No matter: West End audiences have paid for their pews and paid for their ersatz prayer, insisting that their plays be about their own kind, the well-bred, thinly educated echelons of the Establishment, among whom "sex is cellophaned" – as Graham Greene has put it – and the main issues are property and propriety. It was, and still is, a truth acknowledged over lunch at the Savoy that servants and tenants, the lower orders, do not have manners, and certainly do not have glamour. They are "that cretinous boy with the sudden look of cunning in his eyes and that awful painted oversexed girl." They are Irishmen and cockneys; they are quaint, simian, and thigh-slappingly funny.

Joan Littlewood, the director, said not long ago, "In the theatre of those dear, departed days when every actress had roses round her vowels, and a butler's suit was an essential part of an actor's equipment, the voice of the cockney was one long whine of blissful servitude. No play was complete without its moronic maid or faithful batman – rich with that true cockney speech and humour learned in the drama schools."

Actors and directors came out of those schools convinced that the major twentieth-century playwright was William Shakespeare. As Littlewood said, "Even the great English classics were produced and acted as if they had been conceived by Edwardian old ladies seated at their embroidery." These old ladies and actors had secured a certain tone, a certain style. They were glitteringly eloquent even when they were self-deprecating. They indulged in a frigid wit. They pranced. They minced. They had a polished dishonesty. Sometimes they acted like poofters on parade. When they were leaping about the stage with rapier in hand or (as Jeeves) gently jibing their betters, they maintained a fastidious pigeon-toed poise. And a peculiar gallantry that allowed characters to be serious about the frivolous and frivolous about the serious. Either way would do, for as John Gielgud remarked, "When we acted in Chekhov we didn't understand what his plays were about at all." Terence Rattigan sneered at *Waiting for Godot* as Beckett baffled them completely. But caustic or catty, they were rewarded: Sir Ralph Richardson, Sir Michael Redgrave, Sir Alec Guinness, Sir Laurence Olivier, and Sir John Gielgud. With rapiers in hand they could cut silk, but actors do not make a theatre.

Toward the end of the last century, no writer of significance – with the exception of the Irishman Oscar Wilde – was working in the London playhouses. Audiences wanted farce and melodrama, spectaculars and romantic intrigue. And they got it. But on the Continent and in Ireland, Ibsen, Strindberg, and

Chekhov, Pirandello, Hauptmann, and Synge had arrived. Their plays had the bite of truth. Sometimes the bite festered and the truth was an open wound. Shaw and O'Casey left Ireland for England but Shaw soon heaped scorn on the London dramatists and O'Casey was enraged by the English critics who said that he should try to learn stage craftsmanship from Emlyn Williams.

From 1900 to 1930, England stood *en point* with Henry Arthur Jones, Sir Arthur Wing Pinero, Gilbert and Sullivan, John Galsworthy, Harley Granville-Barker, and James Barrie. England then did a turn through another twenty years with Maugham, Coward, Rattigan, Fry, and Greene. Their stalwart audience stood flat-footed in their pews, singing:

The rich man in his castle.
The poor man at his gate,
God made them, high or lowly,
And order'd their estate.

As late as 1949 Arthur Miller's *Death of a Salesman* failed in the West End because the London audiences couldn't take Willie Loman with his sample cases full of drummer's goods seriously, and if ever in those heady post-war days a cockney, perhaps a veteran of Dunkirk, got uppity and forgot his place – as in Coward's *Cavalcade* – and spoke of the dark side of his desires, he was promptly and satisfyingly trampled on stage by horses. As one of Coward's characters said with brittle bravado, "Let's be superficial and pity the poor philosophers. Let's blow trumpets and squeakers and enjoy the party as much as we can, like very small, idiotic schoolchildren."

Then, in 1956, *Rhinoceros* and *Waiting for Godot* were performed in London and John Osborne presented *Look Back in Anger*. Kenneth Tynan gave *Look Back in Anger* an extravagant review in *The Observer*. Jimmy Porter, the angry, complaining hero, was certainly in bad taste; there was no table for him at the Savoy; propriety was not his strong suit; he had no social grace or sense of place. Rather than trivial and flippant, he was brash and bellicose.

All at once there were men and women writing plays who had little education and owned no property, workers who paid their own way. Shelagh Delaney, an usherette, had not completed grammar school. Brendan Behan, the Dublin import, was a Borstal boy, ex-IRA man, and a house painter. N. F. Simpson was a London schoolteacher. And there were Jews. Harold Pinter, like Osborne, had been a minor repertory actor. Bernard Kops, whose father was a shoemaker, sold books at a street stall. Arnold Wesker, son of a communist tailor, had worked as a plumber and a pastry cook. These playwrights, like the gypsies of John Arden's play *Live Like Pigs*, left no hollyhock unturned as they overran the sensibilities of decent reticent people, and treated them like pigs.

Joan Littlewood, embattled, on her toes, and ready to step on someone else's, too, opened the Stratford Theatre Royal by introducing Behan and Delaney, and Behan's play *The Hostage*, set in a brothel, found its aggressive energy in smart bog talk and Sinn Fein music hall routines:

Who fears to speak of Easter Week,
That week of famed renown,
When the boys in green went out to fight
The forces of the Crown.

For six long days we held them off,
At odds of ten to one,
And through our lines they could not pass,
For all their heavy guns.

And deadly poison gas they used,
To try to crush Sinn Fein,
And burnt our Irish capital,
Like Germans did Louvain.

They shot our leaders in a jail,
Without a trial, they say,
They murdered women and children,
Who in their cellars lay,

And dug their grave with gun and spade,
To hide them from our view.
Because they could neither kill nor catch
The rebel so bold and true.

After this song a negro paraded through the brothel carrying a placard: KEEP IRELAND BLACK. The actors, black Irish in their hearts – and wanting to extend the rebellion – improvised on stage so that all their play books were altered from night to night, causing the censor to lose his strict control of scripts, his strict control of the stage – his strict control of the tramps and labourers, prostitutes and junior clerks, negroes, worn-out vaudevillians, and homosexuals. They were no longer ugly and funny. The funny people were the paying customers parked in their plush seats, and they were so funny that the lunatics of Charenton, after they had finished their performance of *Marat/Sade,* lined up on stage and mocked them, giving them a round of applause as if they were trained fur-bearing animals.

Journalists tagged the new dramatists, along with novelists like John Wain, Kingsley Amis, and John Braine, "the angry young men." After Arnold Wesker said "For Shakespeare, the whole world was a stage; for me it's a kitchen," the critics slanged the new drama, calling it "theatre of the kitchen sink." P. G. Wodehouse held his nose and wrote: "I wish the boys who are writing today would stop being so frightfully powerful and significant and give us a little comedy occasionally. I am all for incest and wrecked lives and tortured souls in moderation, but a good laugh from time to time never hurt anybody." Wodehouse and his ilk turned positively grumpy when Sir Laurence Olivier played the lead in Osborne's *The Entertainer*, and he became an old grouse after Arnold Wesker's trilogy was performed at the Royal Court Theatre. When Harold Pinter wrote *The Caretaker* it seemed to Noel Coward and the Savoy lunch crowd that Gorky's grim "creatures who once were men" had come to the West End not just to visit but to nest in the house.

The critics who admired these "kitchen-sink" writers went off half-cocked. Kenneth Tynan had no sooner said (accurately) that Fry's *The Lady's Not for Burning* had the effect of a swimming instructor giving lessons in an empty pool than he turned around and wrote that *Look Back in Anger* would remain a minority taste, but "what matters is the size of the minority. I estimate it at roughly 6 733 000, which is the number of people in this country between the ages of twenty and thirty. And this figure will doubtless be swelled by refugees from other age-groups who are curious to know precisely what the contemporary young pup is thinking and feeling. I doubt I could love anyone who did not wish to see *Look Back in Anger*. It is the best young play of its decade."

The London critics and audiences were spellbound by zest – but it was the zest of performance, of wit without tears. Gielgud and Olivier were joined by Robert Bolt and Joan Plowright, who made *Roots* seem so compelling, and Albert Finney, who managed to hold John Arden's *Armstrong's Last Goodnight* together, and Nicol Williamson, who transformed Osborne's bad play – *Inadmissible Evidence* – into good entertainment. And if there was zest upon the stage could nobility be far behind? Nigel Dennis said that Wesker's *Chips with Everything* was "one of the noblest tributes to the English fighting man since *Henry V*," and after he completed his trilogy, Wesker was hailed as the English Brecht by Robert Wraight, who wrote, "I have already called the author, twenty-seven-year-old Arnold Wesker, a better writer than John Osborne . . . I have no hesitation in calling him the best of the new generation of British playwrights." The English critics had gone to the tea party, the hatters were in business, but Wesker himself warned that "the danger to all of us young playwrights is that we are being treated as masters of our craft, whereas, in fact, we are only just starting. If we are getting rather more notice than usual, it is because the general standard of play writing is so abysmally low. We should not be treated as geniuses. We are only youngsters just beginning."

Noel Coward, of course, readily agreed. In his play *Present Laughter* he had his mouthpiece, an old playwright, Gary, spritz a young playwright, Roland:

> To begin with, your play is not a play at all. It's a meaningless jumble of adolescent, pseudo intellectual poppycock. It bears no relation to the theatre or to life or to anything . . . If you wish to be a playwright you just leave the theatre of tomorrow to take care of itself. Go and get yourself a job as a butler in a repertory company if they'll have you. Learn from the ground up how plays are constructed and what is actable and what isn't. Then sit down and write at least twenty plays one after the other, and if you can manage to get the twenty-first produced for a Sunday night performance you'll be damned lucky!

A. Alvarez dismissed Coward out of hand and said Wesker had set out not only to record "the history of a lively radical East End Jewish family, but to write the political chronicle of the last quarter century . . . Wesker is the first young writer to attempt a whole portrait of the age."

Nonsense. There is a woodenness to Wesker's plays: he is earnest; he won't let his characters be who they are. He has bigger ambitions for them than they have for themselves. In his plays, vacuous comedy has given way to vacuous preachifying. And after all is said, the class system, the dreaded estates, are still in place. Except now it is the butlers who are mincingly affected in their pessimism, cloying in their self-pity, and opportunistic in their sense of preferment. Once again the stalwart are standing flat-footed in their pews, but this time they are singing:

What's it all about, Alfie?
Is it just for the moment we live?
What's it all about when you sort it out, Alfie?
Are we meant to take more than we give?

Arnold Wesker has drive, he has talent. So have Pinter, Behan, Osborne, and Arden. But not one – with the possible exception of Pinter (who Tynan, astonishingly, has recently dismissed as a "cool, apolitical stylist") – is a dramatist of the first order. They are deeply indebted to Genet, Beckett, O'Neill, Brecht, and Williams. The English stage is still an island affair, only the boot is now on the butler's foot.

The Telegram, 1966-1973

ALAN SILLITOE: PIP IN OUR TIME

Alan Sillitoe slumped in his chair and let his head hang to one side. His long hair fell over his forehead. He was staring at the floor, a small man hunched up in himself, and then, like a hair-trigger had been hit, he let loose a clip of words: "I have a sort of feeling in England that there is a potential of revolution which may one day break forth. You see, England is difficult from the point of view of doing anything that seems worthwhile and everyone is totally fragmented and made to seem quite useless and they feel some sort of destiny of insignificance. Therefore a sort of anarchy comes out of this but it's an anarchy not of positive values, but a – I don't care – half-hearted pathetic destructiveness."

His hands, his arms, his legs, his face . . . there seemed to be a simmering anger in his bones, but only his quick, tight lips moved. And he seldom looked at me. His eyes flitted between two points on the floor and then he shied back and away as if sensing a threat in the air. But it was not the gesture of a frightened man; there was something wary and cold and tough and intransigent behind his monotone, an irascible, resentful energy that he managed to keep muffled.

"When I was fourteen I stepped into a factory and there was a great sense of anarchy and the world belongs to me and I'm a worker so therefore I have the right to enjoy myself, and anyone who tries to stop me, well, you know, they don't know what they're talking about and I'd show them and tell them. That was my attitude and it's an attitude I sympathize with because they're people who have a hard life. I enjoyed work in a factory because it gave me a terrific amount of self-respect."

His head jolted back again, as if he had been cold-cocked, clipped on the jaw, and then there was a rising, shrill challenge in his tone as he stuttered and fell into a reflective sullenness. He said: "I suppose there's plenty of violence around. You see, it depends. It's a very difficult situation. If you're writing about people whose normal method of resolving problems is not by discussion or argument, then sooner or later violence is bound to occur. This is only to be realistic. You always have this final flashpoint in mind, because it happens in life."

I read to him from *Saturday Night and Sunday Morning*, read his hero's bawling defiance: "Factories and labour exchanges and insurance offices keep us alive and kicking – so they say – but they're booby-traps and will suck you under like sinking-sands if you aren't careful. Sweat factories sweat you to death, insurance and income tax offices milk money from your wage packets and rob you to death. And if you're still left with a tiny bit of life in your guts after all this buggering about, the army calls you up and you get shot to death."

He lifted his head, and he seemed to be looking at my eyes rather than into them. "That is," he said, "in fact, shall we say, my basic ethos."

We went on talking about his novels, his admiration for the Russians, his loathing for the slumminess of England, about anarchy and the class structure. It all seemed flat, swallowed up in the determined blandness of his presence. But then, bland is not quite the right word, because there was coiled energy in his body, something maniacal about the hurried precision of his words, the detached but precise way in which he talked of violence, those eyes, soft brown and friendly, but furtive, on the move. He left me feeling as if he had ridden sidesaddle through the conversation, as if he – or, more unsettling – as if I had been only half there.

After reading Sillitoe's new collection of short stories, *Guzman Go Home*, I have come to understand something about his work, something about the feel of that afternoon conversation.

Sillitoe's successful stories have a strange power. There is a thrust at work in them. Of course, much of that thrust comes from his extraordinary flow of, and ear for, the language "as she is spoke," his rhythms, but this is only a partial explanation for the drive the reader feels. There is more than the energy of the language itself, and the answer I think is this: Sillitoe's adult characters live in the world of the terrified child, as I understand that world in the work of someone like Dickens. In *Great Expectations*, for example, Pip and others are continually assaulted, pummelled and pounded not by ideas but by actual blows and bodies that come out of nowhere like cannonballs. This pounding is gratuitous, or at least it seems so to the victims, who are defenceless. Even worse, men and women are able to express their emotions only in terms of detached, mechanical movements, like a wagging finger or a mouth that opens and shuts like a mailbox. And as these men become more mechanical, nature comes alive with a vengeance: the fog chokes, weeds clutch, the dampness clings, the air coils . . . This is a fragmented and splintered world full of threat and chagrin in which the adult, like a child, is buffeted by forces too large to comprehend, too swift to avoid. Money is the motor and the matter. Dickens' characters become terror-ridden, neurotic, and dissociated from themselves. Too often they are so out of whack with themselves and the world that they either build moats around their homes and disappear into a dream idyll or commit grave acts and only become aware of their crimes long after the deed has been done. The same is true of Sillitoe's characters. They inhabit a child's world of fear and, like children, they are unable to cope with the unfairness of the inexplicable outside world. And there is little or no respite in Sillitoe's world. There is no Little Nell or Little Dorrit, ready to forgive, bolster, and comfort.

In the story "Revenge," a couple well on in years get married. No sooner is their wedding reception over than some perverse force takes hold of them. He insults her, unable to brake his tongue. Then he discovers that in the midst of their sniping he has actually bitten his tongue; he knows this only because blood has filled his mouth. Confronted by the table of wedding presents, he is compelled to smash them to pieces with a poker, and, when done, he muses wonderingly, "I must have taken my time over it, because Caroline had her coat on, a suitcase by her side that she'd gone to Butlin's with the year before. 'Right,' I said, sitting exhausted on one of the stools, 'going home are you?'" These newlyweds have no choice but destruction, of themselves and each other, and each blow they deliver is a fresh surprise, unanticipated, and undefended by either of them.

Dickensian touches abound in "Revenge," and all the other stories: a man is "one four-eyed bowler hat," "the eyelids of the traffic lights lifted," "his reactions would mesh into gear," and so on. But the ghastly situation is summed up in a story called "Chicken." A young man named Dave has stolen a bird, brought it home, and cut off its head. The chicken fights "harder now for its life than when it still had a head left to fight for and think with." Pumping blood into the air, the bird charges all over the yard and into a neighbour's kitchen, causing havoc and enmity. This maimed bird is like one of Sillitoe's characters: zigzagging through life with a mindless cunning and a desperate energy in the blood – an energy, even as it flows, that is cut off from awareness. This is Pip in our time, a headless chicken.

The Telegram, 1966-1970

COUNTING MY STEPS: JAKOV LIND

I can see behind you in the doorway,
The police cap and the white-faced concierge.

Men refuse to believe they are going to their deaths. They put on clean underwear, they pocket a photograph. And slip a fob watch into a pocket, too. They shake hands with the policeman after he has closed the door. They congratulate the executioner, they hope for the best. They step into a crowded room, are promised a shower, and, too late, they die screaming. And the outside air, in the shadow of the smoke, turns sweet. And then sour. Sour with the shame of those who say they should have put up a fight. Those who've never been arrested in the night. Those who've never stood in their bare feet on a cold floor in front of men who have all the guns.

In Israel, out on the Abu Gosh road, a young Israeli paratrooper – my driver – said to me, "You know, we Jews here do not speak Ashkenazit Hebrew. We speak Sephardic, because we loathe the ones who went to die with no protest, and Ashkenazit and Yiddish is what they spoke. We will never be like those Jews."

He looked at me. Hard. Unflinching. I looked at him. "They liked too much their cake," he said. He sounded angry. Personally affronted. He was handsome, he had shining teeth. He wanted me to believe that he would never shake hands with his killer, that he would survive or die behind a gun. "Yiddish," he said "What do you expect? A mongrel language."

Jakov Lind is a Viennese Jew who was brought up in the *echt Deutsch* lower middle class before the war. He was the son of a travelling salesman who did not care about money or religion or his family, a salesman who sat in cafés and felt smug and superior, a Viennese boulevardier in galoshes. His son Jakov was bred in the father's image. Then the Nazis decided to clean up the *refuse* in their Thousand-Year Reich, clean up the vermin, the Jews, gypsies, cripples, etc., etc. The Nazis went from house to house. They were punctual, they were precise. Sometimes they were polite. They were nothing if not efficient. Who could believe such normal, clear-eyed, middle-class men could want to be so good at killing?

Young Jakov Lind was not fooled. He believed the Nazis were killers, serious Jew-killers, and he hated those among his neighbours who did not: "Chairs and armchairs were covered with sheets to protect the furniture from dust, as they might not be back for some time. They had washed up the kitchen and polished every pot. The empty milk bottles were neatly lined up on the doorstep. That's the way they wanted to go . . . like the clean and correct citizens they'd always been. That's why I stayed behind. I wanted to have nothing to do with these people, this bunch of remote relatives . . . Living for generations among people who wished to wipe them out, the Jews were ready to be wiped out. They, too, believed in this final solution . . . I began to hate the Jews. Not only the orthodox, but all of them . . . They were a rotten lot and one should get rid of them . . . I had to hate because I love life. I love to remain among those who breathe."

Jakov went into hiding. Scared to death, he got inside his own skin and he became Jan Gerrit Overbeek, he became a *goy*, a Dutch boy labourer. As Overbeek he grew reckless, he dared to say loud and clear to all and sundry that he hated the Nazis. They were beasts. He became an overbearing Dutch patriot; he narrowed his soft eyes and stared policemen down. It was insane. He felt safe feeling insane: "It's insane to walk about freely when you're supposed to be sitting in some camp. Insane maybe, but it also makes one contented and happy to be that insane. Schizophrenia did not hurt for a change. To be schizophrenic is to be normal; unreality is reality. I was both – Overbeek for the world and Jakov Lind for this other world . . ."

Overbeek sat in cafés among doddering old-age pensioners and ate cake. He licked his lips. He ate more cake. He was a freak, but he was a freak determined to survive: "It was good to be alive while being dead." He took to wearing a Gestapo hat. In his Gestapo hat he was sure that he had vanished into thin air, like the Hebrew letters he saw in a synagogue that had been turned into a Nazi dance hall.

Letters. Hats. Papers. Identity. A shadow.

He was anyone, he was no one. Insanity was sanity. He'd moved into a separate state: the state of unsane, where "everything is human, especially wars . . . In a war, nobody's innocent. Or everybody. Innocence is an obsolete concept . . ."

He watched as Jews were rounded up in Amsterdam, The Hague, and Rotterdam. To outfox the police, he went deeper into the state of unsane. He became a whirligig of unpersons, all as normal as they were unreal: he became a farm worker, a sailor boy, a collaborator, an outspoken anti-Semite, and then, once in Germany, he became an outspoken defender of Jews, courting death in Berlin, where – as it turned out – he ended the war as a confidant to a high-ranking Nazi metallurgist. Surrounded by apathy, terror, brutality, and banality, he sensed, with rage, how comic and ludicrous his survival was. Yet he *was* alive, he *was*, living at his nerve ends, and that was better than death.

When the war was over he "had nothing left but my bare skin. Everything else had gone. No Zionism, no idealism. No love and no hatred and no language . . . I simply didn't care for others who emerged from their dugouts. I just couldn't care less. I had dug my own shelter when they went by charter to Auschwitz. I hated them both again – Jews and Germans. The first because they aroused my pity, the second because they could claim my gratitude. I had survived as one of them. I hated myself and them, doubly."

Jakov Lind went to Palestine. He was the last man to get off the boat and, while other Jews hugged and wept and danced on the shores of the Promised Land, he squatted and had a good shit. As for Jerusalem, it "turned out to be another very cramped town, with some rich and very many poor. Just like Vienna . . . In Europe all Jews had belonged to the nice, kind, generous, and tolerant species of man. The coarse, rude, hostile, nasty, and mean people were *goyim*. But suddenly, wherever you go, a lot of *goyim* claiming to be Jews are thronging the streets . . . feverish, anxious, and ruthless . . ."

Jacov Lind had shed the skin of Overbeek the *goy* only to stand – as Lind the Jew – among *goyim* who were Jewish.

But, after all, among Zionists this is how it was intended.

In January 1933, at the fourth conference of the Zionist Histadrut, one of the labour leaders had delivered a message from the platform that went like this: "What is *hachsharah* [Zionist vocational training]? . . . First of all, preparation for Gentile jobs, the self-preparation of the Jewish worker to become a Gentile . . . to do Gentile work . . . to make a profit the way Gentiles do . . . The Jewish village girl shall live like a Gentile country girl," etc., etc.

The purpose of *hachsharah* was, therefore, not only to turn the Jewish shopkeeper into a worker and the Jewish *schlump* into a soldier, but to teach him how to live inside the skin of the Gentile. And if he was to live inside a Gentile, he had to turn away from a *qualitatively* different Jewish existence, turn away from a view of life that had been cultivated by Jews since the destruction of the second temple, when the Jews became – as many holy men have since put it – a spiritual people who not only had an aversion to power as exercised by people like the Romans but – by accepting the role of sacrificial victim – had become agents of the redemption of the world. Consoling the Jews of Yemen in the year 1172, Maimonides wrote:

> Our nation speaks with pride of the virulent oppression it has suffered, and the sore tribulations it has endured, to quote the words of the Psalmist, "Nay, but for Thy sake are we killed all the day." The rabbis, of blessed memory, in Midrash Hasita, remark that the verse, "Nay, but for Thy sake" alludes to the generation that undergoes persecution. Let those persons exult who suffered dire persecutions, lost their riches, were forced into exile and were deprived of all their belongings. For the bearing of these hardships is a source of glory and a great achievement in the sight of God. Whoever is visited by these calamities is like a burnt offering upon the altar. We may also apply in commendation the verse to them, "Consecrate yourselves today to the Lord, that He may also bestow upon you a blessing this day."

More explicit was the Midrashic comment to which Maimonides referred:

> As the dove is chaste, so are the Jews chaste. As the dove stretches out her neck to the slaughter, so do the Jews, for it is said, "Nay, but for Thy sake are we killed all the day." As the dove atones for sins, so do the Jews atone for the nations, for the seventy oxen which they offer on the festivals represent the seventy peoples, so that the world may not become depopulated of them, as it says, "In

> return for my love are they become my adversaries, but I pray." As the dove, from the hour when she recognizes her mate, does not change him, so the Jews, from the time when they recognized the Holy One, have not changed Him.

This revolutionary redemptive tradition has been cast off by those who have taken power and exercised power in Israel since 1948. "Never again," they said, and still say. "We will never be like those Jews," my paratrooper said. All that an anti-Zionist philosopher like the German Jew Hermann Cohen could say in return was, "Those bums, they want to be *happy*!"

The paratrooper led me up a short flight of stairs and into an elevator (Jakov Lind, having returned to live on the Continent, will never carry an Uzi . . .) and then he led me out of the elevator into a cluttered, unpretentious office, where he said, "And this is Deputy Prime Minister Ygal Allon," whom I knew of as a general in the underground, in the Palmach, which was a striking force, the general who – it was said – had been in charge of the southern command and had fought especially well in clearing out Arab villages in the war of 1948.

He was handsome, not lean but trim. He had a surprising lack of sternness for a soldier. Still, he was tough in the eyes, though there were laughter lines at the corners of his eyes. He spoke warmly, openly: "In a way, yes, we have become here a normal nation. Everything is Jewish. Farmers are Jews. Workers are Jews. Philosophers are Jews. Soldiers. Thieves. Everybody is a Jew. Fine."

"It's a bit of a shock," I said, "to see Jewish prostitutes in the country. I'd never seen a Jewish prostitute in my life."

"I'm surprised, my dear, that you discovered them so quickly." With a rollicking laugh he went on, saying, "Anyhow, in spite of being normal in every aspect of the word, there is one aspect in which we are still abnormal. We are the only one, the only nation on earth that cannot afford a defeat, because if we are defeated in war we are finished."

"There are differing kinds of defeats . . . moral defeats . . ."

"Look, in the Palmach we attached tremendous importance to the moral education of our members. In the planning of our operations we did our best to avoid unnecessary killing. Today, with the new strategy of nuclear weapons, there is the expression *overkill.* We," and he said this with no hint of the sanctimonious or piety, "we did our best to *underkill* . . ."

"I would ask, if – by stressing moral values – if now you are not making it more difficult for your soldiers to kill?"

"It's true."

"Every time they pull the trigger they are aware of what they are doing. Whereas normally one assumes that with most soldiers they get in the habit of it."

"No, my dear, as long as they feel embarrassed whenever they have to kill it is good. I don't want them to do it in a professional way. Of course, they are all well trained and very professional as far as the regular skills are concerned, but as long as a soldier feels that he has to justify what he has done – to himself, not necessarily to his commander – it is a very good sign. I believe this protects us," he said, reaching toward me, the *goy*, with both hands, "from becoming beasts."

He smiled. "Would you take some tea?"

Caught off-guard, I said nothing.

"Tea?"

"Yes."

An assistant, a young soldier wearing a short-sleeved army shirt open at the throat, brought tea to the desk that was between us. The tea was in clear glasses on white saucers, slices of lemon on the saucers. The glasses were burning hot. He leaned over his glass and inhaled.

"Fine. Good," he said.

"Good," I said.

Out of the corner of my eye I saw, standing in the doorway, my driver, the paratrooper. For some reason there was a little curl of disapproval to his lip.

The Telegram; CBC's *Israel,* 1969-70

STEPHEN LEACOCK: OUT IN NO MAN'S LAND

Many intelligent men and women make pilgrimages to Stephen Leacock's estate at Old Brewery Bay near Orillia. It is a quiet unsheltered and shallow bay that opens up to Lake Couchiching, with a pretty boathouse on a point and, back up a gentle slope, under tall elms, a big house. There are many rooms in the house and many windows look out on the bay, but there is, strangely enough, not a lot of light in the rooms. They seem to retain light rather than let light in. This gives the house a curiously constricted feel, suggesting that Leacock himself might have been constricted, retentive, even dark, yet the wide, sloping lawn down to the water suggests only ease, a welcoming of whatever might come in off the open water. The fact is, the estate is a place of hints, not hard truth.

We know too little about Leacock. But now David Legate has written a biography that is a stolid report on the man's life and to some extent on his work. The biography is a report because Legate has held his man at a distance. His book is packed with information, but certain incidents have been sidestepped. For these we have to go to *The Man In The Panama Hat*, a reminiscence by Leacock's niece Elizabeth Kimball.

❦

In England the Leacock family had been successful in the Madeira wine trade and they had lived in luxurious Oak Hill, close to Osborne House, Queen Victoria's favourite palace. In his little blue boat the pampered young Peter Leacock had drifted out on still river waters with a girl named Agnes Emma Butler, the daughter of an assiduous man of the cloth. They were secretly married on New Year's Day of 1867. Seven months later they had their first son.

There was a standard provision in the family manuals of staid Victorian patriarchs: a son who was so improvident as to pursue the bottle or an ill-planned marriage was packed off to a quickly purchased pasture in the colonies. There it was hoped he would not only learn discipline but also earn a fortune on the backs of the children of Ham, the blacks. Peter and his bride were sent to a cornfield and cattle ranch in the South African colony of Natal, but the farm failed and Peter came back home; clouds of locusts, it was said, had killed the crops, and plague had killed the cattle. Then he was sent off to another farm in Kansas; it failed, too, and there was talk of ravenous grasshoppers.

The last resort for the family was a one-way ticket to Upper Canada and a poor scrub farm south of Lake Simcoe. There this man, whose whole life had once been croquet, cricket, and gentle words while spooning in a little blue boat, settled into an ugly squared-cedar-log house covered with clapboards. For neighbours he had mosquitoes, blackflies, groundhogs, and dour Scots. Nine box stoves burned about the house in the winter, but these stoves – for which cords and cords of wood had to be cut – were never enough. In one hallway there was always ice on the floor in the winter and the children skated down the hallway. "We took for granted that the water would freeze in the pitchers every night and the window panes would cover up with frost . . . For light we had three or four coal-oil lamps, but being just from England, where they were unknown, we were afraid of them . . . All the light we had was one tallow candle in the middle of the table . . ."

Peter became dissolute, a wastrel. It took little to persuade him to travel the road west, alone, hoping to find his fortune in the first Manitoba land boom. He came back to his family broke and a drunk. Once he had loved gardening and gay talk about England, but all that was gone. Over two decades his life had become more lousy than savage; he was a sick-drunk in the scattered encampments of log huts and the taverns of Simcoe County. He had a dutiful wife who cooked horrible cannonball puddings and burned beef. He had eleven sons and daughters. He was violent and despairing and brutal. Distressed, he drank and lay about, too tired and drained for work, bottling up a blind rage. One December night he went after his wife with a knife and she leapt through a window into a snowdrift. Then, one morning in the summer of 1887, he somehow came into possession of an amount of money and he said that he was going to go away. He did not say where he was going. He allowed that he might come back.

His seventeen-year-old son Stephen drove the family cutter down to the train station. He and his father waited for the train. They did not speak. Then the train came in and his father mounted the stairs of the day coach to Toronto. Stephen, white-faced and waving the buggy-whip at his father, said: "If you ever come back, I'll kill you."

He never came back. He went to England and then to Nova Scotia and, through fifty-three years, he and his son never spoke again. The old man died at ninety-two, known on the Nova Scotia south shore as Captain Lewis. He left a legacy for his children of eight thousand pounds.

The deserted family was not penniless. The farm was stone-picker poor but periodic legacies from England had allowed Agnes Emma Leacock to preserve a certain queer gentility in the backwoods. Though she was hardly the Dowager of Sutton, on Lake Simcoe, she permitted her children to play only with a nearby English family, and not with any of the common Scots, and in the summer her children were not allowed to go barefoot. It was, so her son Stephen said, "A question of caste and thistles." She made it clear that her children were to speak with a refined and even rarefied English accent. They were English and not Canadian. She had not only a nursemaid but also a private tutor for her sons, and they soon were sent south, where they entered Upper Canada College, a fashionable boys' school for colonial gentlemen-in-the-bud. Said Stephen: "There came a day soon after I entered when the principal called me up to be questioned and a junior master wrote down the answers. 'What,' he asked, 'is your father's occupation?' I hesitated quite a while and then I said, 'He doesn't do anything.' The principal bent over towards the junior master who was writing and said in an impressive voice, 'A gentleman.' A sort of awe spread around the room . . ." In 1887 Stephen became head boy and he was jealously proud of this position, and that was also the year that he waved his whip at his father and told his father that if he ever came back he would kill him.

By the turn of the century, after graduate school and a master's position at Upper Canada College, Stephen Leacock became a professor in Montreal. He also became a performer. He'd turned himself into a character in the classroom: "When we entered the classroom for political science, we were all agog with curiosity. Up to the professor's desk shuffled an untidy, disheveled figure, apparently just risen from a night on a park bench, none other than Stephen Leacock, known to us students as Leaky Steamcock. Before he said a word we all wanted to laugh. Sometimes brilliant and scintillating; often, perhaps after a bad night, serious and deadly dull, his flow of words was as tangled as his mussy hair."

Leacock, appointed to McGill in 1903 in the department of economics and political science, liked to carp and sneer at intellectuals and almost anyone else who posed as a scholar, and he liked to publicly poke fun at his own PhD; at the same time, his PhD was one of his proudest achievements and scholarship was his initial ticket to prosperity. The truth is, he liked to publicly belittle what he had privately banked on; he liked to poke fun at his own professorial person, but behind the puffing on his furnace pipe and the deliberate parade he made in his tattered academic gown, behind all his clowning, his professorial station at McGill was, for him, the mark of a select man. It gave him a special satisfaction, being there among other select men. Years later he wrote that a state university such as the University of Toronto "has to teach everybody. McGill doesn't have to teach anybody . . ."

Leacock wrote and published a scholarly book, *Elements of Political Science* (1906). It was a publishing success and brought him stature. As a political scientist, however, he was predictable, and he knew next to nothing about economics. Dr. Jacob Viner, a Leacock student and later one of Roosevelt's Brain-Trusters, said: "His teaching of what he thought advanced economics was a farce, and I'm afraid some of us gave him a rough time, until the girls in the class, out of pity for him, asked us to lay off." Others viewed him "as misguided and shallow at best and fraudulent and subversive at worst." He was of no scholarly account. He was by no means stupid, but when he wrote of the non-Anglo-Saxon races and general immigration, he was an intelligent and shrewd man who did not know very much:

> A little dose of them [Russian and Galician immigrants] may even be variation, do good, like a minute dose of poison in a medicine . . . I am not saying that we should absolutely shut out and debar the European foreigner, as we should and do shut out the Oriental. But we should in no way facilitate his coming . . .
>
> For all the [peoples of the] Orient, however, the only policy is and must be exclusion. Where we cannot marry, where we cannot worship, where we cannot eat, there we cannot live. The Eastern and Western races cannot unite. Biologists tell us that where they intermarry their progeny is an ill-joined product, two brains rattling in one skull. Nor could we institute in the Empire, certainly not in the temperate Dominions, a servile class, a race of coolies . . .
>
> The red man would not work: he would rather die. The acceptance of death and the scornful tolerance of pain

> were among the redeeming features of a race whose fiendish cruelty for cruelty's sake forfeited their right to live. Those who know properly the history of such a tribe as the Senecas – cruel, filthy and cannibal – will harbor no illusions about the noble red man. But work the red man would not. The black man will work when he has to, but not otherwise. The white man cannot stop working . . .
>
> Mankind was presumably evolved in a fairly warm climate and has groped its way northward in the dark. The easy luxuriance of the tropics bred, in the long course of countless generations, races of men habituated to torrid heat and saturated air, and colored by the overhead sun. Crowding and conquest moved others northward. The rigor of the cold and the stimulus of effort bred the white races whose superiority no one must doubt. The Aurora Borealis and the starlight – or something else – bleached them out white again to remake them as the northern race. After a period, again of uncounted centuries, the white races have come back to the tropics as conquerors . . .

Presumably he was not thinking of his father's failure in Natal.

Many a colonial layabout and/or gent held such views in Canada during Leacock's limelight years. In Montreal and Toronto, at those clubs in which men assumed a sergeant major's Saxon celibate air, ensconced in leather chairs under heraldic crests and oak-beamed ceilings, flushed with port or Scotch or ale, Leacock's views were accepted coin. One of his most intimate friends in Montreal was Andrew Macphail, a prominent professor of history and medicine at McGill, and it was said among their cronies that few friends knew each other's minds so well. Together they might have laughed at the idea of the Japanese ever having a beauty contest, but when it came to the question of immigration, there was no laughter, and Macphail wrote: "The melting pot means that instead of the pure race from which we have come, we shall have a mongrel race, and this mongrel race is making itself known in Canada . . ."

Macphail was a strange man, marked by a military orderliness of mind, an air of gloom and deliberation, a lurking violence, and a fondness for uttering mystifying epigrams that no one understood. He was stern, a man who lived alone, and it was a man's house that he lived in, with nothing allowed out of place from cellar to second-floor study. The explosion of a heated bottle of soda water made him blind in one eye and doctors told him to prepare for the coming years of complete and unending darkness. He said he was prepared, and he and Leacock regularly had supper in that orderly, gloomy house, bound together by their bigotry, their sour, sneering laughter, their faith in the English imperial idea, their knowledge that only an unending darkness lay ahead.

There is a lurking violence in Leacock's work, an explosive meanness in stories that have no point other than the reporting of a death that is pointless; sometimes these stories are macabre, sometimes they have an incredible deft coldness, as if murder were no more than an afterthought (in other hands – André Gide's, for example – such gratuitous death suggests a frightening motiveless malignancy; in Leacock it leads only to a contemptuous chuckle).

There is, for example, his story about a man standing on a street who, when asked for a match, searches wildly for one, knowing that somewhere in his clothing there is wood, buried, waiting to be found, and at last, shivering and with his clothes strewn all around him in the snow, he produces the piece of wood triumphantly, and it is only a toothpick. The narrator who had asked for the match reports: "Yielding to the impulse of the moment I pushed him under the wheels of a trolley car and ran." END.

Then there is the story of Gustavus Adolphus, a child. It is a story that has the surreal possibilities of the great fairy tales. Gustavus has swallowed a pill containing three hundred and fifty pounds of dehydrated Christmas dinner, and, though he is still hungry, he explodes, he goes *BOOM*, and the narrator, staring at the exploded body of the child, reports only that he had "a lingering smile worn by a child who had eaten 13 Christmas dinners." That's it. Death without meaning; banal, empty buffoonery.

All these tales are strangely remote in technique and temper from the literature of Leacock's time; he is no Ring Lardner; he is much closer to Thomas Haliburton and Artemus Ward than he is to Wodehouse, Walpole, Maugham, Max Beerbohm, or Wolcott Gibbs, and his work is a pale shadow of the writers he said he admired, Dickens and Twain. There are certainly comic burlesques and moments of buffoonery in Twain and there are streaks of raw violence in Dickens, but Leacock ignored the fact that Dickens and Twain had sought the source of the pain that is in laughter and the laughter that is in pain; they had stepped inside their characters, they had loved their characters. Leacock does not love his characters. He sneers at them, mocks them, ridicules them. He felt superior to them, as he felt superior to Shakespeare, to Ibsen, to everyone except Dickens, and he didn't understand Dickens at all.

Of *Hard Times* he said: "*Hard Times* has no other interest in the history of letters than that of its failure. At the time, even enthusiastic lovers of Dickens found it hard to read. At present they do not even try to read it." Those who think that Leacock might have become a novelist are ridiculous. He was a lightweight, almost entirely unaware of the writers of his own time, and certainly unsympathetic in rather stupid fashion to what he thought they were doing: "It is well known that the modern novel has got far beyond the point of mere story-telling. The childish attempt to *interest* the readers has long since been abandoned by all the best writers. They refuse to do it. The modern novel must convey a message, or else it must paint a picture, or remove a veil, or open a new chapter in human psychology. Otherwise it is no good." He said that "the wholesome days of the Eighties and Nineties" had been replaced by a brand new invention of the twentieth century – filthy books: "Many of our so-called best-sellers merely sell because they contain every here and there a patch of dirt. The readers gather just as horse-flies do along a road where a well-fed horse has passed." Leacock not only knew nothing about Joyce, Lawrence, Tolstoy, Hemingway, Eliot, and Auden but he knew nothing about the eighties and nineties, a period that reeked of hothouse decadence.

What he was interested in was money. He would publish anything as long as it paid. He had a fine, spare style, sometimes transparent in its simplicity, but he became a hack. He turned out tired tales, sifting again and again through the same material, most of it shallow and trite. He stumped from stage to stage as the hilarious self-deprecating academic, his routines a thing of delight to old ladies, travelling businessmen, and students. In his last years he happily pumped out promotion material for banks and for ore companies and airlines. He wanted the money. In his latter years he made more money than the prime minister. He felt a special satisfaction in that; his wealth gave him the secure sense of place that he had sought since his stone-picker farm-boy days. As it turned out, the great pain in his life, the really enraging pain, the dirty blow, came when he was told he had to retire from the university. He greeted his retirement – and the loss of income – with a towering, sullen rage – but he was well prepared; he retreated to Old Brewery Bay, Orillia, back to his boyhood, where there'd been only log houses and clapboard; he moved into a mansion of many rooms banked by velvety lawns, a country estate.

But for all his money and all his purchase on the public, what is felt in Leacock and in his work is a deep sense of loss, as if – from the beginning – he were coming home to a dream too late. At the end of *Sunshine Sketches of a Little Town,* Leacock is taking a last surreal trip into a dream of sunshine in a land where there is only darkness. He is going back to Mariposa, back to where he had begun, and he asks himself, as if it were all over,

> Do you remember how when you first began to make money you used to plan that just as soon as you were rich, really rich, you'd go back home again to the little town and build a great big house with a fine verandah, – no stint about it, the best that money could buy, planed lumber, every square foot of it, and a fine picket fence in front of it.
>
> It was to be one of the grandest and finest houses that thought could conceive; much finer, in true reality, than that vast palace of sandstone with the porte cochère and the sweeping conservatories that you afterwards built in the costlier part of the city.
>
> But if you have half forgotten Mariposa, and long since lost the way to it, you are only like the greater part of the men here in this Mausoleum Club in the city. Would you believe it that practically every one of them came from Mariposa once upon a time, and that there isn't one of them that doesn't sometimes dream in the dull quiet of the long evening here in the club, that some day he will go back and see the place.
>
> Hundreds of them know that there is a train that goes out at five o'clock, but they mistake it. Ever so many of them think it's just a suburban train. Lots of people that take it every day think it's only the train to the golf grounds, but the joke is that after it passes out of the city and the suburbs and the golf grounds, it turns itself little by little into the Mariposa train, thundering and pounding towards the north with hemlock sparks pouring out into the darkness from the funnel of it . . . wait a little, and you will see that when the city is well behind you, bit by bit the train changes its character. The electric locomotive that took you through the city tunnels is off now and the

old wood engine is hitched on in its place. I suppose, very probably, you haven't seen one of these wood engines since you were a boy forty years ago, – the old engine with a wide top like a hat on its funnel, and with sparks enough to light up a suit for damages once in every mile.

Do you see, too, that the trim little cars that came out of the city on the electric suburban express are being discarded now at the way stations, one by one, and in their place is the old familiar car with the stuff cushions in red plush (how gorgeous it once seemed!) and with a box stove set up in one end of it? The stove is burning furiously at its sticks this autumn evening, for the air sets in chill as you get clear away from the city and are rising up to the higher ground of the country of the pines and the lakes.

Look from the window as you go. The city is far behind now and right and left of you there are trim farms with elms and maples near them and with tall windmills beside the barns that you can still see in the gathering dusk . . . but they are fading fast in the twilight. They have lengthened out the train by this time with a string of flat cars and freight cars between where we are sitting and the engine. But at every crossway we can hear the long muffled roar of the whistle, dying to a melancholy wail that echoes into the woods; the woods, I say, for the farms are thinning out and track plunges here and there into great stretches of bush, – tall tamarack and red scrub willow and with a tangled undergrowth of bush that has defied for two generations all attempts to clear it into the form of fields.

Why, look, that great space that seems to open out in the half-dark of the falling evening, – why, surely yes, – Lake Ossawippi, the big lake, as they used to call it, from which the river runs down to the smaller lake, – Lake Wissanotti, – where the town of Mariposa has lain waiting for you there for thirty years . . . Already the conductor has changed his glazed hat for an ordinary round Christie and you can hear the passengers calling him and the brakeman "Bill" and "Sam" as if they were all one family.

What is it now – nine-thirty? Ah, then we must be nearing the town, – this big bush that we are passing through, you remember it surely as the great swamp just this side of the bridge over the Ossawippi? There is the bridge itself, and the long roar of the train as it rushes sounding over the trestle work that rises above the marsh. Hear the clatter as we pass the semaphores and switch lights! We must be close in now! . . . and as the train rounds in and stops hissing and panting at the platform, you can hear above all other sounds the cry of the brakemen and the porters:

MARIPOSA! MARIPOSA!

And as we listen, the cry grows fainter and fainter in our ears and we are sitting here again in the leather chairs of the Mausoleum Club, talking of the little Town in the Sunshine that once we knew.

In March of 1944 he died of cancer of the throat. He was in his seventy-fifth year. He left approximately a quarter of a million dollars. He had been a satirist, an economist, a parodist, a historian, a public performer, an ironist, a political scientist, a burlesque artist, a tippler, a fisherman, a politician, a gardener, a parent, an administrator, a sailor, an actor, and, in the minds of some, a potential novelist. He was, above all, the country's favourite humourist. It was a remarkable display. He had fought all his life to get "above the average" and he had accomplished that, but at no time was he ever a master of anything.

There is a great hollowness of spirit behind his work. Words that he wrote before he died seem appropriate: "Give me my stick. I'm going out on No Man's Land. I'll face it."

❧

Burial in cheap pine boxes was the Leacock family tradition. They called it their "fifty-buck box," and old Harve Taylor, the Sutton undertaker, had buried from four to six Leacocks, beginning with old Mrs. Leacock herself, and they had all gone down in fifty-buck pine boxes. There were no headstones over their graves either; their names were chiselled where there was room on their mother's headstone. The only flourish they allowed themselves was the colour of the cloth casket-cover. Mrs. Leacock had been put down under lavender, the same shade as she had used for her morning dresses and her knickered swimming suits. On the other hand, Aunt Dot had been borne to her grave with a cloth of deep Persian blue in a jacquard weave. This family burial drill had been worked out over the decades.

But Leacock broke with this country disdain for display. He chose, so his niece tells us, "a big show-off casket instead of a fifty-buck box. His was a monstrous affair of mahogany or oak – I cannot remember which – but it was ostentatiously grained and burled, with big, horehound taffy sworls and swirls, all varnished and veneered over till the whole contraption shone as if it had just come from the confectioner's tray." The pallbearers did not know, as they staggered under their hardwood and brass-handled burden to the family plot that lay beneath a twisted monkey-puzzle tree by Sibbald's Church, that they were engaged in one last grim Leacock joke; the weight they shouldered was only a fashionable funeral parlour's gewgaw. Leacock had arranged to be cremated. The box held only the few grams of his ashes.

Charles Leacock was a brother. He had come out of hospital for the funeral. Over the years he had suffered fits of mental depression and, though he was a trained and skilled engineer, he had been idle most of his life. After the service he sat by a fire in the fireplace with the family, and he began to tell one of his brother's stories. Apparently there was a strong resemblance between Stephen and Charles, not only in their faces, but in their voices. As Charles went on telling the story, he stepped into the person of Stephen. It seemed to the family that he became Stephen. They heard Stephen's voice coming from the tortured Charles, and there were the same blue-grey eyes of the dead man staring at them, and it was as if the newly dead walked among them.

> The words that broke forth from the mouth were terrible words, for, as if driven by this goad of memory, Uncle Charlie vented forth thoughts he had never allowed himself to utter before. Frightful feelings were expressed . . . uncertainties, doubts . . . hatred, bitterness . . . fear, shaking, white fear . . . thoughts and words which, indeed, Uncle Stephen may never, in reality, have allowed past his lips, but which Uncle Charlie, with his inside track to his brother's mind, divined as clearly as if they had been spoken. And they issued from Uncle Charlie's lips in Uncle Stephen's voice, there could be no mistaking it. Not a note, not a shade that was not exactly true . . . Uncle Charlie said of Uncle Stephen, "He was a man, I tell you, of terrible despairs . . ."

The Telegram, 1971

BECKETT: I CAN'T GO ON, I'LL GO ON

In *Waiting for Godot* there are two tramps in tattered clothes and broken shoes who break the silence by the side of a country road. They are standing under the bare bone of a tree. They are waiting. That's what they do. They wait. For a man named Godot who is to come and ease their acedia. They eat turnips, a carrot, and dark brown radishes. They take their hats off. They put their hats on. Then two strangers pass under the lean shadow of the tree. One is a lout, Pozzo, who is driving, at the end of a noose, his slave. His name is Lucky. He shouts:

> Given the existence as uttered forth in the public works of Puncher and Wattman of a personal God quaquaquaqua with white beard quaquaquaqua outside time without extension who from the heights of divine apathia divine athambia divine aphasia loves us dearly with some exceptions for reasons unknown but time will tell and suffers like the divine Miranda with those who for reasons unknown but time will tell are plunged in torment plunged in fire whose fire flames if that continues and who can doubt it will fire the firmament that is to say blast hell to heaven so blue still and calm so calm with a calm which even though intermittent is better than nothing but not so fast and considering what is more that as a result of the labors left unfinished crowned by the Acacacacademy of Anthropopopmetry of Essy-in-Possy of Testew and Cunard it is established beyond all doubt all other doubt than

> that which clings to the labors of men that as a result of the labors unfinished of Testew and Cunard it is established as hereinafter but not so fast for reasons unknown that as a result of the public works of Puncher and Wattman it is established beyond all doubt that in view of the labors of Fartov and Belcher left unfinished for reasons unknown . . .

And on he goes, staggering, shouting, for reasons unknown. Night falls, the earth turns on its axis, darkness passes into day and day passes into darkness. The tramps wait. The two strangers pass by once more, only this time the master is blind and the slave dumb-mouthed. They fall in a heap, plead for help, and get up and push on. The master, Pozzo, has no idea why the slave keeps trudging on, bearing his bag of sand and accepting the lash. The two tramps are left alone again, inert, on the lip of despair, or maybe it isn't despair, maybe it is just the lip, the edge of an abyss. And sometimes they are wacky and have a dour kind of fun on the lip. There's nothing else to do but flap the loose sole of a shoe or twirl a hat and roll it by the brim along an arm as the arm reaches out . . . hoping Godot will come to them.

These two desolate tramps, Vladimir and Estragon, are nettled by dreams, feeble memories, and snippets of erudition. Their muttered comfort for each other is shaded by gallows laughter. They have their tricks and ploys with hats and a wry deadpan pleasure in conundrums. Suicide is a temptation but they do not commit suicide. They keep going though they are standing still. They seem shell-shocked, tossed up and out of time, men lacking faith but ready to believe anything, capable of a doleful plaint, a quip, a joke, prattling self-pity.

Early in the play the two tramps have this conversation:

> VLADIMIR: Ah yes, the two thieves. Do you remember the story? . . . Two thieves crucified at the same time as our Savior . . . Two thieves.

One is supposed to have been saved and the other . . . damned.

ESTRAGON: Saved from what?

VLADIMIR: Hell . . . both of them abused him.

ESTRAGON: Who?

VLADIMIR: What?

ESTRAGON: What's this all about? Abused who?

VLADIMIR: The Savior.

ESTRAGON: Why?

VLADIMIR: Because he wouldn't save them.

ESTRAGON: From hell? Imbecile. From death.

ESTRAGON: I thought you said hell.

VLADIMIR: From death, from death.

ESTRAGON: Well what of it?

VLADIMIR: Then the two of them must have been damned.

ESTRAGON: And why not?

VLADIMIR: But one of the four gospels says that one of the two was saved . . .

Herein lies an abiding Christian loneliness. Christ through his blood saved all who believed in him, saved those who had the faith. How did they come to have the faith? How did Ezekiel come to see those wheels of fire in the sky? The answer: "The big wheel run by faith, the little wheel run by the grace of God"? Faith alone. Arbitrary grace. It is a grace that comes as a pastille to those of Adam's children who are in God's palliative care. They are sick from sin (grace operates in the same way in the lives of men and women in Mauriac's novels). They wait. Salvation by faith alone. They wait.

This is the Calvinist's condition of salvation. It is Luther's argument, a last-ditch hope. Faith is a gift, and God gives his gift to whom he pleases. And as for those who believe, they believe because they do believe. Or, as Tertullian said, "I believe because it is absurd." And so one sinner may be saved and the next damned, one thief given eternal life and the other eternal death. It is arbitrary – and terrifying, if that is where you live in your heart.

Who are the elect? St. Augustine said, "Do not despair: one of the thieves was saved. Do not presume: one of the thieves was damned." The elect man is the select man, the master. He is Pozzo, and the other, the damned man, he is the addled slave at the end of a noose, Lucky. In anybody else's hands all this would be talking text, dry bones, theatrically tight. In Beckett's hands the language wears loose shoes.

Vladimir and Estragon are isolated. They say so. They know so. But in every conversation – no matter their isolation – they are talking to each other. It may be a new form of stage talk, but it is talk full of affection, wonder, concern, bewilderment, panic, mockery, sulks, jokes, pouts, complaints. In other words, they may be isolated but they have a relationship, and it is often a knowing and very funny relationship, as when they play "After you, Alphonse":

VLADIMIR &
ESTRAGON: [*turning simultaneously*] Do you –
VLADIMIR: Oh pardon!
ESTRAGON: Carry on.
VLADIMIR: No no, after you.
ESTRAGON: No no, you first.
VLADIMIR: I interrupted you.
ESTRAGON: On the contrary.
They glare at each other angrily.
VLADIMIR: Ceremonious ape!
ESTRAGON: Punctilious pig!
VLADIMIR: Finish your phrase, I tell you!
ESTRAGON: Finish your own!
Silence. They draw closer, halt.

VLADIMIR: Moron!

ESTRAGON: That's the idea, let's abuse each other.

They turn, move apart, turn again and face each other.

VLADIMIR: Moron!

ESTRAGON: Vermin!

VLADIMIR: Abortion!

ESTRAGON: Morpion!

VLADIMIR: Sewer-rat!

ESTRAGON: Curate!

VLADIMIR: Cretin!

ESTRAGON: [*with finality*] Crrritic!

VLADIMIR: Oh!

He wilts, vanquished, and turns away.

ESTRAGON: Now let's make it up.

VLADIMIR: Gogo!

ESTRAGON: Didi!

VLADIMIR: Your hand!

ESTRAGON: Take it!

VLADIMIR: Come to my arms!

ESTRAGON: Your arms?

VLADIMIR: My breast!

ESTRAGON: Off we go!

They embrace. They separate. Silence.

VLADIMIR: How time flies when one has fun!

They are having fun. Anyone who does not play this scene as fun is misreading the language. The problem is, what is fun? It is a very peculiar state of being. The trumpeter Miles Davis once asked: "What is fun, I mean philosophically; what do white people mean when they say they're having fun?" Vladimir and Estragon are the answer: they're having fun by killing time.

And they are having fun as only lovers can. They may not know it (and they might be terrified if they did), but they love each other, and that is their tragedy as they stand so comically alone in the middle of nowhere –

Beckett is surprising about love and yearning . . .

For example: When Winnie, buried up to her neck in sand in *Happy Days*, cries, "Was I lovable once, Willie? . . . Was I ever lovable?" she means it. She yearns for love, she echoes Ophelia and Juliet. Her husband, who has been hiding behind a mound of sand, crawls out on all fours. He tries to scale the mound. It is a long crawl. A lot gets said: "Is it me you're after, Willie . . . or is it something else? . . . Do you want to touch my face . . . again? . . . Is it a kiss you're after, Willie . . . or is it something else?" That something else, a thwarted yet taunting need, conveys the menace that is in Strindberg and Chekhov and Ibsen, except that the menace in Beckett is distilled . . . to the point where even silence has a voice . . . to the point – and this may be at the heart of his genius – where he can make a monologue sound like conversation.

In Beckett, the lone voice is never alone.

Because of this lone voice, often filled with manic energy, and a manic dark laughter ("Some people are lucky, born of a wet dream and dead before morning"), there are some who say that a fundamental despair and nihilism lies at the heart of Beckett, that the great metaphysical beliefs lie in ruins in his work, that his characters are clownish, pathetic, meaningless, absurd, provisional . . . lacking even a biological optimism. But this is not what emerges out of the unnameable silence:

> . . . the silence, the end, the beginning, the beginning again, how can I say it, that's all words, they're all I have, and not many of them, the words fail, the voice fails, so be it, I know that well, it will be the silence, full of murmurs, distant cries, the usual silence, spent listening, spent waiting, waiting for the voice, the cries abate, like all cries, that is to say they stop, the murmurs cease, they give up, the voice begins again, it begins trying again, quick now

before there is none left, no voice left, nothing left but the core of murmurs, distant cries, quick now and try again, with the words that remain, try what, I don't know, I've forgotten, it doesn't matter, I never knew, to have them carry me into my story, the words that remain, my old story, which I've forgotten, far from here, through the noise, through the door, into the silence, that must be it, it's too late, perhaps it's too late, perhaps they have, how would I know, in the silence you don't know, perhaps it's the door, perhaps I'm at the door, that would surprise me, perhaps it's I, perhaps somewhere or other it was I, I can depart, all this time I've journeyed without knowing it, it's I now at the door, what door, what's a door doing here, it's the last words, the true last, or it's the murmurs, the murmurs are coming, I know that well, no, not even that, you talk of murmurs, distant cries, as long as you can talk, you talk of them before and you talk of them after, more lies, it will be the silence, the one that doesn't last, spent listening, spent waiting, for it to be broken, for the voice to break it, perhaps there's no other, I don't know, it's not worth having, that's all I know, it's not I, that's all I know, it's not mine, it's the only one I ever had, that's a lie, I must have had the other, the one that lasts, but it didn't last, I don't understand, that is to say it did, it still lasts, I'm still in it, I left myself behind in it, I'm waiting for me there, no, there you don't wait, you don't listen, I don't know, perhaps it's a dream, all a dream, that would surprise me, I'll wake, in the silence, and never sleep again, it will be I, or dream, dream again, dream of a silence, a dream silence, full of murmurs, I don't know, that's all words, never wake, all words, there's nothing else, you must go on, that's all I know, they're going to stop, I know that well, I can feel it, they're going to abandon me, it will be the silence, for a moment, a good few moments, or it will be mine, the lasting one, that didn't

> last, that still lasts, it will be I, you must go on, I can't go on, you must go on, I'll go on, you must say words, as long as there are any, until they find me, until they say me, strange pain, strange sin, you must go on, perhaps it's done already, perhaps they have said me already, perhaps they have carried me to the threshold of my story, before the door that opens on my story, that would surprise me, if it opens, it will be I, it will be the silence, where I am, I don't know, I'll never know, in the silence you don't know, you must go on, I can't go on, I'll go on.

This is the conversational prose of tenderness – a tenderness that lies in the lull of language itself – a tenderness as deeply felt as Molly Bloom's waking reverie, her *yes*, and *yes, yes*. It is as affirmative: "There's nothing else, you must go on, that's all I know . . . I can't go on, I'll go on."

The Telegram, 1967-71

STEINBECK DEAD: 1969

As a young man I used to walk late at night in the summer past the downtown rooming houses on Church Street, where tired women in cotton dresses sat on the front stoops drinking beer and bingo wine in the humid night air, and one night a woman with her stockings rolled at her calves said, "Sit down, boy, and sip with me a while." She said, "Jesus, I crossed half of this whole damn country, just sipping here and sipping there . . ." I said: "You got the turtle in you," and she said, "Kid, I ain't seen a turtle since it was years ago . . ."

I've always had the turtle in my mind, Steinbeck's turtle, crawling and clawing and boosting his shell, boosting his horny, dumb, amused head up, crossing highways, pressing a few seeds inside his shell just as a smart-ass trucker is trying to run him down, catching the tail of the shell and flipping it into the air, but when it landed the turtle scrambled on, dropping spearhead seeds in the ground, dragging dirt over the seeds, going on down a dust road. That was the story of the Joad family, those Thirties country people driven off their dust-bowl lands, carrying inside their shells the seeds of their own worth, crossing the country to California, a broken down truckload of hillbilly sucker bait for hustlers and troopers and goon squads, but they went on enduring and disappearing down along some dust road.

There is always that writer who seems, when you are young, to have caught hold of life as you feel it. Suddenly people in the streets, their eyes and the shape of their mouth, tell you stories. What I saw in the streets of the city that I still carry with me – my own city, so different from Steinbeck's California – were stalwart men and women blinking back tears on the lip of their own grave. Stalwart, side by side with their confused sorrows. I don't know why. That's what their faces told me. Stalwart in sorrow. But I suffered no dismay or disheartening. I believed also that making her way down Yonge Street was Rose of Sharon, her child born dead and her breasts full of milk, and at the end she would take some man's head, some malnourished man unable to feed himself, and she would nurse him as if he were a child.

I have argued since with men of refinement about that scene in *The Grapes of Wrath.* Crude, they called it. Crude and melodramatic and cheap. Of course they read and admired Henry James, they fussed and fidgeted in their own lives, incapable of large, straightforward gestures, suffocating in the circularities of their own lives and their own prose. Those circularities told a more careful truth. I would learn about circularities in my life soon enough. But I was too young to be careful, too brash to be circular.

I remember sitting in a bar on Bloor Street with a girl younger than I was, and I wanted to love her. I wanted her so much that I swarmed all over her with affection and slowly she withdrew, terrified and bewildered, sinking down into her chair, and I knew I was losing her, but I didn't understand why, and I didn't know how to stop.

Later, when I read the story of big, dumb Lennie in *Of Mice and Men*, petting his mouse or a puppy, brimming over with the strength of his affection, his dreams of childish pleasures, I understood how dangerous insistent demonstrations of love can be and are. Lennie always killed the things he loved – and his friend George was obliged to shoot him to keep him from being lynched. All the powerful yearning of people was in Lennie, the terror of loneliness and the compulsion to love, so inarticulate, so guileless, yet so overwhelming; and it was after reading that story (*Of Mice and Men* is a perfect story) that I felt for the first time that I'd lived through a crooked year and come out with a crooked heart, because I knew I'd do the same kind of loving again, and probably again I would scare away those I wanted to love because I believed in Rose of Sharon and the beauty of her gesture. I hated the nitpickers who never came out of their pinstripe postures. But there was Lennie, unaware in his largeness, and murderous in his purity. I learned to fear the pure of heart. I learned to fear what was best in myself.

This was the great thing about Steinbeck as a writer, at least as I read him as a young man. He gave shape to my emotions in his stories. When wiser men dismissed Steinbeck as ham-fisted and clumsy in the construction of his novels, I was angry. Once, standing in my father's kitchen, he tried to convince me that Flaubert was the real writer, but I brushed off Madame Bovary as a dippy broad and gave him an earnest lecture on violence, survival, big business and humble virtues, and on and on, and at last he said, "That's beautiful, that one writer should do all that for you . . . That's what writing should be . . . but, you'll discover, there are more turtles than one on the road."

I suppose the last time that Steinbeck seemed to be part of my life was when I had turned twenty and was home from college. I'd gone around to one of the Bloor Street haunts, the Chez Paree, for a pre-Christmas drink. Some men I'd met once or twice came in and sat down, and one fell face-first into his oyster soup and waiters carried him out through the kitchen. A tall blonde, aloof but smiling, had come in with them carrying a frozen turkey on her shoulder, and she sat at the table talking to the men, the turkey still on her shoulder. She had an independent gaiety about her so I joined the group and eased in on her, only to discover that she was in love with Steinbeck's little story "The Pearl." We talked and talked about Steinbeck and she put down her turkey, and six years later we married.

And six years after that I separated from her, starting in on the first season of circularities in my life, and then, having another pre-Christmas drink, I was told that Steinbeck was dead. I had not read him for a long time. His last novel, *The Winter of Our Discontent*, had been a terrible failure for me. Also he had become a Vietnam hawk, and I worried that if I reread *The Grapes of Wrath* I'd decide that it was not a radical book at all, that Steinbeck hadn't really wanted to change anything for anybody, not even the Joads. If that were true, then rereading his old books would be like visiting a school girlfriend: all the feeling and the hell-bent risk of those years would be lost in a figure who had turned frumpy and coarse. Or maybe I'd be forced to see that I had grown a little frumpy myself. Anyway, I'm older and wearier now and, also being wiser, I'll find myself admiring Henry James, but Steinbeck's death made me want to walk excitedly again through my streets, discovering straightforward little stories, little spearhead seeds by the side of the road.

The Telegram, 1968

SAMUEL BECKETT AT THE CAFÉ FRANÇAIS

Con Leventhal, Samuel Beckett's closest friend in Paris, was standing at the heavy oak door to his apartment in Montparnasse. "I sent Sam your book, and told him he should see you," he said. "When he reads the book, he'll call. We'll set it up."

"That'll be great," I said.

"Just remember the silences," he said.

"What?"

"He stops talking. Don't feel you have to say anything. Don't say anything . . .

Let the silences be silent."

Samuel Beckett's call came. He was firm, courteous, setting aside the following morning at eleven sharp at the Café Français, in a travelling salesmen's hotel across the road from where he lived. I hung up, remembering a story William Hayter, the great engraver, had told me. He lived only a few blocks from Beckett and he'd told me that one morning Beckett opened his bathroom window and found a sweating, eager-eyed academic clutching the drainpipe, whispering "Beckett, a word." Beckett had shaved as if the man weren't there, and had left him clinging to the outside wall.

I hurried to the Boulevard St. Jacques, the Hotel PLM, Café Français – a hotel for Japanese and Korean software drummers and French provincial *avocats* – the perfect place for Beckett to hole up in, safe from crazed American academics on the prowl. At eleven sharp he appeared.

Lean, tall, willowy, a narrow head, circular smoked-black glasses, deep eye sockets, the sinister insularity of a bird; in the glare of morning light reflected in the plate glass, he seemed to be cast in negative. A firm, modulated voice: "Mr. Callaghan," diction deliberate. He had a liquid, slow-moving elegance, head cocked back, a slight sway to the narrow hips, a light, almost feminine drag at the ankles – more the lope of America than the stride of Paris, the walk of a man who sees a long, straight, flat road ahead, empty space . . . but well tailored for the emptiness: cashmere sweater, black Cardin shirt open at the throat. Perhaps, I thought, only an elegant man at ease with his elegance can understand real filth . . . dustbins, decrepitude, Krapp.

He took off his glasses. His eyes were ice blue, the radiance that reflects off snow, small dark pupils like holes, big ears, long fingers, whitish skin, and a curious movement to his fingers – the long little finger moved in sections, segmented, like a water spider's leg coming down to the water surface; the long little finger lay across his cheek, tapping, touching the nostril; I got a sudden sense of crustacea . . .

He sat encapsulated in silence, calm – perhaps it was a momentary shyness, boredom, inertia, conservation of energy, or the extremity of ease – a silence, it seemed, that was his outer skin, to be penetrated, puzzled over, patiently appreciated; sitting as we were, side by side, our backs to the light, he offered me a small brown cigar and coffee and we sat like two burghers on a bench; I felt woozy; I realized I was batting my eyes, trying to focus . . .

"Hello, hello," I said.

"Hello."

"Hello," I said again.

"I've brought your book – creature called Hogg," he said very quietly. He smiled. "Read it. Very fine," he said, as he looked at the opening epigraphs, riffled to the back, felt the page thickness, thumbed along the page edges until he found the drawings, paused over each, put the book down again, said "Thank you," got up, leaving the book in front of me, and sat on the other side of the table in silence. I wrote: "For Samuel Beckett, on a morning of sunlight over a morning coffee." He picked up the book, read the inscription, smiled, and said, "Thank you very much." Silence.

"Con," he said.

"Con," I said.

"Yes," he said.

"Con," I said, laughing lightly, "a fine man; and, boy, we had a night the other night, a lovely man."

Suddenly, with soft-spoken affection, he said how he had met Con: a Jewish student in Dublin whose father had owned a shop in Mary Street specializing in rosaries and religious paraphernalia, who had held small regular literary soirées, and then he, Beckett, had left Dublin for France to study . . . and then had gone back to teach at Trinity and, disliking teaching, had set out for Germany, where he'd gone to brood, and from Germany – before he'd known he was to be a writer – he'd resigned Trinity to stay abroad, where no one could reach him or interfere with him, and Con, his friend, had been given the same job, his job, which Con had kept all the years till he had retired ten years previously to Paris.

"The night before, two nights ago, we were like two hoboes hobbled by drink," I said. "There we were in the dark, a tall man executing a jig, a shuffling small man on bad feet: Mutt and Jeff, just like you did *Godot* in Berlin."

He smiled. "Except Con has ingrown toenails. No one in the play has such nails," he said.

"Maybe the good thief," I said.

I waited.

"What do you do," he said, "when you're not Hogg?"

I told him. I'd taught. Still did, at the university in Toronto. Been a war correspondent in the Middle East, southern Africa

. . . I liked to gamble, the horses. Silence. I also reminded him of *Exile*, the magazine I'd begun to publish, and "Yes," he said, "it comes out rather irregularly, and John Montague, he contributes poems there. A lot of his work." I reminded him that once I had written to him asking him for his own work, something, anything, expecting nothing, and he'd written back, a very courteous card. "Yes . . . explaining I had literally nothing to offer . . ." His exact words from five years earlier.

I said how peculiar it was to be there with him (he put on his dark glasses); a week earlier, coming in overnight to Paris on the train from Munich, I'd toyed with two images of myself: Watt, hurtling backward with his arms outflung, babbling, into a thorn bush (a muffled croak, Beckett's laughter), and also that moment when Krapp is in his boat, the gentle rocking with the woman in the bottom of the punt, when he's at one with the woman, at one with the water . . . "In the boat, yes," he said, "yes," touched by some recollection. "Yes, the water, the rocking . . ."

He asked about Hayter, how was his health? They had worked together on a portfolio, a short text about his farm in the Marne. I said I'd seen the text, and the engravings. "He has a genius," Beckett said. I said the young artists surrounding him in the atelier seemed poky and plodding in comparison, plenty of get up and *do do do* in the morning, but little daring.

"Done," he said.

"Who?"

He took off his dark glasses.

"Done."

Silence.

I told him how Hayter had told me to come and work with him for a while in the atelier.

"As Hogg or as Hayter?"

"Right," I laughed. "Anyone who works with Hayter ends up imitating Hayter."

"It's not his fault," Beckett said. "And how long have you known Montague?"

"Back to '63 . . . I came to Paris on my honeymoon. I thought if I could ever get him to stand on one leg he'd be like an Irish crane looking for water."

Silence.

He opened the tin of cigars and then closed the tin.

"Does Montague go to Canada?"

"Yes."

A smile.

"You'll never go to Canada," I said.

"No."

He ordered more coffee, thimble cups of espresso, and lit another small brown cigar.

"And your place in the country?" I asked.

"It is a very unromantic landscape in the Marne, a house on a hill; there are workers and tractors in the fields, but a great expanse of sky, an expanse of sky . . ."

Silence.

"It's very interesting, you can watch the complete movement of the sun through the sky; you can watch it come up in the northeast and go down in the northwest and move over you, so you get all the seasons."

Silence.

"Do you travel to Ireland?"

I told him about driving up into the Healey Pass, in the southwest. The rock face, the barren jawbone of stone, the road, serpentine, and getting out of the car, the whole great valley lay before us, me and Claire – the woman I live with – the wind on us, so that we lay down in the crotch of the stone only to look up, in coitus, into the window of a family car slowly putting by, a family of four agape, disappearing in as much roar of exhaust as a little Ford could muster, leaving us laughing.

He smiled.

"Laughter's hard on the sex," he said.

"There we were, caught in the bottom of Krapp's boat."

He slipped the cigar box into his coat pocket. "The landscape that touched me most," he said, "was the hills south of Dublin, the Wicklow Hills. The light."

I told him about stopping at a farm in those hills, asking for water from an old woman, blind, who had a prize pet guinea cock on a string, a silvery, ugly bird. And before I could say it, Beckett said, "She ran everything," as if it had been his own mother, or a favorite aunt. And then, shaking his head, he said, "No, I don't know the place, or the woman." He tucked his pink plastic disposable lighter into his pocket. Slowly, politely, he was closing down the conversation. And then he startled me, asking, "What's the line you like most from your Hogg?"

"'The most abrasive lie,'" I said, not hesitating, "'was the perturbed loving look in his eye.'" He smiled. A wry smile or a polite smile? I couldn't tell.

"Well, I must be going," he said. "You'll come back to Paris; of course you will if you're coming to work with Bill – you'll be back. We'll talk again." He stood, surprisingly tall, his movements measured to the required courtesies. In the street we shook hands, a bony hand clasp, and then his looping turn away, his long legs, the sashay of his narrow hips, the drag and turn of his ankles – elegant, a loose walk, peculiar for a man whose characters are so often up to their necks in barrels and earth . . .

Barrel House Kings, 1999

W.W.E. ROSS: AFTER THE BATTLE, THE DAWN

My father took me across town to a red-brick corner house on Delaware Avenue. I have always remembered the street name because my father was telling me tales at night about the Delaware Indians. He took me there for a girl's birthday party – a girl I didn't know. And there was a tall woman who had three names – Mary Lowrey Ross – a woman whose stride was loose and easy, whose voice was deep, whose laughter crackled lustily out of her throat: too much smoking, Players Mild. She led me into the living room, a clutter of easy chairs, sofas, papers, books, cigarette ash. There were girls everywhere and I insisted I wanted to speak to the father of the house. A girl, Nancy, marched me to the hall. She pointed up the stairs. "He's up there, in the attic. He's up there all the time in the attic." The only attic I had ever seen was at the house of my three spinster aunts: empty picture frames and old death cards and wire dressmaker's mannequins and broken oil lamps, steamer trunks with rusted hinges, the dust floating in shafts of light from a small oval window.

I didn't know why a man would want to work in an airless attic room, so I remember agreeing to hold hands with the girls and we paraded around the dining room table wearing paper pirate's hats. Then, suddenly, there was a man standing over us, square-jawed, dressed in grey, his cheeks furrowed and grey. The sight of his skin felt like ash. He spoke to the tall woman and she smiled a little, and then without speaking to us he went back upstairs.

Years later, on every second or third Saturday evening Eustace Ross arrived at our house. He fascinated me. I almost never heard his footsteps. He would come up the veranda stairs, his fedora plunked on his head, and grin at no one in particular, and then drift sideways into the room, making no noise. He always sat near the fireplace, in an antique chair with thin-boned legs and ribbing, the arms too high for comfort, but he liked to sit in it, stolid, incongruous, his elbows jutting out over the arms. He stretched his legs straight before him, the thick soles of his polished black brogues facing his friends.

He would sit for a long time in silence and, depending on his mood, his depressions, he would take no part in the early quick, bantering talk of the evening, or he would defiantly break in, blurting out something sharp, even hurtful, as if he had been angered, slapped by a hand no one had seen (one night Marshall McLuhan was explaining how important it was to understand that what was missing between images in dreams was the conjunctions – and Eustace, exasperated, suddenly hissed, "Listen, for God's sake, he's explaining Freud to us, he's explaining Freud . . ."). Often he mumbled a terse, clipped aside, a snipe rather than a sneer. He went in for ambush. I tried to sit near him. His quiet words were witty and cutting. They nearly always died unnoticed, and Eustace, his mouth squared by the lines of his jaw, would laugh, a wide and silent laugh. No one heard his joke, no one heard his laugh. Sometimes this made him laugh even more, silently, so that he did not look like a dour, taciturn man who worked all day scanning meteorological maps, incoming highs, lows. He looked mischievous, a little lunatic, a prankster lurking behind his grey clothes.

I remember my mother telling me that she had met Eustace at a party, following him down one of those long, narrow halls in what used to be called railroad apartments, living room at the front end, kitchen in the middle, and sunroom at the back end. The hostess was bending over to get more quart bottles of beer from a box. She was a prig: Eustace, with a chuckle, had given the hostess a slap on the buttocks. "Up the Empire, up yours," he'd cried. My mother, who was not a prig, liked him immediately. She always talked to him. I learned over the years that most women found something attractive in Eustace: the feeling perhaps, that he had secrets to tell only them. Or perhaps – rare among men – he knew how to listen to women. Perhaps that's something he shared with my father, because my father knew how to listen to secrets. Women talked to him all the time. I certainly believed that there were profound secrets between Eustace and Mary. She was open and garrulous and full of confident laughter. She never seemed surprised by any gesture he made.

But there were men who resented Eustace. Bitterly. He was impossible if you were a businessman. He baited them. He brought out their bile. He would nearly always say something insulting. They complained that he was rude, that he needed a good punch on the nose. I somehow believed that his sharp, defiant insults were little revelations of a dangerous, desperate game – perhaps because he always winked at me – revelations of the intense capped feelings of a very lonely man, or rather, a man who felt least lonely when he was as alone as he could be, a man alone in the attic of his head.

I remember as a boy standing on the beach at Lake Scugog, where he and Mary had their summer cottage, watching him lay out oars after a long row in their boat, and I asked my mother where he had been and my mother said:

"He rowed across the lake and back."

"By himself?"

"Yes."

I stood for a long time staring at the dim outline of the opposite shore, like a grey water stain at the bottom of the sky, miles away, and I wondered why a man would row over there – all that distance – by himself and then row back, and what thoughts would he have while rowing that hard all alone? What dark and prankish plans? What sharpening of the eye?

He was a prankster. When great public debates were going on in the city newspapers he would adopt the role of the colonial reactionary he abhorred. He wrote preposterous letters to the newspapers, curmudgeonly letters, bigoted, always supporting the British or Ulster Orange cause, ripe with diatribe and the usual ignorance. He signed them "Old Flag," knowing the Old Flag editors at the newspapers would eagerly print such nonsense. No one, except his Saturday night friends, knew who "Old Flag" was. No one really knew who Eustace was. No one knew that he had fought in the First World War, that he had been gassed in the trenches, that he'd suffered shell-shock. No one knew that he was a mesmerist who believed that during the Second World War he had received messages from spirits, messages that he took so seriously he wrote to the U.S. War Department warning them that there was going to be an invasion of western Ireland. The War Department had written back and told him to leave them alone, but he had studied the note with his philatelist's glass and decided that several typewriter keys had been filed down, and after analyzing the flawed letters he discerned another secret message, this one telling him to disregard the order – it was a deliberate deception – and to carry on! He did, writing poetry and receiving messages, not only from the dead but from Prime Minister MacKenzie King. "What a world," my father said some years later – after we knew more about the spiritualism of the Prime Minister – "King was talking to his dead dog and at the same time he had Eustace on the line."

The only reputation Eustace had was among a few poets, relatively unknown themselves. He was the first modern poet in

Canada – as a radical irrealist (his word) he was years ahead of the *automatistes* in Quebec, he was an experimental Imagist (who made the later *Tish* movement seem derivative, if not redundant) and a formalist who gave new vigour to the old sonnet conventions – yet he was incapable of hustling editors and critics during the twenties and thirties. His work was never published by a commercial house, and in the fifties many editors forgot about him. He began to talk of his work as something he had put behind him, a waste of effort. He was ill at this time, deeply depressed, suffering trench sweats in his sleep, enduring shock treatments – electrodes attached to that attic mind – and after he recovered from this *whopping* of his brain, he refused to discuss his poetry.

Then one Saturday the conversation shifted, from the dopiness of Prime Minister Diefenbaker wanting to "green" the tundra and the polar cap, to the West Coast poets, and Eustace sat in his usual chair – but on this evening his legs were drawn under, tucked, and he was hunched forward; and he took apart – almost line by line – Ferlinghetti's *A Coney Island of the Mind* – "All that kind of so-called surrealism, it's really just a kind of sloganeering, images as slogans, insanity and the end of the world as whimsy. That's its charm, that's why it's so wonderfully lightheaded, it's so available. Surreal slogans." Eustace knew what he knew. He read and translated from the French (Max Jacob became a kind of other self), German (Heine and Hölderlin, whose peculiar lyrical bent – his "impersonal voice of the heart" – he could not quite capture), Italian (Dante, who did not suit his gifts at all), Latin, and Spanish. He had a first-rate eye and a critical mind. The next day I searched my father's library for a little volume I had long ago thumbed through, a privately printed book of Eustace's verse. I found *Laconics*, and *Sonnets* and two ochre issues of *Poetry: Chicago,* one featuring "Irrealistic Verses" by W. W. E. Ross, 1934, and the other – "Modern Thoughts in Disguise" by Marianne Moore, 1933 –

In magazines favorable to innovation, Mr. W. W. E. Ross is conspicuously one of the writers of this day. It is therefore not surprising that these sixty-nine sonnets (privately printed) should have freshness, responsibility, and authenticity of locality. They are about the oak, the pine, the lake, the river, the Indian, injustice, the supernatural, death, art, the Muses. In being proffered, some of them as imitative of Dante and of Italians before him, their modesty is appropriate but only conduces to an augmented conspicuousness. It is plainly "one of the writers of this day" who gives us sonnets *1* and *2*, *To the English Language*, and no one could have made the following sonnet without having boldly faced the difficulties that to verse belong:

Prometheus, bound in adamantine chains
To the grim rock stark-lifting from the sea,
Watching with eyes that wandered ceaselessly
The sea and sky, the sky and sea; whose pains
Not yet become a torment in his veins
Were still sufficient, while in tension he
Awaited the strong hand of deity,
Expectant of some increase to his pains; –
Bound as he was, his eyes were growing dim;
Discouraged, he relaxed the effort vain
Of rude rebellion on that fatal day, –
When, like the dolphins in their lively train,
Gliding toward the rock in bright array,
The sea-nymphs sang encouragement to him.

There is present the Spenser-Sidney-Milton-Wordsworth elegance, and an ingenuity with dactyls, which recalls the Melic poets. To so staggering a roster of consanguinities with an occasional defect, one may demur, but poetry with the unforced note is rare.

The next Saturday I told him I thought his poems were fine. He didn't want to talk, but persisting, I finally said, "Goddamn it, Eustace, they're good! What have you been doing up in that attic lately?" He invited me over to Delaware Avenue for drinks.

I felt silly on the evening. After all, Mary and Eustace had once stood over me as I stumbled around their dining room table, unhappily holding the hands of their little adopted daughters. They had watched me grow.

Eustace gave me drinks, nervous, prowling from chair to chair, awkward in his eagerness. Mary presided, a little bewildered that a young man should be so interested in forgotten images. We drank. We quipped. At last I asked for the poems, and Eustace, hesitating only for a moment, disappeared up the stairs, and that was the only time I heard noise when he walked – those black brogues clumping up the stairs.

He showed me four ledgers filled with poems neatly written in ink, workbooks, the quality uneven, but many of the poems excellent. He seemed to have kept everything, hoarded each thought. I read aloud the poems I liked, and some I found astonishing:

> *After the battle the soldiers danced and ate up the*
> *enemy's dead. No one tried to stop them. Help!*
> *cried one of the corpses before it was devoured. The*
> *way lay clear before them. Action dictated solely by*
> *considerations of self-interest and one's own stomach*
> *consisted in doing just one thing. So that corpse*
> *too was eaten and the dance continued.*

We drank a lot of Scotch and he prowled back and forth, saying little, but he was pleased.

Some weeks later I spoke about him on the radio, and read some of his poems . . . *the music that was heard Beyond antiquity.*

And sweeter than the call of bird in Spring's Iniquity. But there was little or no response. Certainly none from the editors in town. Eustace had listened, and he told me, "You read them the way I would have read them." I was silly, he said, to expect any response.

Eustace was sick. My father muttered about "those damned shock treatments." But curiously, he seemed more at ease, more jovial, more like an amiable elf than a big clawing cat. He had been to death and back a couple of times. He was coming out of himself. Other poets were looking him up – a young fellow had come all the way from the prairies – and Eustace was full of strut, small strut, but strut. His face was no longer grey but white, which made the red stand out on his cheeks, and he seemed alive and over his depression. But the white was the colour of cancer, and suddenly, Eustace Ross died.

It is a curious fact that Imagism, as a movement, got kick-started in Canada. T. E. Hulme, the English literary theorist and poet, boarded a cargo boat for Montreal in July of 1906. Hulme crossed the Ontario north and the prairies. Struck by the vast forests and flat spaces, and knowing that the language of rumination and reverie had gone to seed on the sceptred isle, he decided that what was needed to capture a landscape so raw was a language pared down and precise.

Hulme returned to England. Within a few years the Imagists had broken the back of *airy, fairy Lillian* and her limpid retinue on the Oxford Road. It was a time – among those who cared – for Pound, H. D., Moore, cummings, Williams, and Amy Lowell. When Eustace began publishing in the *Dial* (1928) and *Poetry: Chicago* (1934), he had turned not just to Pound but to Hölderlin, René Char, Heine, and especially the surrealist Max Jacob – he had turned to images at the point where dream begins, images so spare, so direct, that they could make the dream concrete:

The old maid!
She wears a black silk cape; she arrives with her
lameness which supports her words and her hollow laugh.
She comes into the garden, descending its scarcely marked
slope. They thought she was lying down, very ill.
"Well, since the doctor doesn't come to me, I'm
coming to you, and I wish to say that I died this
morning at . . . but I can't find the words any more . . .
Excuse me . . . if you see a flame in a bowl,
it isn't melted candlewax, it's my soul . . .
yes, indeed!? laughing, always amiable.
"Good health to you all! I'm going away."

Each word, each phrase was exact. There was no deliberate verbal complexity, no comfortable cosmic moralizing. The effect of unforced plain speaking was the essence, what Wordsworth meant when he said "there neither is, nor can be any *essential* difference between the language of prose and metrical composition . . . the most interesting parts of the best poems will be found to be strictly the language of prose when prose is well written." The concentrated eye is the key. Soldiers marching. A beggar. Angels. A flower. Trees, the lake, or a fish spine and rocks, exist in themselves, as "the fact the silence – only the silent fact," not as parts of any ideational design (he was at one with Williams, who said, "No ideas but in things"):

The white gum showing
in the gloom
along the massive
trunk of a great
pine-tree standing
on the hill
with a deep bed
of needles below.

There is a music in his lines, a music based on his ear for stress. It is a stringent music, sometimes not what it seems to be (he had an interest in syncopation, in the Blues monotony of the off-beat), sometimes complex. Try reading "Spring Song" on the down side of the first column – it starts with a stern two stresses per line, a regular marching beat on the 2-4, but try reading the song across, inserting the word *Momma* in the white space until you force yourself to read the space as a silence itself, and you are on the 1-3, the syncopated blues beat:

"Spring Song"

One day	*in the spring*
walking	*walking*
along	*he railroad track*
the railroad track	*near the town*
I passed	*looking at*
a pond	*a pond*
slimy	*of greenish water*
greenish	*a large pond*
From it came	*incessantly*
sounds	*sounds*
of frogs	*frogs piping*
piping	*frogs in the water*
I picked up	*I could not see*
a stone	*any frogs*
and threw it	*I threw a stone*
into the pond	*into the pond*
The stone	*it splashed*
splashed	*a big splash*
and the piping	*and the sounds*
of the frogs	*the frog's piping*
stopped.	

This may seem slight to the casual reader, but it is not. Those silences are how he gave an unforced vitality to the everyday and how he entered into the surreal, too – they are the spaces McLuhan was talking about on that Saturday night, spaces where the conjunctions are left out – silent spaces enclosed/embraced by images that never become vague, images that are always hard. It's true that he had no ideas but in things, but I had never suspected how courtly a lover he could be in verse (who knows in life?), nor how committed he was to the dream made real by the word, nor had I quite understood while he was alive how acts repeated over and over as ideas – the deep plunge into the cold green element – could open up before his very eyes so intensely for him – literally opening up as flowers – and how blooms were not only an affirmation of life renewing itself in a cold land but an intimation of a May-leafing on the side of life that we call death. These intimations erupted out of the earth:

the densed grouped dandelion,
flames breaking patch-wise through
from inner suns beneath the soil . . .

These flowers, these flames, the explosive resurgence of life "alarms" – then strikes "terror" into the minds of those who have "denied this explosion" because the explosion is the spirit made "manifest in the world" – manifest to those who have tried to see a truth, to see

the wind
that blows from outer space
and from beyond,
a wind that
blows in through the hole
that the diggers have made in the wall.

Eustace died, went out through the hole in the wall when he was seventy-two. Among his last poems there is a suggestion that the laconic long-distance Scugog rower – after a life of shock treatments – from little deaths to two great wars – and after a sojourn of being at play with Ezra Pound in the fields of canto land – might be back:

Come ride in a boat past the shelving shore where
the castle stands ruined and the ruins of the castle
show sharp and black in the moonlight. Let us glide
beyond the ruins, beyond the headland on which the
castle once stood, around the headland past the
sleeping village with the roofs of the houses shining a
little in the moonlight; and going on as the boat
glides down with the stream, on its dark surface, we
may come at length to the land that we left once;
and we may come to that land about dawn.

The Telegram; Irrealities, Sonnets & Laconics, 1966-2003

YOUR POINT IS NINE IN POLAR DARKNESS

Ah, Franklin! I would like to find you
Now, your Body spreadeagled like a star,
A human constellation in the snow . . .
I can almost suppose you did not die,
But are somewhere walking between
The icons of ice, pensively
Like a priest . . .
—Gwendolyn MacEwen

There was a time when men dreamed of sailing across polar lines into the land of ice. They dreamed of disappearing into great clefts of whiteness, seeking the silence of the womb, they said, or, if lucky, the Pole itself, where they believed all our compasses spun wildly, searching for direction even though there was no direction. They believed the dense sheen of white ice would be as close as they would ever come to the mind of God, that state of absence that contains all colour.

Some dogged men had tried in the past to find clefts and passages through the ice caps, bundling their dreams into ships and onto dogsleds. They had left their lives out on the floes, their bones sealed in ice, channel markers on the maps of other men who had decided to pursue a cold silence, a silence that was as far as they could get from the gabble of those men and women in their lives who were trying, as best they could, to inch into old age.

I bought myself a ticket on a cruise ship that was going to go through the Queen Charlotte Islands to Glacier Bay in Alaska. It was a sleek white ship called the *Royal Princess* (christened by Diana, Princess of Wales.) As I came into the two-tiered rose red lobby of the ship, which had a staircase of polished brass and elevators inside a brass missile-like casing, I was confronted by a sculpture that was more than eleven feet high, a spiral of burnished steel set in a marble-and-sandstone water fountain; and it bore clusters of nineteen seagulls in patinated bronze, and a man wearing a smart white jacket said importantly, "Each bird weighs thirty-two pounds."

Just then, an elderly man on a "mopie" – a kind of cut-down golf cart or soapbox derby car – sped down the gangway, beaming as he made a wide arc around the lobby, apparently a man with a bad heart. The mopie seemed to have gears; trailed by his wife – trotting behind him wearing jogging shoes and a silk print dress – he saw the elevator doors open, slammed the mopie into gear, and shot into the empty elevator. The doors closed. His wife was left patting the brass doors with upstretched hands. "Albert, Albert," she said softly.

"Thirty-two pounds," I cried, staring at Albert's pleading wife.

"Yes, indeed," the man in the white jacket said.

"How do you figure he stopped inside the elevator?" I asked.

"Head first; these are hard-headed people."

"Are you an officer?" I asked.

"No. A waiter. See you at supper, sir."

As I went into one of the several bars to be among my fellow travellers I had a peculiar sensation. I seemed, by a long shot, to be the youngest person on board ship. I began to suffer slight vertigo, a giddiness, and later, when I sat down to supper, a leathery-skinned woman with little ball-bearing eyes said to me with enthusiasm, "Hi, ahm Ellen Sales an' ahm from Waco, Texas, an' this har's ma mothuh an' she's ninety-two. How d'yuh do?" Wearing many diamond rings, she complained to the waiter that I had been served more vegetables then either she or her mother and she insisted that they be moved to another, more hospitable table, "where the peas would be plentiful."

"Can I buy a bottle of vodka?" I asked the waiter.

"How big?" he asked.

"Big," I said, preparing for a night among the well-dressed and well-heeled in the ship's nightclub, a show that was going to star Mr. Blackwell, a designer who annually chooses the Ten Worst-Dressed Women of the Year.

"Does he sing or dance?" I asked innocently.

"No. He insults," I was told.

"How long does it take to get to Alaska?"

"Two days."

"Make that two bottles," I said.

That evening, men who had the crackle of self-made no-nonsense aspiration about them laughed heartily as Mr. Blackwell asked their wives where they had got their wattles from and why did they insist on roping their "tits" up in so many lines of pearls, and the wives not only laughed but they applauded Mr. Blackwell. I put my head down and drank.

After a sound sleep in my stateroom, I sat out on my deck in the morning sun, staring at the shore, the steep stone slopes, and in the calm water the stone islands in Hecate Strait seemed weightless to me, seemed to levitate in a strange absence of any order that I decided was the order of things in that landscape. And yet – because the air was so clean – I immediately believed that it was a place, it could only be a place, for meditation on stone and ice and the gift of fire and on the northern sun as it falls closer to the horizon – yes, I thought, meditation on the dying of the light.

I took a stroll around the ship. The corridors were strangely empty, and on one of the decks I passed two joggers who had the fixed stare of those who've looked into the wind and blinked and seen nothing. In the weightlifting room, a trim young woman wearing a headband, red with little white hearts, was alone on her back on a padded board, pumping a barbell into the air, watching herself in the mirror.

"Do you really like this?" I asked.

"Why else would I do it?" she said. She had a gap in her teeth.

"What do you like?"

"When I'm done, I feel really drained. Empty."

Along another corridor, past a small bar, I discovered women drinking the Cocktail for the Day: bananas and kahlua topped with chocolate and a "fruity fiesta" – and then I saw that all the comfortable chairs beside the sealed windows had been settled in by men and women wearing golf shirts and polyester slacks. They were watching the dark and densely treed stone slopes slip by as if they were panning shots on television. One of the men, who had a high forehead and the scowl of preferment, touched his friend on the arm.

"What do you think of them trees, Harry?"

"There sure are a lot of them," Harry said, rubbing his hands together.

He had a little diamond ring on his pinkie finger.

"Do you think, Harry, them trees is natural or man-made?"

"I don't know. They must be natural."

"Now that's what I was saying to Edna. They gotta be natural. If they was man-made they could never have got them that close together."

After shopping in the ship's boutique, I went to the afternoon's entertainment, a bingo game in the pink and beige International Lounge, where three or four hundred people were hunched over their cards, some playing several cards at once.

They were a singular group of men and woman – at least they were to me – nearly all of them from Texas, Arizona, or California. They were the children of the dust bowl, the Depression years, folks who had not only survived hard times but had, through grit, become rich enough and easy enough with their own money to play games for a snowball bingo prize of five hundred dollars (but, I thought, probably not too easy on anybody – particularly among the young – who was down-and-out now, anyone having their own hard times). The cruise director called out the numbers: "Under the I, two little ducks – twenty-two." To my astonishment, the crowd cried, "Quack, quack."

"Under the I, one and six, sixteen – sweet sixteen and never been kissed."

"Rubbish," all the men and women cried, snapping the little window numbers on their cards.

"Under the B, one little snake, the number six," Chris the cruise director called.

"Hissssss," the crowd cried.

"Vodka," I told the passing waiter.

The next day the cruise ship dropped anchor at Juneau, the old gold-mining town that is on an inlet under an enormous mountain, and behind it I could see that coastal rain forests stretched for fifty miles to the east, and there were some mountain peaks I was told that were as high as fourteen thousand feet. Two elderly ladies stood at the bar drinking the cocktail of that day – Galliano, peppermint schnapps, cream, and strawberries – but down in the narrow streets of the town, at the Red Dog Saloon, below abandoned mine shafts and the rock face of the mountain, I drank a whiskey, making my own little toast to the old dead and gone sourdoughs and then, because I had the whole afternoon free on shore, I hired a small seaplane to fly me to the Taku Glacier. As the plane lifted off the water I felt a surge of both relief and fear: the small plane passed through a cleft in the hills and climbed into the mountains above the treeline, entering a world where, I was sure, only the ice worms live, a world of brutal serenity: jagged peaks, the broken upper reaches of the earth, and wide valleys bedded with chalk white ice, miles and miles of fretted ice, compressed in places where the frozen water – with all the air squeezed out of it – seizes the light, sucks it in and creates pockets of turquoise that have a strange vinyl sheen.

The plane landed in Taku Lake by the lip of the glacier, its huge, blunt end, I was told, growing at two or three hundred feet a year – and standing there, I thought, This is lifeless growth – lifeless but growing relentlessly as it crossed the water, a growth that would crush the spot where I accepted the invitation to join a fisherman who seemed to be totally alone, a man who had just lit a fire so that he could sit down and eat a salmon he had plucked from the cold lake . . . and as I sat with him, I kept thinking: This is obliteration, and this is the way the world will end, not in fire (that desert vision of God's voice turning within wheels of fire) but in ice, a freezing desert that approaches the image I had of God's mind in these polar climes, approaches because I felt I had not yet crossed into the real and absolute chasms of white silence that cap the world, I had not yet crossed into the place where

> *The ice cannot bear the flesh of men,*
> *The sun will not tolerate coloring,*
> *Where we begin already*
> *To move into the ice to mimic it.*
> *Our Father who art in heaven,*
> *Our Father*
> *Our father*

I sat down. The pilot had declined to sit with us. Standing at the edge of the lapping water, he was smoking a cigarette and staring at something (or nothing) on the other side of the lake. The fisherman – whose cheekbones seemed to be Slavic, but maybe they were Indian, too – forked a slice of grilled salmon steak onto an army surplus aluminum plate, saying "Name?" I said my name, but in reply the fisherman said only that he was glad to meet me, and so I said, "You alone out here, are you . . . ?" After a silence the fisherman said, "Yes and no." We ate together but kept a silence until I stood up to leave and asked, "What is it you do out here besides fish?" The fisherman smiled and said, "I spend most of my time largely looking forward to the past." I said, "Do you now?" We shook hands and said goodbye and the fisherman called out to the pilot, "Be careful, you hear; they're piling up on the other side."

The next day the cruise ship eased into a channel that was banked on both sides by mountain slopes. I suffered an optical illusion. The shores and slopes seemed close, the rock-strewn beaches the length of any ordinary beach. It all seemed strangely intimate, almost human in dimension – until I saw a tent and two tiny figures building a fire. They were minuscule, like fleas on the shore, and I realized that what had seemed so close, so normal, was actually immense . . . beyond comprehension in its massiveness, and then there were telltale chunks of ice in the water, signs of what was to come, walls of ice. The water began to fill with floes, ice reached out from the shore, ice was littered like crumbs on the still surface, and the ship glided between chasm walls into Glacier Bay.

White, I knew, could be blinding – the glare of white, the density of white, snow-blindness – and tongues of packed ice, miles wide, lay in the enormous valleys, their roots in the sky, ice inexorably on the move, a cracking and sudden crashing of huge wedges twenty storeys tall into the water, breaking the silence. The bay was a white womb, and I stood on deck speechless, wondering what anyone could say about something so unapproachable, so dead as it opened into a passage, a strait, a birth canal into zero weather silence . . . And then I believed I understood why the Inuit had always quickened in their imaginations to all and anything that could hold and contain the heat of living. That was why, in their sculpture, they tried not to impose form on stone or whalebone but sought instead to release the inner shape of the spirit, the warmth within, their shamans, their holy men, eagerly surrendering themselves to the spirits that were within all animals, yearning in their stark isolation to be entered into and possessed by each animal's inner fire, and – unlike tribes of the desert sands, whose god I had been brought up with – their god was not a taskmaster mouthing the laws of Leviticus but a god of renewal, the spark of life, god in everything and anything in a white expanse.

Surely this was why, I decided, in Russia so many of those northern Old Believers had thought – and maybe they still did – that each man carries a singular Christ within his own heart, a personal snow-blind Christ who sees everything. In such white wombs as Glacier Bay, faced with obliteration, a man could truly see that he and even the stones contained the gift of fire,

Which burns the night to morning
And cracks the latitudes of time and sleep

I went to the rose red lounge, and because it was late afternoon, I found that three or four hundred people were again playing bingo, the snowball pot at eight hundred dollars. Several men and women had ordered Love Boat cocktails – Galliano, white crème de cacao, tequila, cream, and grenadine – and Chris the cruise director called out "Under the O, twin fives, those Dolly Parton fifty-fives," and the crowd cried, "Oh, so big."

"A big vodka," I said, "a double."

I decided to go along to the casino, and as I passed the boutique, the louche Mr. Blackwell was selling dresses to two fussy women. "Of course we can take out the seams; we always leave lots of room to manoeuvre," he said. The casino was empty except for one elderly man at the end of the craps table. He held his head very high and had a good strong chin. He threw the dice with a stiff-armed swoop. The croupier called out the number: "Hard eight, your point is nine, sir." He had his cane hooked over the lip of the table, and then I realized that it was a white cane. He was a blind man shooting craps all alone, a pleased smile on his face as he picked up the white dice again and blew on them in his cupped hand, giving them heat.

"Coming out," the stickman called, as if the blind man were stepping out into the cold, and suddenly, as the blind man said, "Double my bets," and the croupiers took his money from the rack and laid it out on the green baize, I felt – in that isolated moment – that I knew all the wonder of a human trust in life . . .

a blind gambling trust . . . I knew that one man does not by nature have to steal from another, does not need to wound another, not when a white cane can hang on the lip of a table close to the polar darkness where all compasses spin.

Leisure Ways, 1986

FIRST ICE

In a phone booth, chilled to the bone,
she pulls her flimsy coat close,
crooked lipstick, eyes
puffy from crying.

First ice, telephone talk.
First ice. A cold shoulder.

Blows into her balled fist.
Earrings – jet glass. Fingers – blue.
Slouching home alone, alone
along the icy street.

Frozen tears sting her cheeks –
First winter of the heart.

• Translated from the Russian of Andrei Voznesensky

1972

STEPS: JERZY KOSINSKI

One evening there was a heavy snowstorm. The snow fell into the early hours, thick and wet, and then, at about three in the morning, it got cold. The snow stopped. A crust hardened on the snow, and under the street lamps in the silence of the early hours the crust glistened. I pulled on my high black boots and went out walking.

No one else was in the streets. There were no lights in the houses. There was only the deep white snow settled into smooth banks, unbroken, vulnerable, and I went plodding forward feeling an exhilaration as the crust held and then collapsed and my boots sank into the clinging softness. It was the dry breaking of the crust, the percussive clarity of each step, that I recalled while reading this strange book by Jerzy Kosinski. It, too, is a series of steps, moments of percussive cruelty, told aslant in a dispassionate prose.

Kosinski is Polish but writes in English. He has written one other novel, *The Painted Bird*. It is a novel made up of little stories about a child abandoned to brutality . . . peasant villages during the war. The stories build like a stone-picker's pile in a convict's field . . . a stone, a stone, a stone, horror upon horror. The stories are persuasive because they seem to carry the weight, the gravitas, of autobiography. But the piling up is also a piling on: the horror becomes laboured and dulling. Predictable. In *Steps* the narrator is older; the men and women he meets are not the monsters of a child's eye. He has grown up to become a kind of monster himself, a man stripped of emotion, stripped of remorse, a man who takes a step, a step, and then another step . . .

. . . the day, for example, when he stepped into a barn where the deep stillness was interrupted only by the buzzing of a wasp. He stood among clusters of horseshoes, whips, buckles, and belts hanging on nails and two axes driven into a short, thick tree stump, and then he heard a piercing whine.

> A large cage was suspended from the rafters. Formed of metal grating, it hung down on a heavy rope which passed through a ring that secured it to the roof. The rope fed down the wall and was fastened to a large cleat.
>
> The strange cry came again: my light beat against the cage. A white hand stretched toward me through the bars; behind it a head, dim but clearly framed in untidy tresses of fair hair, caught the light . . . A naked woman sat behind the grating, babbling meaningless words, staring at me with wide watery eyes . . . She stared at me, then began crawling toward me . . .

She is a crazed woman, crazed because the village men keep her caged, keep her to violate her. The village priest knows that they violate her. He does not interfere. She has become the wound that is sin, a suppurating wound. Men with the stench of the wound on their souls offer their sin to the priest: ashamed, they sob, they seek compassion, and they ask for forgiveness – they ask out of the same profound need they would bring to a prayer for a good harvest. It is these sinful parishioners who give the priest his significance. They and the priest are made one by sin, by rituals. And so life is lived, in crime and expiation. The narrator, however – the seeing eye – is connected to no one. The villagers, the priest, feel what he never feels: remorse.

The narrator is, as a storyteller, very much like a soldier in one of the stories, a soldier on military training who casually turns into a sniper. A peasant couple are making their way along the crest of a hill . . . "The soldier's rifle kicked twice and muffled shots cut into the silence. When I looked toward the couple again, they lay in the swaying grass like two surfers suddenly swept off their boards by an unpredictable wave."

Like that sharpshooter, the narrator catches men and women in the crosshairs of his telescopic lens, catches them up close and intimate though he is safely a mile away, a disinterested yet curious seeing eye as he pulls the trigger, all the fragility of life – and death in life – at his fingertip – a fragility akin to the fragility of the butterflies he caught of an afternoon among the ruins of his broken city.

> Like rebellious shreds of a rainbow, the butterflies swarmed high against the blackened walls. My friends and I would capture them by the dozen in our homemade nets. They were easier to catch than the stray cats, the birds, or even the fierce, hungry rats.
>
> One day we placed some butterflies in a large glass jar and set it upside down, its wide neck overlapping the edge of an old ramshackle table. The gap was wide enough to let in air, but too narrow for the butterflies to escape. We carefully polished the glass. At first, unaware of their confinement, the butterflies tried to fly through the glass. Colliding, they fluttered about like freshly cut flowers which under a magician's hand had suddenly parted from their stems and begun to live a life of their own. But the invisible barrier held them back as though the air had grown rigid around them.
>
> After we had nearly filled the jar with butterflies, we placed lighted matches under the rim. The blue smoke rose slowly about the pulsating blooms inside. At first it seemed that each new match added not death but life to the mass of living petals, for the insects flew faster and faster, colliding with each other, knocking the colored dust off their wings. Each time the smoke dimmed the glass,

> the butterflies repeated their frantic whirl. We made bets on which of them could battle the smoke the longest, on how many more matches each could survive. The bouquet under the glass grew paler and paler, and when the last of the petals had dropped onto the pile of corpses, we raised the jar to reveal a palette of lifeless wisps. The breeze blew away the smoke – it seemed as if some of the corpses trembled, ready to take wing again.

These stories, these anecdotes, are percussive steps across a crusted and stricken landscape, a landscape crusted by war, by death camps, a landscape of displaced persons putting one step in front of the other, with no sense of beginning, no sense of end, and the narrator is a witness who has no home, no family; he is a nameless man who carries only the maps of an unnamed country. He is the victim who has stepped out of the concentration camp mirror. He is as pitiless and detached as any concentration camp commandant might be. He is the victim who finds himself staring at a woman caged in the dark, a woman putting her hand out to him – as he notes her every move – as he brings her alive – and he feels no compassion, none at all.

The Telegram, 1969-72

ARID ATTITUDES: HUGH MACLENNAN

Hugh MacLennan, the novelist and essayist, is dismayed by the recent eruptions of street violence in Montréal. He says the mayhem reminds him of Rome and the Vandals. But who are the Vandals – the Plouffe family, or the uprooted Québécois working in the Montréal factories, or the jobless Gaspésiens? Who knows?

He has said: "Rome was once a very tough, puritanical city; suddenly it became very permissive . . . The thing is self-evident to me. People, all of us, are animals and they break loose. I mean a handful do it; and I know if all discipline goes, and society depends on an element of discipline, [the violence] will happen." He has elaborated on this theme, saying that Montréalers and Canadians, are "more bewildered by the change in moral climate than any other country I can imagine. Unaccustomed to affluence, we abused it and lost our perspectives. The authority of religion in Quebec disappeared far more suddenly than elsewhere. The sexual revolution produced a sudden precociousness among the young . . . and of course there was television."

Nonsense.

What we have always lacked is any awareness of Québec based on what French-Canadian intellectuals and especially Québécois nationalists have said about themselves over the decades. Now Professor Ramsay Cook has brought together such material: a collection of essays – three historical interpretations of the French fact and twenty-two other entries made up of manifestos, journalism, pleas, and ideological arguments.

Reading this material, most of it surprisingly well written and well translated, it becomes clear that the recent riots and the terrible violence of the past few years have definite, complex roots in Québec history. One need not look to Rome or to agitators in Cuba or Algeria to understand what has been going on. The question central to French Canadians for the past hundred years has been *la survivance*: "Nearly every other intellectual pursuit – philosophical, religious, literary, historical, social, economic, and political – has been subordinated to, or at least interwoven with, the national question." In other words, French Canadians have diligently recorded and delineated their anguish, their *angoisse*, their sense of frustrated uniqueness.

It is generally agreed that the so-called Quiet Revolution of the sixties had its accidental beginning in the Asbestos strike of 1949. Not only did the strikers stand against the Duplessis police goon squads and those conservative cardinals who were at the political trough, but certain young men came to their defence: Pierre Elliott Trudeau, Jean Marchand, Gérard Pelletier, Jean Drapeau, and René Lévesque. The revolution, once it took up steam, fell into the hands of these men, and since then we have watched them engage in a kind of fratricidal war: federalists vs. nationalists. But what was the emotional and intellectual temper of these men at the time of the strike? Were they optimistic humanists banding together to stave off social injustice, were they ingrown nationalists, were they expedient opportunists, or was there some boil in the air that had to burst?

In 1948, the year before the strike, an art teacher at Montreal's École du meuble delivered 400 copies of a mimeographed pamphlet to the Henri Tranquille bookstore. It was a manifesto signed by sixteen people, the *automatiste* group, led by the art teacher and painter Paul-Émile Borduas, who wrote: "It is nauseating to realize our own cowardice, our helplessness, our weakness, our bewilderment . . . as if there were no future for us." Borduas – and those other artists who signed the manifesto, *Refus global* – saw the Québécois, the intellectuals and the labourers, as not only trapped within fortress walls of fear, walls that had been built up over a hundred years, but trapped also by their dreams and the anguish involved in ever tearing those walls of fear down:

fear of prejudice – fear of public opinion,
of persecution, of general disapproval
fear of being abandoned by God and by a society
that invariably leaves us to our lonely fate
fear of oneself, of one's brothers, of poverty
fear of the established order – fear of absurd laws
fear of new acquaintances

fear of the irrational
fear of opening the flood-gates of our faith in man –
fear of the society of the future
fear of the unsettling experience of love
deadly fear – holy fear – paralysing fear: so many
links to our chains.[1]

Borduas prophesied that those who engaged this violent duality would rid themselves of

---

[1]In English Canada, Margaret Atwood, in her sequence *The Journals of Susanna Moodie,* says in an afterword: "If the national mental illness of the United States is megalomania, that of Canada is paranoid schizophrenia. Mrs. Moodie is divided down the middle: She praises the Canadian landscape but accuses it of destroying her; she dislikes the people already in Canada but finds in people her only refuge from the land itself; she preaches progress and the march of civilization while brooding elegiacally upon the destruction of the wilderness; she delivers optimistic sermons while showing herself to be fascinated with deaths, murders, the criminals in Kingston Penitentiary and the incurably insane in the Toronto lunatic asylum. She claims to be an ardent Canadian patriot while all the time she is standing back from the country and criticizing it as though she were a detached observer, a stranger. Perhaps that is the way we still live. We are all immigrants to this place even if we were born here: The country is too big for anyone to inhabit completely, and in the parts unknown to us we move in fear, exiles and invaders. This country is something that must be chosen – it is so easy to leave – and if we do choose it we are still choosing a violent duality."

the days of debilitating fear
as they entered the era of anguish
. . . And after
the reign of overpowering mental anguish comes
the reign of nausea.

How did such a feeling for life take deep root in Québec?

Québec nationalism took on a peculiar form after Confederation in 1867. Never an aggressive assertion of pride and confidence, it was conservative and authoritarian. The nationalists drew strength from a sterile defence of local traditions – the survival of novenas, fish on Fridays, scapulars over the heart, the ground chill of piety, spoon players, fiddlers, general practitioners, wood whittlers, hockey players, a horde of *petits avocats,* and an equal horde of nuns and priests. Leaders, with a sometimes mystical fervour, kept French Canadians agrarian, aggrieved, ill-read, ingrown, dreaming the stunted dreams of their fathers. Taught by obscurantist priests, they were interested in politics only when Québec's autonomy was at stake; seldom, if ever, did they question the political hierarchy. Aloof from industrialism, commercial technocrats, big business, and the labour movement, Québec remained a retarded province – producing cheap labour and a peasant class, craven politicians, and a clutch of reactionary cardinals.

When the *automatistes* and the Asbestos strikers revolted against this torpor, the intellectuals not only had to find new names (*séparatistes, indépendantistes, souverainistes*) for the movement within federalist Canada, but they launched into an internecine war. The Québécois – nationalists, separatists, and otherwise – have been battling not only English dominance but also themselves. They have been trying to turf out the established political and economic managers, yes – but just as important, they have been trying to shed a clinging fear, an anguish, even a shame – and to shed it with a confidence that is not acquired but authentic, and authentic because it is earned. To describe – as

MacLennan does – what the Québécois are up to – the release from a malaise and spiritual suffocation – as permissiveness, abused affluence, lack of discipline, and a sexual precociousness aided by the insidious and debilitating influence of television – is to mislead an already ill-informed English-speaking community.

The Telegram, 1967

HARAROLD PINTER: *THE HOMECOMING*

Some people have a cold in the nose.
Some people have a cold in the head.
The English have a cold in the heart.
—e. e. cummings

On the surface, each of Harold Pinter's plays seems a comedy of manners: characters are static; their vitality is dependent on verbal wit; they argue over trivialities – the arrival of a new tenant, a cup of tea, a birthday, a son who has returned home with his wife. This is drawing-room comedy down-at-the-heels. Pinter's men and women, seated in high-back chairs in *The Homecoming*, are in rooms that are spacious, grey, and lifeless. There's an undercurrent of violence in their gestures and gibes, there's a hint of strychnine in the teacups.

Talking about violence, Pinter cited a short story he wrote some years ago: "That story dealt very explicitly with two people in one room having a battle of an unspecified nature, in which the question was one of who was dominant at what point . . . a threat constantly there: it's got to do with this question of being in the uppermost position . . . I couldn't call this violence so much as a battle for positions, it's a common, everyday thing . . . the world is a pretty violent place, it's as simple as that, so any violence in the plays comes out quite naturally. It seems to me an essential and inevitable factor."

In Pinter's early plays – *The Room*, *The Dumb Waiter*, and *The Birthday Party* – this inevitable violence, this slow escalation of animosity under the cover of clever repartee, this battle for positions, was expressed symbolically in awkward fashion. Death hovered in a black void outside each character's well-lighted room, death in the form of blind blacks or hired killers. The victims of these killers, like Stanley Weber in *The Birthday Party*, mouthed protests that were paranoid and hopeless. An unknown power had decreed their deaths.

These plays, particularly *The Birthday Party*, were effective because Pinter aroused a deep sense of dread through the figure of the motiveless professional killer. In *The Birthday Party*, the killer Goldberg is at one moment the vulgar East End Jew, a stock character slobbering over mama's gefilte fish, celebrating family loyalty in a fit of nostalgia, and then he is the ruthless hood who has murdered countless men, tallying up his talents with a kind of evangelical enthusiasm. Murder in Pinter's work is macabre because it is offhand. But for the same reason, death lacks important meaning, and as a result life is robbed of significance. All gestures are reduced to the trivial, but paradoxically – because everything is trivial, each object, each phrase takes on ominous significance. A door, a dumb waiter, an old man stumbling through the night, all seem to carry their own menace.

Because violence is the lynchpin for the action and because the violence stems from some unknown malevolent force, the early plays lack internal combustion. The killers, those blind black men who come out of the night, may symbolically represent self-destructive forces within each victim, but the question of who is dominant, as Pinter puts it, is never answered. In the early plays there is no explicit battle for positions. The oppressor is faceless. Goldberg is an agent; he is a zero. His victim is a martyr who does not believe in anything.

In *The Homecoming*, however, Pinter is still dealing with a battle of an unspecified nature, but no force threatens mysteriously from without. There are no cipher-like figures signifying death. The battle is where the heart is, in the home, within the family.

We are introduced to a seventy-year-old North London widower, his three sons, and his brother. The old man, Max, is a retired butcher, full of swagger and nostalgia, full of pecker-pride in his sons at one moment and hatred for each son the next. The youngest is a bumbling muscle-bound construction labourer who is training to be a prizefighter. If he could only master offence and defence, his father says wryly, why, he might have a chance. The second son, Lenny, is a professional pimp, a sometimes surly, sometimes suave psychopath. The eldest son has been absent for years and is a professor imprisoned spiritually within his philosophical discipline. He brings home his wife. She, it turns out, was "on the game" before she bore three boys. Rounding out this family of men is the butcher's brother, an ineffectual, impotent chauffeur.

The Homecoming has no plot to speak of. Each scene makes clear that these men, beneath an urbane air of fellow feeling, are violent. They shift between roles: they are devoted and dutiful, or they are curs slanging each other. The father is a protector and a tyrant, the boxer is impotent, the woman is a mother/prostitute and the meek Lenny is murderous. There are no helpless victims (with the possible exception of the chauffeur brother) and no symbolic death figures. Each member of Max's family is capable of lopping off his own hand or the heads of others. Pinter has caught this in a controlled, spare prose that has its own compelling rhythm, a plainsong. It is brittle music. The object of this music is to make spoken language express what it does not ordinarily express. To find the menace in the flatware. In this Pinter reminds one of Hemingway's very early stories, the *In Our Time* stories. His subject, too, was violence and brutality, driven home through a clean, concise prose that never interfered with the emotion being described. So, in *The Homecoming*, when Max moves close to his chauffeur brother, he begins by talking protectively to him and moves plainly and almost unobtrusively into self-centred, threatening contempt.

> I want you to get rid of those feelings of resentment you've got towards me. I wish I could understand them . . . When Dad died he said to me, Max, look after your brothers . . . his sacred words, Sammy . . . you think I'm joking? You think when my father spoke – on his death-bed – I wouldn't obey his words to the last letter? . . . You're prepared to spit on the memory of our Dad. What kind of son were you, you wet wick? . . . Well, I'll tell you one thing. I respected my father not only as a man, but as a number one butcher! And to prove it I followed him into the shop. I learned to carve a carcass at his knee. I gave birth to three grown men. All on my own bat. What have you done?

These men struggle for dominance in the family, a struggle learned at the father's knee. It is a world lacking maternal force. "I gave birth to three grown men. All on my own bat." A man gives birth. In blood. To rancour. To particular words. Father. Carcass. Obey. Death-bed. Son. Carve. Each polite and agile gesture of considered rage and inconsiderate appetite is tied up in the extremity and loneliness of private lives lived within the family.

The Telegram, 1967

A FACE IN THE MIRROR: THE POETRY OF FRENCH CANADA

End your moan and come away.
—John Webster

Québec is our great gap of unknowing. There has been no volume of translated verse that we could turn to and say, yes, that is the French voice heard through their land, that is how sensitive minds suffered their compulsions, failures of will, their *moments fragiles.* Now we have such a volume, edited and introduced by John Glassco, wry pornographer and the author of *Memoirs of Montparnasse.* There are many mediocre poems included. There are important poems and poets – Paul-Marie Lapointe's "Les arbres," Gaston Miron's "Monologues on Raving Alienation," the works of Eudore Évanturel, and the surrealists, especially Claude Gauvreau – left out (Glassco has no taste for the *joualisants,* or for their working-class argot, the street talk of the Quiet Revolution), but there are sufficient poems for an overall picture.

There have been many movements, many schools, in French-Canadian poetry, but it is surprising – at least in this selection made by Glassco – how coherent and single-minded the experience of these poets has been, no matter their age, their rococo urges, their religiosity, their usurping of Parisian techniques, or how hermetic their quarrels. The nearly fifty poets in this volume seem to have suffered through the same stunted loves in the same sour rooms, the same metaphysical gripes, the same words whispered to the same pallid ghost hiding behind household mirrors.

Apparently François Hertel played a role akin to that of Hugh MacLennan in English letters. Of the same generation, they shared the same urge: limited in imaginative scope, both attempted to set down the social outlines of their country's condition. Both, writing under the impress of the land – writing from the need to belong, the need for *appartenance* – had a natural feel for disinheritance. Hertel:

O, my country!
Motionless, fixed, like an eye of glass
in a robot's head,
You the immutable, your belly
crammed with meats
And promises . . .
The great ones, the mighty ones
begat no children in their image . . .

To think that perhaps I have the blood
of Frontenac in my slender veins,
And my pale forehead could be the
flesh of Madeleine.
When a race dries up, it breeds politicians . . .
My damnation is here and now, and
my crime is to have been born,
But I do not wish to die . . .
No longer can I even formulate
My special formula for damnation on earth.

The poetry shares images with the fiction – fear's yellow beak in their hearts, men haunted by heroic ancestors, a wicked stepmother, and a mutilated childhood, women who hate their doltish fathers, lovers who despise themselves and their God, men and women succumbing to suicidal dreams, and at last, those same men and women rising like angry children in long pants to engage in a revolution. One of the finest of the poets, Saint-Denys Garneau, began as a writer fascinated by the play of light in the paintings of Monet, Sisley, and Degas:

O morning of my eyes on the water.
A luminous bathing-girl has drawn upon herself
all the light of the landscape.

But, like his fellow Jansenist the French novelist François Mauriac – who said he always, as he began to write, heard the angels of Mozart, only to be then invaded by the black birds of Beethoven – Saint-Denys Garneau lost his joy in the play of light and became a morbid mystic whose day-to-day journals are grim, lugubrious reading. As a poet he wrote:

I am a bird cage
A cage of bone
With a bird . . .
He cannot fly away
Until he has eaten all
My heart . . .
He will have my soul in his beak.

With Anne Hébert, a younger cousin of Saint-Denys Garneau (and a poet exquisitely tuned to her own sensibility), you get the image of the dead child, ubiquitous in the literature:

A little dead girl is lying across our doorstep
We found her in the morning, curled on the sill
Like bracken touched by frost.
Now that she is there
We do not dare go out,

This pale child in her frothy skirts, shedding
A strange milky darkness.

Trapped in such a nightmare house, pain is celebrated as pleasure, pleasure as pain, madness is enchantment, and morbidity is enchanting. Again, Hébert writes:

Here is an ancestral manor
Without a table or fire
Or dust or carpets.
The perverse enchantment of these rooms
Lies wholly in their polished mirrors.
The only possible thing to do here
Is to look at oneself in the mirror day and night.

This dry narcissism seems encoded in the generations, even in the poets younger than Hébert, the poets of the *Partis pris* and Hexagone groups of the fifties, those who are now in their thirties. But there is a new note, too, a glimmer of resentful aggression. Yves Préfontaine, like Hertel (and with much the same talent), writes of his country as a lost land, but there is anger in the *angoisse*:

My country is quietly strangling under a snow of fatigue . . .
I am rooted in a people that has lost its root . . .
walk with the ghost of race
brushed off like an uncomplaining whore.
Round and round I go in this wilderness, ringed by a
cloud of white and furious faces.

Fernand Ouellette, more hermetic, more layered in his effects, takes the fury further:

One evening, hope being quite dead
bodies turned into stones, hurled
themselves into their nightmare.

Paul Chamberland (influenced by Kerouac and Ginsberg and the *Californie* movement) announces the actual revolution, the destruction of the birdcage and the breaking of the mirror on the wall:

I've broken the mirror of poetry shattered that
image on the wall
I'm casting my eyes my forehead
and my bare fists in the mould of
a naked wind howling through
chinks of anger
And nothing nothing can shield me
ever again from the anguish of my people.

For the effete effect of the mirror he has substituted the shrill virility of the Soviet wall poster:

I am the poster from which your blood has spurted
my comrades
spattering the night of traitors
And revenge's peep of day.

Finally, André Brochu, a child of street bombast and dynamite sticks, has turned history into agitprop in the nursery:

Mother, you handed me naked into the thorns
Broken from my seasons
You poured your kerosene and neglect on the faggots
of my destiny
You left my soul a gaping wound defenceless
I was riveted to the terror of my rabbit-warren
Evilly walled away in the cages of frost.
But also now and still
There's the thundering threat of the children's bombs.

The glass eye in the robot has blinked, the dead child has risen, he is quick on his feet, angry and boisterous, with a bomb in his hands. His poster face is on the wall, his teeth are bared, he is a sloganeering child transfixed by his own revolutionary image, crying *OUI OUI OUI* all the way home. This is the story of a cradle inside a coffin, the story of weakness seeking the prestige of strength. As a result, much Québécois poetry continues to follow the politics and social ferment of Québec, to suffer the limitations of François Hertel – the earnest moan of poets barnacled to a beleaguered politics – but, and we should be aware of this, there are several poets – Nelligan, Saint-Denys Garneau, Hébert, Miron, Lapointe, Ouellette, Brault – who have stepped through the mirror of nationalism and religiosity, and they have come out on the other side writing a poetry that moves us beyond the moment.

The Telegram, 1970-71

PORTNOY, SON OF A JEWISH JOKE

Whumpf.

She was a mother. A Jewish mother. Weeping, she grated her own horseradish, she lit candles for the dead, she sewed, she darned, and when her little son would not eat, her little son who was going to be a doctor (God willing), she sat down beside him, a long breadknife in her hand, murmuring love words, *whumpf whumpf,* and she held the knife at his throat, asking whether he wanted to be a man or a mouse.

She loved her son, she loved every hair on his head, every loose elastic string in his jockey shorts; she loved him, she loved him with only the pain a mother can feel, only the tears a mother can shed. He fled into the bathroom. Behind the locked door he took hold of the only thing he could call his own in that house.

Whumpf whumpf whumpf.

Alex Portnoy, approaching middle years, is on his doctor's couch. He is complaining, pleading, mewling, as he confesses his dirty little secret: he still masturbates day in and day out. He is haunted by the superstitious, hysterical love of his Mama, her watch-its and be-carefuls, you're breaking the law. "What law, whose law . . . ?" he wants to know.

His father was no help. He *schlepped* after his son into the bathroom. He, too, locked the door. He struggled to move his bowels, but Mama was up against the door, whispering, begging: "How's it going . . . How's it going . . . ?" As an insurance salesman he has suffered ignominy, he has been insulted in a *goy* world, so that – driven in upon his innards – he has only one conversational subject: the tribulations of the New Jersey Turnpike.

"Dr. Speilvogel," Portnoy cries, "this is my life, my only life, and I'm living it in the middle of a Jewish joke. I am the son of a Jewish joke – only it ain't no joke. Please, who crippled us like this? Who made us so morbid and hysterical and weak? . . . sucking and sucking on that sour grape of a religion! Jew Jew Jew Jew Jew Jew! It is coming out of my ears already, the saga of the suffering Jews!"

Portnoy pours out his life: In the perambulator he was pinched, he was prodded and cooed over; in school he had a scholastic score sheet of straight As but he struck zero as he lusted after candy floss *shikses*; at home, in the house, there was a model son who'd lived downstairs, a thoughtful, courteous boy, but that model son had hanged himself from a shower nozzle.

Whumpf whumpf whumpf.

In his college days, Portnoy's passion for the handle he had on himself did not abate. He became a voyeur, an exhibitionist, a fetishist who hated himself, hated his world, and hated the *goyim*: "The outrage, the disgust inspired in my parents by the gentiles, was beginning to make some sense: the *goyim* pretended to be something special, while we were actually their moral superiors. And what made us superior was precisely the hatred and the disrespect they lavished so willingly upon us. Only what about the hatred we lavished upon them?"

But he wanted their *shikses*, he wanted their golden hair, their bobbed noses, their refined manners.

Whumpf whumpf whumpf.

"America is a *shikse* nestling under your arm whispering love love love love!"

He wanted love.

The last of his *shikses* is a woman so dumb her tits are in a trance. Her name is Monkey. She is as lascivious and puerile as Portnoy is puerile and ludicrous, but, like his mother, she bristles with accusations, blaming him for her depravity, driving him, guilt-ridden, to his sore muscle and then, at last, to an El Al plane for Israel, Promised Land, land of freedom.

In Israel Portnoy feels expansive; he is no longer the outsider. The hotel clerks, the cab drivers, the cops, the girls on the beaches, they're all Jews, and happily he ends up in the sack with Naomi – the Jewish Pumpkin, who is six feet tall, an army girl on leave from patrols along the Syrian border. Self-reliant, strong, she reminds him of his mother. Immediately he loves her, he wants to marry her.

"'You,' she says incredulously, 'there is something very wrong with you . . . All day long the same thing. In some little way or other, everything is ironical, or self-deprecating . . .'

"'Oh,' he says, 'self-deprecation is a classic form of Jewish humour.'"

She turns on him.

"'Not Jewish humour! No! Ghetto humour!'"

He is, he is told – Israeli to Jew – the epitome of the *gonif* from the *galut,* a frightened, defensive, self-deprecating, unmanned, self-hating, whining, hysterical man. His life disgusts Naomi, the Uzi-toting heroine of the desert hills. He is left muttering to himself: "I had been made to understand that I was the epitome of what was most shameful in the 'culture of the Diaspora' . . . gallant Sabra! You go be a model for mankind! Fucking Hebrew saint! . . . The work-molded legs, the utilitarian shorts, the battle-scarred buttonless blouse . . . 'Look at you,' I said, 'way up there . . . Look at you – how patriotic!'"

Portnoy's story – given as a self-deprecating confession that concludes with his doctor's ironic punchline – has the character of a saloon joke modelled on Henny Youngman or Myron Cohen or a host of other Catskill troupers who snipe every other week at their wives and mothers on the *Ed Sullivan Show.* This does not mean, however, that Roth's hyperactive savagery is without point, for the rambling Portnoy has constructed a handjobber's handbook – a Mrs. Mendel's Book of Regular *Galut*

Etiquette – a guide to ghetto morals and manners, observations that are sometimes burlesques, sometimes revelatory: the prevalent, casual contempt for *goys, shikses,* and *shvartzes*; the fear of entering into non-Jewish life that leads the Portnoys of America to become faux kibbutzniks in Israel – not to stay as Zionists and to work, but to thrill in stories of pre-emptive military strikes; and the effect of kosher laws that involve more than discipline (because certain foods are forbidden, the Jew learns early lessons of renunciation and suffering, and because the *goyim* eat unclean foods, Jews learn that the *goyim* are contaminated and corrupt and the *goyim* therefore are despicable, and hence, suffering and moral superiority are served up at every Jewish meal).

As Portnoy becomes a despicable, uptight, whining, narrow-minded little creep – at home on the psychiatrist's couch rather than a creep hunched over a hand job on the toilet – his witty one-liners and his manic eloquence turn mean and cloying, the joke runs out.

WHUMPF WHUmpf Whumpf wh. The self, the seLF, the SELF.

As D. H. Lawrence once wrote, "within the vicious circle of the self . . . a self-absorption is made public . . . The vicious circle of masturbation! The vicious circle of a self-consciousness that is never fully self-conscious, never fully and openly conscious, but always harping on a dirty little secret."

The Telegram, 1969-72

MARGARET LAURENCE: ENGLAND, 1965

Went today to visit Margaret Laurence, who lives in a grey stucco cottage, Elm Cottage, in Penn, just outside of London. Small and set back from the road, difficult to find, flanked by larger homes, trees, vine-covered walls. The rooms cramped, damp and dark like a doll's house (and if they seem so to me, think of her – from the prairies . . .), but the low ceilings hold the little heat at shoulder level, an electric heater in a brick-trimmed fireplace in the sitting room, and a little stove in the kitchen/eating room.

Laurence is frenetic. She bolted into the room (the sitting-room is at most ten by ten, with a tiny alcove to the side), shaking hands quickly, eagerly. She dropped two packages of Cadets onto a side table (Cadets, she said, because they are cheapest), then picked a package up, fumbled for matches, said, "Let's have no formality – call me Margaret," and when I jokingly replied, "I'll go further . . . a hello kiss on the cheek," she said, "No, no, not that friendly," and lit up, throwing the matches onto the table. Though there seemed to be stern resolve in her open and direct almond-shaped eyes, her hands were shaking, ashes spilled over her black dress, a simple wool dress, square necked. She flicked the ashes off her small breasts, always moving, hands waving, her head bobbing, ashes falling, brushing them away, hunched forward in her chair, swinging back, shifting from side to side, lighting up again, always talking, trying to control a tremor, apologizing, excusing herself, but articulate, with a firm stare.

"Why did you have to go to Africa," I asked, drawing my chair close to hers, sitting in front of her, "before your imagination really stirred?" Her legs were crossed, and she has good legs, a trim body, and her hair was short, pulled into a French twist at the back, with firm little curls at her temples.

"Well, probably because that whole countryside seems somehow less real than your own country and therefore terribly exotic. This was tremendously exciting in a way I couldn't believe the Canadian prairies could be exciting. I realize now that this is nonsense, of course."

"What seems to have quickened your imagination was the Somali struggle to stay alive, primitive struggle, staying alive with just a little dignity."

"I think this is absolutely true," she said, leaning forward in her chair, "and I think that you find – sort of unknown to yourself – that the same themes tend to emerge all the time in your writing. But when I was writing about Africa, the struggle to survive was strictly a physical struggle, whereas in *The Stone Angel* Hagar's struggle is not only to survive physically, but also to survive in an inner sense. The book I've just finished, *A Jest of God* – I can see the same theme, survival with some dignity, but it's more a question of survival of the personality in a world filled with enormous strains and tensions; survival becomes spiritual."

"What about politics and the novel? You've written about the struggle between blacks and whites, and a number of short stories in the same context. Can the artist really deal with politics, get involved in actual political situations, without seeming to deliver messages?"

"Personally, I think not. I think very few writers, maybe none, can be novelists and political propagandists at the same time. I think they find themselves writing propaganda. It becomes propaganda rather than a novel because when a writer becomes highly political, he thinks he knows the answers and wants to make you hold the same political point of view, whereas a novel is almost always a kind of discovery. I don't think the writer herself knows entirely what's going to happen, or what's going to emerge, and she has to be prepared for the unexpected. In fact, you partly write to discover something you didn't know before." She laughed and lit another cigarette. "I think there's a very strong sort of evangelical strain in most political writers."

"What do you think of Doris Lessing in this respect? She's written about Rhodesia, you've written about Ghana . . ."

"Well, I think that when Doris Lessing writes about relationships between people, whether they're Africans or Europeans, she's fine, she's at her best. But her political writing I find quite quite dull, really. Where she is absolutely super is in this terrific ability for self-analysis; she is tremendously honest."

"And the English writers in this country who've come out of the lower classes: Alan Sillitoe or Arnold Wesker . . . is the laying on of a political point of view – in someone like Wesker – is that an attempt to cover up for a fundamental weakness?"

"I think with a great many writers whose obsession is a social or political theme, this is a kind of evasion, an attempt to look away from inner things. In other words, you focus entirely on the outside world." She shifted her black-rimmed harlequin glasses. "The outside world is terrifying, but not quite so terrifying as the inside world."

She lit another cigarette. She seemed suddenly tired . . . or emptied, not of energy but of words. She stared straight at me. *Gainsay Who Dare*, I thought, remembering tough Hagar Shipley and the Shipley family epitaph, but then there was also some terrible vulnerability in her. That fluttering of her hands. She touched the elegant brooch at her left shoulder and then gave a wide, silent sweep of her arm toward the walls. The bookshelves. The room was book-bound: hundreds, nearly all contemporary, many African. On one wall, a highly polished purple hand in some kind of stone or glass. On the mantel, a wooden fawn-coloured urn and a carved ebony head. Margaret said the urn was used in Somali religious services; after prayers the Somalis urinated in the urn. She added, if they had no urine they could substitute sand. The head was from Ghana, one of the few good heads she thought available, and the hand on the wall, also African, was used to ward off evil spirits – she hoped, suddenly talking again with good openness; and she seems incapable of assuming a public face, a role, or perhaps a natural heartiness is her role, her defence. Within the time we had been talking she was greatly gentle when listening or defending her thoughts. And perhaps the cottage atmosphere had much to do with my impressions, but she is a countrywoman – bold, even brash in her shyness, with plain, rough hands, fingernails bitten back to the quick, and adjusted to her circumstances.

"You know," she said, "I think that I came to the point, writing about Africa, where I felt that if I continued to write about Africa I would be writing strictly as a tourist, and in fact might be spending the rest of my life as a tourist. I didn't want that. I started writing about Canada; it was very much a coming home, mentally, for the first time an attempt not to evade my own past and childhood. Essentially, the same thing very many writers do, come to terms with what you are. This came out in *The Stone Angel.* There are many things, many discoveries I didn't like, in fact I deplore, but these things are also in myself, and this is where I came from, this is what I am. You don't get very far unless you come to some kind of terms with it. I don't really want to write anything any more except about people that I can know a bit from the inside."

"And you've just finished a novel!"

"Yes, I'm very happy, deliriously happy about this: *A Jest of God.* What it's about is an unmarried schoolteacher, a woman in a small prairie town, Manawaka again, a person who doesn't really make very much contact with the rest of the world, who is very withdrawn and shut in, and it really is the story of her attempt to break out of this kind of shell and also to break away from the influences of the past . . ."

"Is this the same survival . . . ?"

"It is really survival, yes . . ."

"Getting a little dignity by breaking out . . ."

"That's right, and also finding even in the most personally appalling circumstances that sometimes you discover dignity at the very depths of the pit, as it were," she said, her gaiety gone, turned inward. "You know . . ."

"Well, you've gone back to Manawaka in your imagination, and now your Manawaka woman's trying to break out, but you're still here living in England. Why is that?"

"It's just sort of chance, really. At the moment I like it here. I like living close to London. I've gained quite a bit through having met a number of English writers and publishers and so on, but I don't intend to stay here for the rest of my life. I'll go back to Canada."

"What do you make of the whole business of Canadianism? I remember one of the reviewers of *The Stone Angel* said that the real merit of this fine new book was its Canadianism."

"Really, I feel so . . ." and she closed her eyes, as if in pain, "I feel so strongly against that point of view. I think the thing that matters least about a novel is whether it's Canadian or American or English or African, or what it is. I think the only thing that matters is whether it's a good novel, and I hate really to have my writing talked about as Canadian writing. I mean, it is Canadian writing because I'm Canadian, but this is not the central thing. This is not important for me to try to be a Canadian writer – I wouldn't dream of trying – but the only thing that one wants is to be a reasonably good writer. And I think, If only Canadians could quit talking about Canadian writing. We're far more sort of self-conscious about this than other people are . . ."

"Don't you fear, when you come back to Canada, getting caught up in the whole business of being a Canadian writer, promoting Canadian culture?"

"I don't know whether this is a tactless thing to say or not, but I really am very much afraid of this. In one sense, this is a reason why I'd rather stay here for the moment, because I do think that with the best will in the world, in Canada the writer gets too much recognition for too small a body of work. This sounds so terribly ungrateful, but I'm not ungrateful, you know. I'm terribly pleased that my books have sold well in Canada and so on . . . but I don't think it's a very good idea for a young writer – not that I'm all that young – but a beginning writer to have a great deal of attention given over one or two books. The whole thing is, can you continue, can you go on to where you've written maybe three, four, five novels, and then we can see whether you're a good novelist or not. This is really all I want to do."

We sat down to lunch in the kitchen/eating room and were joined by her children. Her daughter is a pretty, very English girl of fourteen wearing glasses; her enthusiasm is horses. (Margaret hopes she will get over this, hopes she will not become one of those "terrible horsey women" – and then she worries that her daughter will meet no boys in England. Boys and girls, she said, never seem to meet in England until they are adults, and then, like children coming together for the first time, they have no idea of what to say to each other – exactly Dickens' description: people do not meet, they carom off each other.) The boy is ten, apparently very clever with his hands, and is building transistor sets in his room.

The casserole was frugal: macaroni, peas, and chicken chunks. She served no dessert, though the boy complained, gave her a setting out because they seldom had dessert. She is worse off than I thought. There are not enough cups to go around.

She went on talking with animation about Canada, and how the idea of "the land" has been overplayed and what interests her is people, not poplar trees. She remembers her little town not as picturesque or as landscape, but as the home of her domineering grandfather, a man hated by his children and his children's children. That experience, she insisted, was far more interesting, overpowering, than any mound of rock, clump of trees, or CPR train track across the tundra.

When I left she seemed a little sad, though she was hearty and abrupt in her farewells. She had relaxed completely during lunch, sitting back in her chair, picking her teeth with a wooden match. Smoking, smoking. The two little curls were still firmly pressed against her temples. She shook hands. She called good-bye and turned back into the cottage.

I drove away under a grey sky. It was drizzling. I looked back, the cottage almost hidden by half-dead autumn foliage, a frail wisp of smoke from the stove. I felt she was very alone and vulnerable there, that she should come home and settle.

Books In Canada, 1987

SOUL ON ICE: ELDRIDGE CLEAVER

Eldridge Cleaver, the Minister of Information for the Black Panther Party of Self-Defense on the West Coast, is an inmate of the California state prisons of San Quentin, Folsom, and Soledad. His essays, written in jail, are a chronicle of a man who has put himself through a spiritual shakedown, trying to become civilized. Civilized is not to be confused with becoming white or anything like an Oreo cookie. (Perhaps it is still necessary to point out that *Western white* and *civilization* are not necessarily synonymous.) By civilization I mean that Eldridge Cleaver has written essays in order to give a shape to his experience that approaches parable; to save himself from pandering to white men and from retreating into self-destructive hatred – "The price of hating other human beings is loving oneself less." Cleaver craves self-respect; he is presently in jail.

He was eighteen years old, in Folsom Prison on a marijuana charge, when he suffered his first crisis in becoming. He had, of course, always known he was black, but he discovered he preferred white girls. A terrible guilt came over him, and he vowed vengeance. He would become a rapist of white women. When he got out, he practised on black girls, and then set out to send "waves of consternation throughout the white race." What he found, however, was that he lost his self-respect. "My pride as a man dissolved and my whole fragile moral structure seemed to collapse, completely shattered. That is why I started to write. To save myself."

Back in prison, Cleaver went through a series of religious experiences and became a Muslim convert, then a Muslim preacher of eloquence, and then a follower of Malcolm X. There are few in the white community who understand how powerful a figure Malcolm X was, and is. They know neither the depth of his religious experience nor how important his break with Elijah Muhammad was to white society, let alone to blacks, nor how unique is his *Autobiography*, nor how tragic was his murder.

Cleaver states the Muslim attitude toward white and black succinctly and places much recent history in perspective: "The New Testament parable of Jesus raising Lazarus from the dead is interpreted by the Black Muslims as a symbolic parallel to the history of the Negro in America. By capturing black men in Africa and bringing them to slavery in America, the white *devils* killed the black man – killed him mentally, culturally, spiritually, economically, politically and morally – transforming him into a 'Negro,' the symbolic Lazarus left in the *graveyard* of segregation and second-class citizenship. And just as Jesus was summoned to the cave to raise Lazarus from the dead, Elijah Muhammad had been summoned by God to lift up the modern Lazarus, the Negro, from his grave."

Jezebel, the white seductress, was a constant taunt, the white woman who could never be possessed by black Lazarus in his chains:

> The white man made the black woman the symbol of slavery and the white woman the symbol of freedom. Every time I embrace a black woman I'm embracing slavery, and when I put my arms around a white woman, well I'm hugging freedom. The white man forbade me to have the white woman on pain of death . . . Men die for freedom, but black men die for white women, who are the symbol of freedom. That was the white man's will, and as long as he has the power to enforce his will upon me, force me to submit to his will in this instance or in any other, I will

> not be free. I will not be free until the day I can have a white woman in my bed and a white man minds his own business. Until that day comes, my entire existence is tainted, poisoned, and I will be a slave – and so will the white woman.

This, of course, is Cleaver as Lazarus – Cleaver back when he first admitted to himself in his prison cell that he preferred white women. But his conversion to the Muslims was a first step out of the Lazarus death: the whites became devils and black was beautiful. White devils were the enemy of Allah; they were to be hated and destroyed.

But then Malcolm X, apostle of Elijah, committed heresy. He went to the Holy Land and wrote back: "You may be shocked by these words coming from me, but I have always been a man who tries to face facts and accept the reality of life . . . I have eaten from the same plate with people whose eyes were the bluest of blue, whose hair was the blondest of blond and whose skin was the whitest of white . . . and I felt the sincerity in the words and deeds of these 'white' Muslims that I felt among the African Muslims of Nigeria, Sudan and Ghana."

Many blacks were shocked and outraged. This was schism; but for Cleaver it was liberation from a doctrine of hate and racial supremacy. Malcolm X had special meaning for Cleaver. He, too, had been a prisoner and had risen from the lowest depths to great heights of self-awareness. Then Malcolm X was assassinated by other blacks. Racism triumphed for the moment. "The bootlickers, Uncle Toms, lackeys, and stooges of the white power structure have done their best to denigrate Malcolm, to root him out of his people's heart, to tarnish his memory." But Malcolm had given blacks like Cleaver their manhood; they no longer needed Jezebel. Malcolm's sense of freedom from hatred within himself was his resurrection from the dead, and Cleaver and others have not surrendered that resurrection: "We shall have our manhood."

"I have," says Cleaver, "washed my hands in the blood of the martyr, Malcolm X, whose retreat from the precipice of madness created new room for others to turn about in, and I am caught up in that tiny space, attempting a maneuver of my own."

That manoeuvre, an evangelical release rooted in self-respect, has allowed Cleaver to re-enter American life with fervor. Predictably, perhaps, he observes: "Over the past 12 years there has surfaced a political conflict between the generations that is deeper, even than the struggle between the races . . . What has suddenly happened is that the white race has lost its heroes. Worse, its heroes have been revealed as villains and its greatest heroes as arch-villains." What is not so predictable is Cleaver's realization that it is among white youth that the greatest change is taking place. They are experiencing, he says, a psychic pain as great as any suffered by blacks: the awareness of their fathers' villainy.

These white youth, he says, now move in a gulf of fear, hostility, mutual misunderstanding, and contempt. So it is that Cleaver sees the white rebellion as a moral revolution in conjunction with the black pursuit of freedom. As a result, he can write about himself and his country:

> Individuality is not nourished in prison, neither by the officials nor by the convicts. It is a deep hole out of which to climb . . . I was very familiar with the Eldridge who came into prison, but that Eldridge no longer exists . . . I have come to feel what must be love for the young people of America and I want to be part of the good and greatness that they want for all people. From my prison cell, I have watched America slowly coming awake. It is not fully awake yet, but there is soul in the air and everywhere I see beauty. I have watched the sit-ins, the freedom rides, the Mississippi Blood Summers, the teach-ins, and the mounting protest over Lyndon Strangelove's foreign policy – all of this, the thousands of little details, show me it is time to straighten up and fly right.

Cleaver is talking about the fine line between barbarism and civilization, and that line is the moral awareness that allows a man to condemn without hatred and love without sentimentality. Our times are charged by singular hatreds, singular sentimentalities. The history of white North America continues to be charged by hatred and sentimentality. Eldridge Cleaver has been able to make of the realities of his life a meaningful parable and, as such, his essays encompass much that is sick and much that is beautiful in American society.

The Telegram, 1968

NO EXIT: EXPO '67

Montréal, Wednesday

Major poets from every continent are expected: Ezra Pound, Robert Lowell, Pablo Neruda, George Barker, Shih-Hsiang Chen, Robert Creeley, André Frénaud, Irving Layton, Simeon Kirsanov, Czeslaw Milosz, Denise Levertov . . .

The Dupont Auditorium on Ile Ste-Hélène: precast concrete walls, deep relief holes drilled in the concrete – and, like a rear-view blank mirror, a glaring white screen hangs above the rostrum; the sloping room feels like a last-ditch refuge.

Poets straggle down the aisle, and some, especially the continental French, have the air of insurance brokers, corseted in double-breasted suits. A knot of American poets are all in herringbone, as befits East Coast professors. There is something meek about their intermural nattering. Only Robert Creeley, with his black beard, his damaged eye and loose-limbed walk, and Robert Lowell, who seems permanently damaged, command attention.

Earle Birney says, "They wanted me to read a paper. But who wants essays at a poetry conference? Let the poets read their poems. They're poets, after all." Though lanky, Birney is curled into his chair, his white hair ruffled, his skin a buffed pink. He is staring at the holes in the rough cast concrete. Ezra Pound has not shown up.

André Frénaud speaks in French and the English fumble for their plastic headsets. He plods head down through pages piled between his elbows. Frénaud's poetry is sensuous, ironic, erotic, and he once wrote, "I assert, I proclaim man's right to be

God," but now, with the light catching his steel-rimmed glasses, he speaks in the tone and style of a public works official as he analyzes the obligations of the poet to society.

Irving Layton is hunched forward, intent on his own bluff irritation. George Barker, from England, fiddles with the volume button. He is wearing dark glasses. With a mild grunt he flips the clear plastic plug from his ear, leans back, nods and dozes.

Judith Wright of Australia follows Frénaud. She apologizes for being "a minor poet from a minor country," and her voice quavers, and her right leg shakes badly. She talks of the terrors of science and technology. Czeslaw Milosz of Poland holds her with his glittering eye, his heavy eyebrows combed up to a point. He has the presence of a front-line officer. He talks about exile, revolution, war.

As Milosz concludes, the chairman calls for other poets seated in the three front rows to come forward and comment. Robert Lowell slides down into his chair, his chin on his chest. Panic crosses the chairman's face. There is silence and a shuffling of feet. He looks like a teacher pleading with students to speak out.

Pierre Emmanuel of France strides to the microphone. Hardly pausing for introduction, he lauds all the poets for their suffering, alienation, commitment. In the midst of a final rhetorical flourish he asks for care and precision with words. Words, he says, are sacred and not to be wasted. Words are magic. The woman beside me mutters, "What a windbag." No one moves to the microphone.

The chairman, with his hand to his brow like the watchman in a crow's nest, gets Layton to the floor. The bottom buttons of his shirt are undone. His bare navel is a dark zero. He is amiable, cocksure, ironic. He scorns the laurels that Emmanuel has heaped on the poet's suffering. Get in touch, he charges them, with something concrete – like the thirty-eight poets in Czechoslovakia who, in a signed letter smuggled out of the country, cried out for aid of any sort. "Any sort."

George Barker is napping again. Layton, arms folded across his chest, looks distressed. Denise Levertov rushes to the microphone and explains that her whole life has been lived in a time of war, and now there is Vietnam, and the poet, she says, must engage these problems, put himself on the line and initiate effective action. A poet asks – how effective, in the face of technology, of science, of war, can the individual poem be? The American Mr. Cox, who is black, rises to say: "I read my poem about a black on a radio in New York and now that black man's face is going to be on a stamp."

The chairman brings this first session to a close. He is bedraggled but pleased. Leaving the auditorium, Layton says, "You see, you see why the French have de Gaulle. Someone has to come along and tell them to shut up. No more speeches. Shut up."

I ask, "What difference do you think Pound would have made?"

"Difference? I never expected him to show. And what would he have to say to such people? He would have wanted to read his poems."

The poets pile into a sightseeing bus. A military band prepares to play for the poets. At the first bugle blast the bus pulls away. The bandmaster stops wagging his baton. He looks furious.

Thursday

Czeslaw Milosz, grown vehement, has apparently argued with Robert Creeley. Milosz says he believes Creeley is on his way back to Buffalo, in a snit. Earle Birney says, "There's going to be one poetry reading, one afternoon of poetry at least, and the officials didn't want that one." A. J. M. Smith, the poet and professor, says, "You must understand. The reading of poems would not seem respectable. All the money and expense, all the time and organization – for them to make such an investment, and then have only the fleeting experiences of a poem: never. They want good solid prose, the more pedestrian the better, essays that can be weighed like butter."

Simeon Kirsanov – who survived Stalin – is wearing a worker's denim shirt with a loud floral tie, his hair white and close-cropped like a medieval soldier's skullcap. He speaks French with a Russian lilt, an imp, darting about the rostrum. He is nimble among platitudes.

Denise Levertov is earnest and speaks with great conviction, insisting the time for commitment has come – "Anguish is the source of poetry and . . . we have a choice. To go down into darkness, talking, talking, talking, or to discover what peace is and be against war . . . The time has come for poets to put their bodies in front of the war machines." She smiles, gap-toothed, wearing a horrid print dress of crimson flowers. She is applauded. There are bravos. She is against war. She is for peace.

Robert Lowell says he wants only to point out that good poetry has been written in support of bad causes. "The two poets not with us – Neruda and Pound – surrounded bad causes, one superficially and the other profoundly. Both were better poets for it." He sits down. Ranaivo of Madagascar, in exquisite French, stands up and explains that the poet is above all coarse matters, such as war.

Words.

Harindranath Chattopadhyaya of India sports darks glasses. His hair is black on top, grey on the sides. He seems to have suffered a bad dye job. He is scowling, moaning, keening, chanting, celebrating himself and "his new music added to the harp strings of humanity." To a roar of mock bravos (some are also hooting in disgust), Chattopadhyaya burbles.

Robert Lowell reads three short poems as if possessed by weariness (if Eliot was too much "an aged eagle," then Lowell drags his heavy wings across the floor) and he calls out, "We are a lot of wild spiders crying, but without tears."

Layton sprints down the aisle. He is damned tired, he says, of listening to poets tell him what it is like to be a poet. "Poets have replaced the discredited priests, rabbis, and ministers – new poets dish out uplift and self-adulation. You are specialists in uplift. Not once in these sessions have I heard one word of abuse. We have talked not about poems but about poetry. The mood of the speeches has been solemn, pompous . . . making me think of those high-school teachers I suffered years ago. I said yesterday that this was the first great conference since Homer. Well, let it be the last until another Homer appears."

The American poet Paul Goodman places his lips against the microphone and *pop*s as he explains that "There is a *pop* poetry renaissance going on that is *pop* part of the common *pop* people and the *pop* political revolution among the young who *pop* protest the war, which is *pop* part of that revolution."

Frank Scott of Canada says he is terribly disappointed, the poets seem so afraid of technology. He says there was an eclipse of the sun over Montréal. Editors in the newspapers had warned against staring at the sun. He had written a poem about his own refusal to be intimidated:

I looked at the sun straight in the eye.
He put on dark glasses.

He sits down, mighty pleased with himself.

Friday

The mood is serious. Frénaud whispers, "Such cheap grandstanding by Layton the Canadian." When he is angry Czeslaw Milosz has the look of the henchman in his eye. He is angry at Layton, too. As an exile, he says, he knows all about political awareness, but then he says, "Poets do not speak out because they fear public misunderstanding. We must be actors in public." Milosz is followed by Emmanuel, who says, "Milosz – the poet is not afraid of the public, the public is afraid of the poet." Eugène Guillevic of France says, "Faced with the enemy, faced with the world, let us adopt a resolution." A resolution! There is something of the fellow traveller in his tone. Someone tells me he is a Stalinist.

Chattopadhyaya bellows, "Tatti, Tatti, Tatti," unaware that the audience is shuddering in fits of derisive laughter. Levertov utters brief, controlled images of war. She smiles. Cox reads. He confirms that he is banal. Layton, alone with his poems, is flat, ineffective. Frénaud and Karel Jonckheere of Belgium emerge as fine readers. Jonckheere, smoking a twisted black cigar, says: "Gentlemen, we have said much about the poet. I will give a short definition: the poet is witness of his own resurrection from the dictionary, this is his magic, a man who also has the courage to keep his feet on the ground."

A petition is circulated on behalf of the Czechoslovakian poets; those who had called for commitment refuse to sign.

Saturday

As poets amble and bump their way into a hotel dining room, I remember that my father once asked me, "Who killed Harry Houdini?" and when I said I didn't know he said it was a Canadian who killed Harry Houdini – he just stepped up out of nowhere in a crowd and punched Houdini in the stomach and killed him.

"But why," I wanted to know, "would a Canadian need to kill the magic?"

"Well," Morley said, "it's a complicated story."

He never did tell me the story. He just told me who had killed the magic, and I was trying to tell this to George Barker as we sat down in the Windsor Dining Room, one of those silverplate hotel eating halls with huge acorn-shaped chandeliers, heavy white tablecloths and clumsy cutlery, the knives and forks you used to find in the dining cars of trains when trains had dining cars. Barker, still wearing dark glasses, is disgruntled. "Now we get the rubber chicken," he says. We get rubber beef instead but that doesn't cheer him up. He mumbles a lot and seems not to hear anything I say. Then he realizes he is still wearing his Sleep Well earplugs. He takes them out and then complains about the noisy clashing of cutlery and plates. He is a hard man to please, but he does say, "Not terribly easy, trying to have a conversation with me." As he jabs his spoon into a frozen-froth dessert there is the clinking of a knife against a glass, and Barker, out of the corner of his eye, sees that someone has risen to speak. He pours cognac over his froth and keeps on eating. But then he stops and turns to listen. A trim, sinewy man, hair cropped to his skull, is talking in an off-the-cuff fashion about writing and art. He has a natural grace that finishing schools cannot teach. After listening for five minutes, Barker asks "Does he write good verse?"

Realizing he thinks the speaker is a poet chosen to welcome the lunching poets to Montréal, I say, "Poetry . . . I have no idea. He's the new Minister of Justice."

"You mean he's a bloody politician?"

"Yes."

"Uncanny. The man knows what words are."

Barker is so bemused by his own pleasure at hearing Pierre Elliott Trudeau talk about the language of poetry and the language of politics and how a failure of the imagination for both the poet and the politician always takes the form of pandering to the public, he makes me a present of a little magic, his own resurrection from the dictionary, new poems:

I see the idiot fishes play
like zanies in the sea,
millions and millions night and day
delighting so to be.

And by the shore, host upon host,
the unborn children stand
each one as silent as a ghost
holding a ghost by the hand.

Note: Houdini died on Halloween in 1926. He was in Montreal to perform at the Princess Theatre. The illusionist was assaulted by thirty-one-year-old McGill theology student, J. Gordon Whitehead, whose unprovoked punch was powerful enough to rupture Houdini's appendix. The great performer died nine days later from peritonitis. Whitehead disappeared.

The Telegram, 1967

TRUDEAU AND QUEBEC: 1967

We must distinguish between "that which is established because it is right from that which is right only because it is established."

—Samuel Johnson

In his *Memoirs*, Vincent Massey – who had an eerie presence: tough and sinewy but his grey skin unattached, loose – said there was no place he felt more welcome as Governor General than in Québec. He was often a guest at the stolid Garrison Club, and "as the principal social club in Québec, it naturally has a bilingual atmosphere. One of its traditions is the reservation of one room for English-speaking members and another for French-speaking members, with a communicating door between the two which is always opened on New Year's Eve; the rest of the club is, of course, common to all its membership. The arrangement of rooms illustrates the important principle that there are natural differences between French- and English-speaking Canadians."

Those elegant rooms, so appealing to the Massey temperament, may be a pleasing metaphor for our language relations, but as Pierre Elliott Trudeau has pointed out, the French and English have never resided in equal rooms in our country: democracy in Canada has been a tale cynically manipulated by the French and cynically exploited by the English. As Trudeau says, the authors of our constitution "created a country where French Canadians would compete on an equal basis with English Canadians . . . but French Canadians have not really believed in democracy for themselves; and English Canadians have not really wanted it for others. Such are the foundations upon which our two ethnic groups have absurdly pretended to be building democratic forms of government."

English Canadians became aggressive cannibal-kings, bellicose, cunning, and oppressive. The French, on the other hand, ended up defeated, occupied, belligerent, leaderless, and banished from commercial enterprise. The French, constantly outmanoeuvred by the English minority in their own province, made politics a desperate means of guaranteeing racial and religious survival. They created a nation-state, if not in political fact, then in their minds. In their reserved rooms, both sides became intolerant and discriminatory. They called it compromise and made it a national virtue at the Garrison Club, with Vincent Massey as doorman.

It is fair to say that the French allowed their civic sense to atrophy so that their spiritual condition might flourish. The French were Catholics in an authoritarian Catholic state. Abandoned by France after being beaten by the English, they saw themselves as alone and encircled by enemies – English Protestants preaching liberalism. The priesthood, seldom challenged by their flock, were determined to defend the faith. In doing so, they defended the culture. Because the Church was the lone French power capable of resisting the English, the parishioners of Québec placed their political and spiritual lives in the care of their pastors. The Church maintained the integrity of Québec on one hand and wielded federal and provincial power on the other. It was a mixed blessing. It is Trudeau's argument that the English power group, not interested in encouraging the large French community to discover and put into action their political rights, recognized the Church as a force with which they could come to agreement. The French people, politically craven if not corrupt, incompetent, and unaware, were citizens of what was, in effect, a totalitarian nation-state within another nation-state.

To understand how bleak, crippling, and anti-democratic the atmosphere in French Canada was, and to some degree still is, we have to consider the influence of Jansenism, a crooked branch of Catholicism transplanted to Québec from Port-Royal.

Jansenism is an extreme dualism: the division of the spirit and the flesh into absolutes of purity and corruption. If we turn to French Canadians writing as the articulate expression of intellectual and emotional experience in Québec, we discover Jean Le Moyne: "It is forbidden to love and be happy because – guess why? – because it is a sin. Any means are valid to ensure that this edict is respected; sickness of various sorts, especially TB, noble sacrifice, family tortures, murder, incest, suicide . . . When I say love, I mean first of all, the most difficult kind, the love of self, and after that the love of others and the love of things."

The individual, if Québec literature is any mirror, has been robbed of his faculty for happiness. He cannot believe in himself. He has been led to associate being happy with a sense of unpardonable guilt. The political implications of this literature are profound, for if the individual is caught between absolutes, obsessed with his unworthiness and unable to believe in personal happiness – in effect, alienated from himself – it is impossible to imagine that person ever embracing the principles of responsible government.

Politically, what would be most natural to such an individual is some form of absolutism, and that, as Trudeau suggests, is the current character of separatism, so that – rather than being a revolutionary force – separatism is counter-revolutionary, and counter-revolutionary at a time when "the dogmatism of Church and State, of tradition, of the nation, had been defeated. Authority had returned to its proper place in a free system . . . Professors could say 'no to the Jesuits' without being barred from the university . . . Students could try to impose their views . . . The Family itself had lost its power over young men and young women. In 1960, everything was becoming possible in Québec, even revolution."

Hurrah for revolution and more cannon shot!
A beggar on horseback lashes a beggar on foot!
Hurrah for revolution and cannon come again!
The beggars have changed places, but the lash goes on.

The contemporary young, by refusing to enter into dialogue, by making it clear that they are intent on imposing the will of the few on the many, have turned to a new dogmatism, a new absolute, a new lash. Religious sectarianism has become national sectarianism. As Trudeau relates, "Scarcely a week passes without a handful of separatist students coming to tell me they are against democracy and for a single party system, for a certain totalitarianism and against the freedom of the individual. In this they are in the pure tradition of all that our society has always produced that was most traditionalist, most clerical, most monolithic, most reactionary . . . They are in sole possession of the truth."

It is Trudeau's contention that English Canada shares the same intolerant, close-minded, authoritarian approach to individual liberty. This will gall Anglo-Saxons, but Trudeau describes the situation as he sees it:

> The point remains that the English-speaking Canadians, rightly considering that self-government is the noblest way of regulating social relations among free men, proceeded to claim its benefits for Canada, but only after serving standing notice on the French that such benefits were not for members of a subject race . . . English-speaking Canadians have never given up their condescending attitude to their French-speaking fellows . . . At Ottawa and in provinces other than ours, this nationalism could wear the pious mask of democracy. Because, as English-speaking Canadians became proportionately more numerous, they took to hiding their intolerance behind acts of majority rule; that was how they quashed bilingualism in the Manitoba legislature, violated rights

> acquired by separate schools in various provinces, savagely imposed conscription in 1917, and broke a solemn promise in 1942.

These strong-arm English tactics are well documented, but Trudeau's case will seem less partisan if we think for a moment about that particular and peculiar Canadian "democratic" concept, a concept that has been cultivated and praised by the Anglo-Saxon minority – the Canadian mosaic. The mosaic means that immigrants, when they arrive in Canada, are not assimilated, or "melted"; any melting, as Vincent Massey and others of his ilk insisted, would have led to Americanization, a vulgarization of society, intermarriage, a thinning not only of the blood but of power and influence. So we have an insidious policy: hyphenated groups, no matter how large (the Italians in Toronto – in their "ghetto" – are the third-largest Italian-speaking community in the world), are encouraged to fuel-inject only one or two representatives into the Anglo-Saxon elite power group. The rest are encouraged, if not paid off through grants and other government gestures, to continue to speak in their "foreign" tongue, to publish newspapers in their "foreign" tongue – to seldom be more than landed foreigners. This is Massey culture (as opposed to mass culture, Mr. Massey being the pre-eminent representative of the Anglo-Saxon view) and it is essentially one of contempt: a fear that the bloodlines will be contaminated and centres of influence reduced.

Consider the Ukrainians who settled out west. Waves of labourers arrived before World War I; they were encouraged to huddle and cluster and were treated as "the breed" from Central Europe. Clifford Sifton, the minister in the Laurier government responsible for the influx of immigrants, came under fire from other Anglo-Saxons for bringing in "the scum of Europe." Social workers spoke of the "the dilution or contamination of national blood, national grit, national government, and national ideas." When the First War broke out, the "bohunks" had their property stolen from them and they were herded into concentration camps (camps for civilians were invented by the English general "Butcher" Kitchener, during the Boer War) at the insistence of Anglo-Saxon pirates masquerading as petitioners; and then, with the onset of World War II, long-time settled Ukrainian intellectuals were interned once more; they were declared "enemy aliens."

Between the wars, a well-known Montréal Anglo-Saxon economist wrote:

> Canada, especially in its north-west provinces, is badly damaged . . . [as a result of the general foreign immigration before World War I]. From the point of view of the Russians and Galicians, etc. this meant improvement for the north-west. Not so from ours. Learning English and living under the British flag may make a British subject in the legal sense, but not in the real sense, in the light of national history and continuity . . . A little dose of them may even be variation, do good, like a minute dose of poison in a medicine . . . I am not saying that we should absolutely shut out and debar the European foreigner, as we should and do shut out the Oriental. But we should in no way facilitate his coming.

That was from *Economic Prosperity in the British Empire* (1930). The author was, of course, our national humourist, except that he was deadly serious: Stephen Leacock. Vincent Massey, sharing Leacock's view, had no hesitation in quoting in his *Memoirs* from a letter he wrote in 1922: "One thing which annoys me is the lack of interest on the part of the government in immigration from Great Britain. The one thing that would prevent us from becoming Americanized would be a constant flow of good stock . . . our Cabinet, partly, I suppose, because of the French influence, seems very apathetic. In the meantime Sir Clifford Sifton is indulging in rhapsodies about the hardy peasants of Central Europe, of whom I think we have enough."

This is distressing, but I hardly know what to say when I read in Vincent Massey's *Memoirs* that *nothing* touched him "quite so much as this comment in a Canadian newspaper: ' He made the Crown Canadian.' It was too generous a tribute; but that was what I had tried to do." Massey culture! What a preposterous view, what a preposterous denial of the realities of Canadian life. What vanity and what dignity was wasted on that ambition – to make the Crown Canadian. And what a curious admission from Massey – that the Crown had to be *made* Canadian, that is, it had to be imposed on the people.

Trudeau has already made a special mark, not only because of his willingness to engage with unpleasant political and historical facts, but because of his ability to see through the traditional racial and cultural smokescreens. If one accepts Arthur Miller's judgement that "the task of the real intellectual consists of analyzing illusions in order to discover their causes," then Trudeau is distinguished for this reason alone.

But there is more to Trudeau. And as a politician, he is particularly intriguing, because the politician panders to popular opinion. That's how he stays in power. He is the ventriloquist of the people. But Trudeau is rare: he has his "sign of contradiction," his ready opposition to accepted opinions, his constant determination to step away from and analyze whatever group is in power, whatever idea holds favour. In an attempt to explain this "sign," he wrote: "I have never been able to accept any discipline except that which I imposed upon myself – and there was a time when I used to impose it often. For, in the art of living, as in that of loving, or of governing – it is all the same – I found it unacceptable that others should claim to know better than I what was good for me. Consequently, I found tyranny completely intolerable."

It is astonishing that this and other like statements in the preface to his collected essays have roused a worried response.

He finds tyranny completely intolerable. That men should feel threatened by such an assertion of the self tells much about this country and its ingrained failure of faith in the individual. After all, Trudeau is only saying what is squarely in the tradition of Tocqueville and John Stuart Mill. Trudeau's approach reminds one constantly of Mill's *On Liberty*, particularly where that English democrat spoke of the limits of social authority. However, John Stuart Mill raised an interesting question about countries like Canada. He maintained that "free institutions are next to impossible in a country made up of different nationalities. Among a people without fellow-feeling, especially if they read and speak different languages, the united public opinion necessary to the working of representative government, cannot exist."

Trudeau has rejected this argument, boldly, and instead he offers a curious blend of vision and pragmatism. He says that Canadian federalism is not only an experiment of major proportions, but it could become a brilliant prototype for a truly pluralistic and polyethnic society.

This is a grand project that Trudeau believes can be made real if a pragmatic approach is taken, if rational appraisals are made of the different stages of political maturity across the country. If we accept that regionalisms do exist in Canada, and if we encourage self-government, then "the whole Canadian system of government would be improved by creative tensions between the central, the provincial, and even the municipal administrations." In the manner of Tocqueville, Trudeau is recommending a theory of checks and balances, believing that not only regional, but ethnic and language differences, if encouraged rationally, will give rise to competence, progress, individual rights, and self-esteem. Trudeau's theory of politics is very straightforward: separate once and for all the concepts of state and nation, and then create healthy counterweights and reap the benefits.

This is an admirable vision; one can only guess about its taking effect. What interests me for the moment is Trudeau's emphasis upon rational awareness, or, as he puts it, that our hopes reside with "the fully developed man of intellect."

Throughout his essays Trudeau conveys a horror, or, more accurately, a fear of the emotions. He associates the emotions with totalitarianism, the arch-evil in his political universe. Intellectual control, on the other hand, is the guarantee of individual freedom. I suggest that Trudeau is more of a Québécois than we suspect.

Let me put it this way: there are polarities in Pierre Elliott Trudeau's world – the individual who is free unto himself is the individual pitted against totalitarian tyranny. The release into political freedom is through the intellect, while political enslavement is the fate of those who trust their emotions. It is the old Jansenist dichotomy: the spirit struggling against the flesh. Of course, Trudeau is not hobbled by the struggle. But in his own way he is a true believer – in the intellect, in his intellect. This makes Trudeau a potentially great man. It also makes him a potentially dangerous man, for in the refusal to recognize emotional responses, in the belief that he is always acting rationally, lies possible self-deception. I do not mean to suggest that Pierre Elliott Trudeau is necessarily a victim of self-deception. I believe him to be the most articulate and analytical federal politician of my place and time. But there is this curious streak in Trudeau, a streak that is an integral part of his strength, and I suspect that Trudeau's unique understanding of the authoritarian nature of his country stems from tensions that exist within himself. It has been said that English and French Canadians do not have opinions, they merely have emotions. Pierre Elliott Trudeau is determined to prove that there is nothing merely emotional about himself, nor about the people of Canada, if only they will learn to have an honest opinion of themselves.

The Telegram, 1967

KÉBÉKANTO OF LOVE

We'll take off minus bullets and baggage
my tit-propelled tugboat
O migration O tourism
my wives will be left with
only the parings of my heart
from my whittled loves

I'll wheel around on you one night unannounced
I'll be decked out in the door like a suit of armour
breathless I'll hike up your skirts so my hands can see you
you'll cry like the month of never
your heart bouncing off the table
we'll do the iceberg float in mulberry redcurrant wine
dead drunk as a skunk
in the OK affairs of the heart and bread

when death comes between two breast-strokes of the heart
at the crucial moment
we'll pretend we're stone deaf
the last card you'll lay on me like a love-nip
on the neck will be the queen of spades
and torn apart by a thousand fan-tailed curses
I'll take off after my mothers and fathers
on the eternal
search for chokecherries

when I go ass over teakettle
one autumn evening or wherever
I'll cover your neck at choker-time
with a basket of little white lamb kisses
and when I settle like stale milk
to the left of the wood-stoking stove
come what may in my cherrywood rocker
you'll be the only reason my little sweetie
that my rocker croaks
like a heart
once I'm off in the by and by of my mothers and fathers
on the eternal
search for chokecherries

my basket of lambs will run down your neck like scales
every evening after supper
at the hour when I usually
pop up at your place
like a jealous lover

buzz off buzz off death will tell me
I've cocked an eye on your life for one last time
like a snared bird my insane eyes swoop from sink to stove
intrepid traveller I'll snap you up everywhere
by the fistful
and torn apart by a thousand fan-tailed curses I'll take off
too little too late
but pleased as the blue pea-souper
under the midnight sun

you'll find me again between the pages
of my phrases joualesques *a pressed black flower*
we'll sup together again

on mulberry redcurrant wine
between two baskets of kisses soft as our shawl
on official nooky nights

• Translated from the Québécois French of Gérald Godin

Exile, 1985

HEMINGWAY: *IN OUR TIME*

I heard his name in conversation around the house. Not a lot. Just from time to time when my father was talking about writing and writers. "We were walking up Yonge Street," he said, remembering when he was a young reporter at the *Toronto Daily Star* and Hemingway was a reporter, too, "and Hemingway told me, Don't forget, it was Tolstoy who said that the basis of all great writing is good reporting." I took that as true and sat down and read a story by Tolstoy that my father told me to read, "The Death of Ivan Ilytch."

Then one day when I was in high school I asked my father why some lousy writers were known by everybody and some good writers were hardly known at all, and he said, "Well, when Hemingway was going back to Paris I told him I was losing my reading public of one – him, and he said, 'No, there are always four or five people in the world who are interested in good new writing.' Hemingway had just told me that my first real story, 'A Wedding Dress,' couldn't have been done any better by Tolstoy, and though nobody talks to me now about that story, I'm sure those four or five people are out there."

Four or five people. That didn't seem like consolation to me. And I didn't offer him consolation. It was ten years before I read "A Wedding Dress." But after that talk with my father I was told I had to read a new novel by Hemingway, *The Old Man and the Sea*. It was published in *Life* magazine. A priest, my English teacher, made all his students buy a copy. I still have it: September 1, 1952, twenty cents, and there is Hemingway, head and shoulders on the cover, handsome, fleshy, with a grey moustache, a reporter's eyes, regarding the world with interested, sardonic warmth.

But I had an argument with the priest in class about *The Old Man and the Sea*. I thought there was something phony about the book. I thought there was something phony in the way the old fisherman talked to himself, and to the fish. In the story the old man has been out alone in his boat, he has the biggest fish he has ever seen on his line and his left hand, holding the line, has become a cramped claw.

> It will uncramp though, he thought. Surely it will uncramp to help my right hand. There are things that are brothers: the fish and my two hands. It must uncramp. It is unworthy of it to be cramped . . . He is much fish still and I saw that the hook was in the corner of his mouth and he has kept his mouth tight shut. The punishment of the hook is nothing. The punishment of hunger, and that he is against something that he does not comprehend is everything . . . I'm clear enough in the head, he thought. Too clear. I am clear as the stars that are my brothers. Still I must sleep. They sleep and the moon and the sun sleep and even the ocean sleeps sometimes on certain days when there is no current and a flat calm.

That's the way Hemingway had the old man thinking and talking.

"Nobody thinks like that," I said to my priest.

"Nobody?"

"Nobody I know."

"That's Hemingway, and Hemingway's not a nobody."

He got the Pulitzer Prize for *The Old Man and the Sea* and a couple of years later the Nobel Prize, and his photograph was everywhere all the time. In those photographs I tried to look him in the eye again, looking for that sardonic reporter's attentiveness, but this time he wasn't looking back. He had been Karshed by

Karsh. Everybody loved that photograph: the big head, the big turtleneck sweater, the beard . . . but his eyes, his eyes were upward, fixed on some outer destiny, not a reporter's eyes (this was the beginning of my disdain for Karsh, all those set-piece Portraits of Greatness). That photo is the mark of Karsh and it is the mark of bunk, I thought; and besides, Hemingway looked strangely morose to my eye. Like he was his own man but nobody's brother. All that sun, moon, two brother hands, and the fish with his fish feelings of comprehension was sentimental rhetoric. I didn't know enough to call it sentimental rhetoric; then it was just phony like I thought Karsh's photograph was phony.

In college I read *The Sun Also Rises.* I still hadn't read much of my father's work. I had not yet become one of his four or five. But he didn't mind. He was pleased that I was reading Hemingway. He said: "I can't tell you how thrilled I was when he sent me that book. It was a new thing, a fresh way of seeing. I felt nothing but possibilities after reading that book." Maybe I was discovering the possibilities in Hemingway, too, but I was going backward in his work to do it. I was beginning to see where he had begun, and I saw where Hemingway had been coming from when he was young, doing something like what Charlie Parker and Dizzy Gillespie had done with horn players – doing something so singular, so influential, that he made many good writers turn over into bad writers.

And I understood something about good writing and bad writing, good reporting and bad reporting, too, after reading *The Sun Also Rises*, because there is a moment in the novel when Jake Barnes (Hemingway's mouthpiece) is in Pamplona for the running of the bulls. He's explaining that some few bullfighters have *afición*, and those who go to the fights and can see this *afición* in a fighter are aficionados:

> I sat beside Brett and explained to Brett what it was all about . . . so that it became more something that was

> going on with a definite end, and less of a spectacle with unexplained horrors . . . She saw how close Romero always worked the bull, and I pointed out to her the tricks the other bull-fighters used to make it look as though they were working closely . . . Romero never made any contortions, always it was straight and pure and natural in line. The others twisted themselves like corkscrews, their elbows raised, and leaned against the flanks of the bull after his horns had passed, to give a faked look of danger. Afterward, all that was faked turned bad and gave an unpleasant feeling . . . all the bull-fighters had been developing a technic that simulated this appearance of danger in order to give a fake emotional feeling, while the bull-fighter was really safe. Romero had the old thing, the holding of his purity of line . . .

This is not just a statement about bullfighting. It is also a statement about writers and writing (think of the shrieks of derisive laughter we'd hear if anyone now applied this aesthetic to the corkscrew prose of Tom Wolfe, or to Martin Amis, for that matter). Reading this passage in *The Sun Also Rises* I remembered an afternoon when my father took me to a baseball game, the old triple-A Maple Leafs, who played in the stadium at the foot of Bathurst Street nestled between a Joy gas station, the Tip Top Tailors elegant art deco building, and the wartime housing project for displaced Norwegians, Little Norway.

There was a centre fielder on the team that year whom everybody loved. He was spectacular, his little legs churning as he ran. He was always making running, diving catches. Crowds came to see this young man, Bobby Del Greco, and sportswriters said he was a sure thing to make it in the big leagues. As an eleven-year-old boy I, too, cheered Del Greco. But around the third inning, my father said to me quietly, "You watch him, he cheats. Great centre fielders take off at the crack of the bat for a fly ball. But Del Greco always starts late and then, because he's so fast, he can catch up and make what should have been an easy play look like a great and spectacular play. The great ones make it look so easy you hardly notice what they're doing. Everybody notices Del Greco, but what the sportswriters should be writing, if they were really looking, really reporting, is how he's a fake. He'll never make it in the big leagues, and all these fans will wonder why."

Del Greco never did make it. But I didn't wonder why. My father had told me something true about baseball, but I didn't understand that he had also told me something about writing, about art, until I read *The Sun Also Rises*. Suddenly, everywhere I looked I was looking for *afición*, so that when I first saw Willie Mays play centre field I knew he was no Del Greco, he was no show-boat trying too hard. He made everything look easy. He certainly had *afición*: he was straight and pure and natural in his line and gave real emotion that stayed with you and didn't turn sour.

Then I went back to the root of what Hemingway was, back to the beginning of Hemingway, to his little stories, *In Our Time*, written when he and my father were young and walking up Yonge Street talking about Tolstoy and reporting, trying to see – as intense aficionados – things for what they were, without tricks, without the turns of style that some now like to call "prose that is poetry" – or is it "poetry that is prose"? (Or is it, as with Michael Ondaatje's *The English Patient*, rhinestone prose?) I read those old stories of Hemingway's and found them new and striking (Walter Canby of the established *Saturday Review* had said Hemingway's stories and *The Sun Also Rises* signalled the death of American prose!), striking because of the way he set things down in a clear ordering of observations, as if an incident was happening under your eyes:

> We were in a garden at Mons. Young Buckley came in with his patrol from across the river. The first German I saw climbed up over the garden wall. We waited till he

> got one leg over and then potted him. He had so much equipment on and looked awfully surprised and fell down into the garden. Then three more came over further down the wall. We shot them. They all came just like that.

And that's the way he wrote, just like that. He hadn't done enough writing yet to call himself Papa and to admire himself as Papa. There were no brother moons and suns and brother hands and no old fisherman's plaintive cries of "How do you feel fish?" It is true that there are very fine things in *The Old Man and the Sea*, for the canny old fisherman knows about centre fielders. The old man knows there is Joe DiMaggio, who made it all look artless and easy, but the old man learns, too, that a shark will always come through the dark waters to take the aficionado's great fish and strip it to the bone before he can reel him in (in Hemingway's life, he allowed in *A Moveable Feast*, the sharks were always the rich, tempting him, leading him astray, ruining his relationships). That's life, just like that. But in *The Old Man and the Sea* Hemingway, with his stilted talk, was verging on the ludicrous, he was about to leave the early stories far behind, and the terrible thing is that he soon became his own shark. He became a self-conscious stylist, imitating his own style , and his own style ate him alive so that he ended up as a parody of himself as he made what should have seemed easy into a mannered awkwardness, even – during the last ten years of his life – talking to friends and reporters in his own curious cobbled pidgin English, Papa's English. Perhaps, like Francis Macomber, his last great character, he had shed fear as a young writer and had truly risked danger, and then – having done that – he'd nowhere to go. Anyway, he killed himself.

Strangely enough, this all fell into place for me three years after his suicide, in 1963, when I was reading Solzhenitsyn's *One Day in the Life of Ivan Denisovitch.* The great Russian writer, then new to us all, was getting the details and incidents of life in a subarctic Gulag prison camp down without artifice – as if life were speaking for itself – and when Solzhenitsyn, in that grim world where every word counted, where each word had to "say" the thing as it was seen, actually mentioned Hemingway – the Hemingway of the early stories – I was delighted, my father was delighted. It seemed absolutely right.

But then, later on in Solzhenitsyn's story, several prisoners are discussing Eisenstein's films *Potemkin* and *Ivan the Terrible*, and one says, "'Or the scene with that baby carriage coming slowly, slowly down the steps?'"

> "The trouble is we're rather spoiled by modern close-up techniques."
>
> "It gives you a cockeyed idea of life in the navy."
>
> "Yes, those maggots crawling in the meat were as big as earthworms. They couldn't have really been that size, could they?"
>
> ". . ."
>
> "But one must say in all objectivity that Eisenstein is a genius. Now isn't Ivan the Terrible a work of genius? The oprichniki dancing in masks! The scene in the cathedral!"
>
> "All show-off!" K-123 snapped. He was holding his spoon in front of his mouth. "Too much art is no art at all. Like candy instead of bread! And the politics of it is utterly vile – vindication of a one-man tyranny. An insult to the memory of three generations of Russian intellectuals! . . . don't call him a genius! Call him a toady, say he carried out orders like a dog. A genius doesn't adapt his treatment to the taste of tyrants."

In the end, Hemingway had a tyrant inside his head. I don't know who the tyrant was. Nobody does. But maybe his tyrant was that man called Papa, that failed reporter, that face in Karsh's crowd. He had ended up playing to the *oprichniki*, playing the crowd; he had lost his straight and pure and natural line. I suspect he killed himself because, as an aficionado of his own work, he knew he no longer had *afición.* But he'd had it, he'd had it like few have had it, big time and in our time.

The National Post, 1999

UNDERSTANDING ME, DEAH: MARSHALL MCLUHAN

One evening when the dew was on the pumpkin a shy, befuddled little man lifted his head and looked into a television camera and declaimed, "A poem by Henry Gibson":

Marshall McLuhan
What're ya doin'?

The little man looked, he waited. Marshall McLuhan does not watch television. He explains television. He did not answer Henry Gibson. I sent Henry Gibson a telegram:

What Marshall McLuhan
Says He's Doin'

I'm jest a poe Fool
A Spectator with Spectacles
To his Ears detached

McLuhan is a pithy man. Playing on words – what he calls "the breakdown as breakthrough" – is his particular way of making you see things as you've never seen them before. So –

Jest: play on the word gist, suggesting not only Marshall's knack for getting to the gist of things but his cultivated role as corporation court jester.

Poe: play on "poor boy," his agrarian boyhood, his attachment to the Ciceronian tradition of the agrarian south, and the crucial place that Edgar Allen Poe holds in his thinking.

Fool: in lieu of a King Lear, he probes the likes of Pierre Trudeau, offering palindromes and paradoxes to princes who do not believe that they are mad but think they are isolated and alone on a heath.

Spectator: referring to the eighteenth-century writer Addison (The Spectator papers); as Addison did, McLuhan reflects and shapes his world in his unique essay form.

Spectacles to his Ears: McLuhan's bridging of the perception gap (tactile television, etc.); his world is essentially a conflict arising out of dialectical interplay (hot media vs. cool media; high sensory, low participation vs. low sensory, high participation).

detached: his determination to never state a moral position nor utter a value judgement though he is an authoritarian moralist.

If it is true that McLuhan, a conservative convert to Catholicism, is an apocalyptic moralist who, behind his playfulness and punning, is deeply dismayed by our contemporary lives, how does one prove it? Where, buried in his metaphors and convolutions, are his roots, intellectual and emotional?

The literary figures he is attuned to are in the tradition of Renaissance humanism: Erasmus, Pope, Joyce.

The heart of the matter for these men is rhetoric, the art of persuasion. Essentially, there are two rhetorical styles – the Ciceronian, which produces a gentleman interested in politics, law, the arts of expression, and of course the associated humanistic values – and then the Senecan style, which produces a language of aphorism and short statements conducive to the exchange of value-free information between technologists and financiers.

In the United States, the North produced entrepreneurial Senecans and the South produced gentlemen Ciceronians. McLuhan – sounding like a Senecan – took his intellectual ease among agrarian Southerners, as did his man Ezra Pound.

Though Ciceronian, he is by no means a Southern isolationist. He is – like a Northerner – an entrepreneurial freebooter. He has, we might say, Senecan ambitions. Hence his attachment to Edgar Allan Poe's story of the mariner in a maelstrom, the isolated mariner who, in a state of detached rationality, observes the scattered fragments of a world that has come unlatched in a whirlpool, and thus discovers the pattern that saves him from drowning.

McLuhan the mariner speaks, in the aphoristic style appropriate to that destructive whirlpool, of the electric age. That is, he attempts to speak persuasively to the people in their own language. In so doing, like Erasmus, Pope, and Joyce, he seeks to achieve a position of affective balance .

He is, therefore, a kind of Addison, a popular essayist, a gadfly and PR man to the crass mercantile class. He is trying to enlarge their awareness, not confirm their values. He is, like Erasmus, a teacher, but beyond that, he is a Thomist.

This suggests that there is a dualism to all McLuhan's procedures: Ciceronian/Senecan; North/South; Ancient/Modern; typographic/graphic; tribal/individual; hot/cool; faith/reason.

McLuhan appears to the unsuspecting to be torn between dualities, torn between apocalyptic contradictions: on the one hand, he is permissive and liberal; on the other, he is authoritarian and conservative. But, because McLuhan's understanding of life is rooted in the psychology of Thomas Aquinas, he seeks a balance between contradictions through what Aquinas meant (not what we mean) by common sense, that is, an electrical insight into the essential nature of things that is arrived at through a synthesis of the five senses.

The five senses, the five wounds.

Synthesis, not the synthetic.

The movement from Aristotle's empirical *nihil in intellectu nisi prius in sensu* (nothing in the intellect that is not first in the senses – the cognition of universals from particulars) to *facit universale intus in anima* (cognition as partly extrinsic and partly intrinsic to the soul, whereby the soul sometimes induces universal phantasms prior to the particularity of sensory experiences) is the rational conviction that underpins McLuhan's faith. It is a faith rooted in *Posterior Analytics* – that Thomistic bridge between Plato and Aristotle – the faith of a rational man who has confirmed for me on two occasions that he believes in angels and that they can be found, if we could only see them, on planets, asteroids, etc., a rational man of faith who is given to seeing the world through Thomistic correspondences: The medium is to the message as the ground is to the figure.

Out of these correspondences containing contradictions and paradoxes has come a poet *manqué* – a modern mariner who has created his own aesthetic form, an *essai concret.* His *essais* alert us to insights and bursts of scholarship that are singularly compelling, sometimes wrong-headed, often brilliant.

The Telegram, 1971-78

THE EYES HAVE IT

Every writer I know is interested in *Huckleberry Finn*, interested in how the story is told, and by the story I don't mean *l'histoire*, the actual events, but what the French call *discours* – the telling – and by and large there are two ways to tell a story.

There is the story that is told through the omniscient eye of the author. That's the way Tolstoy does it, so you get Tolstoy's eye. In *Anna Karenina*, Karenin prepares to tell Anna that he knows she loves Prince Vronski:

> And everything that he would now say to his wife took clear shape in Alexey Andreyevich's head. Thinking over what he would say, he somewhat regretted that he should have to use his time and mental faculties for domestic consumption, with so little to show for it; but nevertheless the form and train of thought of the speech he would make shaped itself clearly and distinctly, like an official report.

Tolstoy has told the reader what Karenin is about to tell Anna. This telling has its own intimacy, but Tolstoy – like a shadow inside a mirror – always stands between Anna as seen by Vronski and Vronski as seen by the reader.

Then there is the telling of the story through the eye of the "I" – a telling that has all the persuasive intimacy of the confessional, a confession in which the outward world has become a unique inward necessity. This eye, Stendhal said, is the eye of the egoist. In one of his letters he tells a story through the eye of a Lieutenant Louaut:

Two days ago I was walking towards the pont d'Iena, in the direction of the champs de Mars. There was a high wind, the Seine was turbulent and reminded me of the sea. My eyes followed a little boat, laden to the gunwales with sand, which was trying to pass beneath the end arch on the other side of the Seine, near the quai des Bons-Hommes. Suddenly the boat capsized. I saw the boatman trying to swim, but he was making a poor fist of it. "The clumsy fellow will drown," I said to myself. I had some idea of jumping into the water; but I am forty-seven years old, and I have attacks of rheumatism; it was piercingly cold. "Somebody will jump in from the other side," I reflected. I watched despite myself. The man came to the surface and shouted. I rapidly made myself scarce. "It would be crazy," I said to myself. "If I were nailed to my bed by an acute rheumatism, who would come to see me? . . . Why did that silly brute become a sailor without knowing how to swim? Besides, his boat was overloaded." I could still hear a shout from the drowning man, calling for help. I quickened my steps. Suddenly I said to myself: "Lieutenant Louaut . . . you are a shit. In a quarter of an hour this man will be drowned, and all your life long you will hear his cry for help." . . . "Shit, shit," said the side of prudence, "tis easy to say that. What of the sixty-seven days when rheumatism kept you in your bed last year? Devil take him." I walked away very quickly . . . Suddenly a voice said to me: "Lieutenant Louaut, you are a coward!" This word startled me. "Ah that is serious," I said to myself and started running toward the bank. I was the happiest of men. "No, Louaut is no coward. Not a bit of it." The upshot of it was I saved the man . . . my rheumatism came back . . . I began to think of the motives that caused my heroic action . . . upon my word it was fear of contempt. It was that voice saying to me, "Lieutenant Louaut, you are a coward." . . .

> As soon as I realized that I could save the poor clumsy fellow, it became my duty to do so. Had I not jumped into the water I would have despised myself.

Louaut's eye is the reader's eye, and so this little story creates an immediate reality, an immediate intimacy. This is exactly what happens in *Huckleberry Finn* when Huck sits down and holds a debate with himself about Nigger Jim. What goes on in Huck's mind is what goes on in the reader's mind. "I was a-trembling, because I'd got to decide, forever, betwixt two things, and I knowed it. I studied a minute, sort of holding my breath, and then says to myself: 'All right, then, I'll *go* to hell.'"

But being this intimate with what goes on in Huck's mind also has its limitations – because Huck's life is a narrow life: he is who he is, an illiterate country boy. He has to talk the talk of a country boy and can see only as far as a country boy sees. He's no Tolstoy, and he can't try or pretend to be.

But by talking the talk of his story, by sticking to who he is, he has become real – so real that he is life, and since men and women – his readers – are able to make of life what they want, T. S. Eliot may be right when he says that Huck Finn is as big as Ulysses or Faust or Don Quixote or Hamlet, and Lionel Trilling may be right when he says that Huck is the river and the river is a god, and Leslie Fielder may be right when he says that Huck's relationship with Jim is a pure, homosexual, interracial marriage, a mythic story that is the hindside to the American moon.

All of this may be true, but none of this is of the first importance to the writer.

The way the story is told is what's important. The *discours.* That is why Hemingway complained about the end of the story, that is why he said that Huckleberry's story ends in the Phelps episode, where Nigger Jim is stolen from the boys. That is where the story, the talk of the telling breaks down, where the inner necessity is lost, because suddenly Tom Sawyer is doing the talking, suddenly Tom Sawyer's little Rotarian eye has become the reader's eye. He is doing the seeing. And the eyes have it: Huck's reality is turned to farce because farce is the tiresome world of Tom, and life may sometimes be tiresome but that is not Huck's story. With Tom in charge of the story, in charge of the town's talk, Huck does what every Huck since has done: he strikes off alone into the wilderness.

CBC's *Audio*, 1964

THE EYES HAVE IT

Cousin Smerdikov, a sharp-
shooter, a Grepo garrisoned at the Berlin wall for two years
in a tin-roofed bunker
shinnied up the courtyard drainpipe
carrying a knapsack of stollen carp
into her cramped kitchen.
A deserter on the grift, agile, ingratiating,
he kept a live sparrow
in his breast pocket, both wings broken.
It hip-hopped on the old harvest
table, overfed, plump,
peep peep peeping
as she scooped the eyes of potatoes onto a plate,
asking whether we thought carp
with their old priest's whiskers
ever smiled in the dark water
before taking the bait.
"Bottom feeders," Smerdikov said,
talking about the security police,
how they had the look, of drowned men.
The bird ate the eyes.

Hogg, 2001

NORMAN MAILER AND MARIO LANZA

Contradiction is perhaps the subtlest of all spiritual forces

—ALBERT CAMUS

On the weekend of October 21–22, 1967, Norman Mailer and thousands of the amorphous New Left marched across the Pentagon north parking lot. They were protesting the Vietnam War. Mailer was looking dapper in a pinstripe suit and vest and a regimental tie, stripes of wide dark blue and wide maroon. In his face there was – so he said of himself – "the softness of a man early accustomed to mother-love." He wanted to get arrested quickly, be released, and make it back to Manhattan for an evening party. At one end of the parking lot The Fugs, dressed in orange and yellow and rose-coloured capes, were chanting: "Out, demons, out – back to darkness, ye servants of Satan – out, demons, out! Out, demons, out!" Mailer, accompanied by Robert Lowell and Dwight MacDonald, mused that "an entire generation of acid-heads seemed to have said good-bye to easy visions of heaven, no, now the witches were here, and rites of exorcism, and black terrors of the night – hippies being murdered."

Paunchy and small, calling out, "Hey, let's not lose our cool," Mailer walked in the first line and faced

> the symbol, the embodiment, no, call it the true and high church of the military-industrial complex, the Pentagon, blind five-sided eye of a subtle oppression which had come to America out of the very air of the century . . . yes, Mailer felt a confirmation of the contests of his own

> life on this march to the eye of the oppressor, greedy stingy dumb valve of the worst of the Wasp heart, chalice and anus of corporation land, smug, enclosed, morally blind Pentagon, destroying the future of its own nation with each day it augmented in strength.

Confronting the ranks of the military police and U.S. marshals, Mailer – in the Hobbesian cave of his imagination – believed that he and the country were on the verge of a twenty-year civil war – the issue: whether America would become a great nation or a totalitarian tyranny. In this first skirmish he saw that his function was "to be arrested – his name was expendable for the cause."

Mailer headed across the grass to the nearest MP. To his great surprise, the MP was trembling. Mailer darted like a scatback past two lines of petrified policemen, and then he was jumped. At last, comic as it might be, he was in the land of the enemy, the keepers of the rule of law, the police, and he got to see their rural American faces: with his singular capacity for getting hold of the explosive contradictions in everyday street shit, he concluded that cops

> are attached umbilically to the concept of honesty, they are profoundly corrupt. They possess more physical courage than the average man, they are unconscionable bullies; they serve the truth, they are psychopathic liars . . . their work is authoritarian, they are cynical; and finally if something in their heart is deeply idealistic, they are also bloated with greed. There is no human creation so contradictory, so finally enigmatic as the character of the average cop . . .

As the long arm of politicians who have defence plants in their districts back home reached out and put Mailer in jail along with hippie kids and academics from MIT and preachers and

Leninists, the New Left went ahead and played out its political aesthetic: "Their radicalism was in their hate for authority – authority was the manifest evil to this generation . . . because the authority lied." While admiring the young men who had handed in their draft cards in protest, young men who were "committing their future either to prison, emigration, frustration, or at best, years where everything must be unknown . . . The terror to a man so conservative as Mailer was that nihilism might be the only answer to totalitarianism."

But Mailer is not so much conservative as cataclysmic.

And in America, though there are terrible outbreaks of cop law, as a state it is not totalitarian.

Behind Mailer's bravado, his flourishes, there is a great yearning. He wants to report on his own rapture. In that rapture, in the white light of his own concentration, he will find himself to be magnificently articulate – his prose will be a revelation – the explosive apocalyptic moment will be as Big a piece of writing as the Bang itself!

Instead, as happens in the ordinary run of life, even at its most extreme, there was no bang; he was fingerprinted, processed, and booked. Supper in Manhattan was out. He slept the night in jail. Next day the commissioner sentenced him – as a "mature man" who exerted an influence on the young – to five days in prison. A quick-footed lawyer named Kirshkop, flitting from court to court that morning, outfoxed the commissioner and got Mailer out on bail, to Mailer's breathless relief: "Since the assassination of Kennedy, no political prisoner could necessarily trust an American jail again, not even a political amateur for a routine five days."

Political prisoner!

Assassination!

Kirshkop!

That was Mailer's weekend. Out of it has come what he calls his non-fiction novel. Though he presents himself as a character who is likeable because he is so ludicrous, a character who ruminates and rummages through his own mind, *The Armies of the Night* is no novel. It is no rapture. It is a compelling blend of history, confession, and literary sniping. As for reportage, he observes and orders facts out of a wonderfully idiosyncratic, outraged point of view. In an act of embattled confession, he admits to the vulgarity of his breast-beating. As a literary sniper, he tries to, and sometimes does, annihilate – with his cannon – the lesser writer that he holds in his crosshairs. Through it all you can feel what he wants. He wants to be both the chronicler *and* Henry the King, the king urging his people to feed off his own fury at Harfleur:

Then lend the eye a terrible aspect;
Let it pry through the portage of the herd
Like the brass cannon; let the brow o'erwhelm it
As fearfully as doth a galled rock
O'erhang and jutty his confounded base,
Swill'd with the wild and wasteful ocean.

There is bathos here, because all too often he takes himself more seriously than the serious situation, bathetic in his pinstripe suit and regimental tie – a guerrilla only in the literary back alleys of his mind, where he slaps leather and calls "Draw" and guns down unarmed poets, applying, of course, the word *existential* to his every act as if it were Pond's beauty cream.

Like his bogeyman Hemingway, who blamed his failures of imaginative nerve on the rich, Mailer reports on the public event but also ridicules and patronizes his four wives, blames and ridicules his critics, blames his country and all others who have done him dirt, and all of them somehow end up as emissaries of that blind five-sided oppressor the Pentagon, this heavy deadweight of wonky generals and wives and literary dirt-bags that has kept him from the larger promise of his life, the great novel.

It is an astonishing performance, a confessional tract very much for the times, touching in the way that Mario Lanza was touching: Mailer aiming at chandeliers, trying to break glass.

The Telegram, 1968-72

HEAR THE CLOPPING OF THE HORSES

While others fish with craft for great opinion
I, with great truth, catch mere simplicity.
—Troilus and Cressida

Two books: Isaac Babel's stories and Robert Lowell's *Notebook 1967–68*. Babel . . . a shadowy figure in Russian letters. Gorky published his first stories in a little magazine, *Letopis*. The police learned about him. He learned about the police. He was charged under Article 1001 with writing "works detrimental to public morals." Then, after a stint in the Czar's army and, subsequently, the Soviet army – on the Romanian front and in the Odessa Cossack cavalry – he published four stories in *Lef*, a magazine edited by the poet Mayakovsky. This led to a collection of stories, *Red Cavalry*. The stories were stark. They were stripped of sentiment. These were soldiers who wanted to kill, and if they didn't know how, they wanted someone to teach them how to kill. *Punct.* Babel became a celebrity. "Babel is the rage of Moscow," Konstantin Pedin wrote on July 16, 1925, to Gorky. "Everyone is mad about him." Stalin himself was intrigued and allowed him to go to Paris and then allowed him to come back – and then he waited and waited for him to produce stories for the Party. Babel, for his own purposes, wanted everyone to believe he couldn't write a lot of stories because he was blocked by contradictions and doubts. In 1935, knowing that the secret police were reading his letters, he wrote to his mother to partially mislead her, but to deliberately mislead the police:

> In a country as united as ours, it is quite inevitable that a certain amount of thinking in clichés should appear and I want to overcome this standardized way of thinking and introduce into our literature new ideas, new feelings and rhythms. This is what interests me and nothing else. And so I work and think with great intensity, but I haven't any results to show yet. And, inasmuch as I myself do not see clearly how and by what methods I will reach these results (I do see my inner paths clearly, though), I am not sure myself where and in what kind of environment I ought to live if I am to achieve my goal, and this is what causes my reluctance to drag anyone along behind me and makes me an insecure and wavering man who causes you so much trouble.

Trouble came from Stalin, who was irritated by his reluctance to publish, his silence. Trying to justify himself, Babel said publicly: "*V dvortse tvorchestvo ne tvoritsya* – creativity does not dwell in palaces." Secretly he wrote stories, and many of them were stories critical of the Soviets, critical of the forced collectivization of the peasants. His secrets didn't stay secret for long; stories will out in a police state. He was arrested on May 15, 1939, and taken to Lubyanka Prison. *Ne dali konchit.* His last words as they slammed the gates behind him: "I was not given time to finish." Thirteen years later, his official death certificate was an act of Babelian terseness:

> *Name: Isaac Emmanuelovich Babel*
> *Date of Birth: 13 July 1894*
> *Date of Death: 17 March 1941*
> *Place of Death:*
> *Cause of Death:*

Two years later, the following document was issued:

Military College
The Supreme Court of the USSR
23 December 1954
No.4N-011441/54
Moscow, Vorovsky Street, #13 Certificate

The case in accusation of BABEL Isaac Emmanuelovich has been reviewed by the Military College of the Supreme Court of the USSR 18 December 1954.

The sentence of the Military College dated 26 January 1940 concerning Babel, I.E., is revoked on the basis of newly discovered circumstances and the case against him is terminated in the absence of elements of a crime.

Babel, like Anna Akhmatova, had heard "terror's dry coughing sound . . ." Both had survived the Terror, those years when "only the dead smiled . . ." – when "the railway yards were asylums of the mad," a time when Babel – living in silence and working in secrecy – had written and rewritten his succinct stories twenty and thirty times, striving for the right word, the period in the right place, a period that was as elusive, he'd said to friends, as "the smile on a dying man's lips." He had, speaking of a dying man's lips, tried in 1934 to placate not only the Writers Union but the secret police and Stalin:

> Speaking of the use of words, I must mention a man who doesn't have any professional dealings with words. Nevertheless, look how Stalin hammers out his speeches, how his words are wrought of iron, how terse they are, how muscular, how much respect they show the reader.

> [Applause] I don't say here that we should all write like Stalin, but I do say that we must all work at our words as he does. [Applause]

And then he tried to explain:

> You talk about my silence. Let me tell you a secret. I have wasted several years trying, with due regard to my own tastes, to write lengthily, with a lot of detail and philosophy, striving for the sort of truth I have been talking about. It didn't work out with me. And so, although I'm a devotee of Tolstoy, in order to achieve something, I have to work in a way opposite to his.

Sometimes he stood on his shadow, sometimes he outran his shadow, pausing here, pausing there, pausing for a time in Saint Petersburg. He'd "hidden" as a house guest in people's flats. He'd hidden stories in those flats. Between flats, between friends, he planned to move into a villa in the Peredelkino writers' colony. He announced in letters to his wife, and therefore to the police, that he was sharpening his pencils, he was getting ready to write. Publicly, his lips were sealed. But small stories, hidden or not, like gossip, get around. Small stories can cause big problems. Gorky, who was fairly close to Stalin, had provided some protection, but when Gorky died Babel was left exposed. The witch word was put out . . . he was a Trotskyite, a spy, a black marketeer, a lover of the sister of Yagoda, the ex-chief of the political police. He was picked up. He disappeared into a different silence. After he disappeared the police rounded up a cartload of his working manuscripts. They sealed his house. They sealed his fate. They said that he had died in a labour camp. Time passed. The Gulag grew. Stalin died. Some of Babel's stories were published in a "rehabilitation" edition in Moscow in 1957. More time has passed. Now his daughter, Nathalie, has gathered twenty-four of those stories that he had hidden away with friends . . .

They are stories about thugs, sleazebags, sluts, and soldiers. Some are slight, not fully worked out; others are fragments. Some are like a blow. He could pack a single paragraph with hope, ambition, foreboding, fatalism . . .

⁂

This is the scene: at the end of a day a small boy is sitting with his grandmother. She suddenly explodes at him:

> Study! Study and you will have everything – wealth and fame! You must know everything. The whole world will fall at your feet and grovel before you. Everybody must envy you. Do not trust people. Do not have friends. Do not lend them money. Do not give them your heart.

This is a strident, suffocating atmosphere. Compacted life. Impacted pain. The tone is hard to describe; it's as elusive as that smile on a dying man's lips, full of pity and yet hopeless, jocular and yet jaundiced.

⁂

Babel is about to tell a story.

A character has appeared: a faded, down-at-the-heels old man in a mud-spattered frock coat. He is carrying a sack. It looks like there must be frozen potatoes in it. Every time the old man moves, something inside the sack creaks. Babel begins –

> Here is the story: three days before, at the beginning of our occupation, all civilians had been ordered to evacuate the village. Some had left and others had stayed; those who had stayed had taken to the cellars. Their courage was of no avail under bombardment, stone walls proved a poor defense, and some were killed. One entire family

had been buried under the ruins of their basement, and this was the Marescot family. Their name – such a good French name – had stuck in my memory. There had been four of them – father, mother, and two daughters. Only the father had come out alive.

"My poor fellow, so you are Marescot? It's all very sad. What on earth were you doing in that wretched cellar?" I was interrupted by the corporal: "Looks as though they're starting up, Lieutenant . . ."

This was to be expected. The Germans had noticed signs of life in our trenches. The barrage started on the right flank and then shifted to the left a little. I grabbed père Marescot and pulled him down. My men, as good as gold, got their heads down and sat dead-still under cover; none of them showed so much as the tip of his nose.

"What do you want? Tell me and look sharp about it! You can see that things are pretty hot around here."

"*Mon lieutenant,* I've told you everything: I'd like to bury my family."

"Very well, I'll have someone get the bodies."

"I have the bodies here, lieutenant!"

"What do you say?"

He pointed at the sack. It did indeed contain the meager remains of père Marescot.

"You need not worry . . ."

"But . . . but I have a family vault . . ."

"Very well then, show me where it is."

"But . . . but . . ."

"What do you mean, 'but'?"

"But, lieutenant, we're in it right here."

In 1928 many revolutionaries had been driven into hiding by the organized and ruthless Soviets, who were consolidating their hold by killing anarchists and democrats. In an appalling but poignant story, two agents have found a man named Adrian Sulak, who has been holed-up in a pit in his barn for six years:

> We went in and saw an open pit in the middle of the stable, and a man sitting at the bottom of it. The tiny woman in the white blouse was standing at the edge of the pit with a bowl of borscht in her hands.
>
> "Hello, Adrian," Chernyshev said. "Just having your supper?'
>
> Down below, Sulak struggled with the bolt of his gun; the bolt clicked.
>
> "We're trying to talk to you like a human being," Chernyshev said and fired.
>
> Sulak slumped against the yellow, smooth-planed wall; he groped at it with his hands, blood gushed from his mouth and ears, and he fell down.

⁂

Babel said that "no steel can pierce the human heart so chillingly as a period at the right moment." No superfluous word. Stiletto silences. No wasted gesture. An acute understanding of how full a silence can be, how acerbic, how accusatory a period can be. The pursuit of perfect periods caused his death. To make sure the periods were chillingly right, to give shape and form to violence, he published little, he exasperated Stalin . . . one can imagine Stalin as he signed Babel's death notice, saying, "Babel . . . you're not a dog; we're trying to talk to you like a human being."

Period.

⁂

Since every dog has his day, there must be an hour for skunks.

Robert Lowell remembers lying on his back in his childhood bed, holding his knees, and rocking. "'Stop rocking,' my nurse or Mother would say. I remember this trembling fury . . ." He rocked and rocked. It didn't help his fury. He looked up. In "the sunset hour" he saw a ceiling roughened with oatmeal, blue as the sea. And his Mother, "with new caps on all her teeth," a chic and impulsive woman who knew how to stew in her own fury. Over nothing. Or next to nothing. She stewed as Sarah Stark Wilson, Lowell's socialite aunt, thundered "on the keyboard of her dummy piano . . ." She stewed when the aunt, on her recital day, failed to appear at the concert hall. That was it. Period. Then, a little older, and still in a fury, Lowell looked up and saw his father, who had once been an epauletted admiral on the Yangtze River, get into the family bathtub and sit "humming 'Anchors Aweigh,'" a stunted man dwarfed by "the tranquilized *Fifties.*" Then his mother died. That seemed all wrong. Even the lettering on his mother's coffin – Lowell – had been misspelled "Lovel," and worse, her "corpse was wrapped like *panetone* in Italian tin foil." It was all wrong. He looked up and saw

Spiders marching
through the air,
Swimming from tree to tree that
mildewed day . . .
They purpose nothing but
their ease and die
Urgently beating east to sunrise
and the sea . . .

He came from people of ease, who had little purpose, people who were nonetheless dying on the edge of their nerves, going to pieces in the bathtub or sitting at dummy pianos. It was all very complicated. Dread, a certain menace, hung in the air; the local railroad tracks began to shine "like a double-barrelled shotgun . . ." In the Skunk Hour, love-cars, their lights turned down, lay together "hull to hull, where the graveyard shelves on the town . . ." Because he thought the cold sun was melting, he cried out, "My mind's not right."

He was right.

Travelling fast, he crashed his intended wife into a wall. He turned Catholic. Then he lapsed. Manic and without purpose, and perhaps because he had to respond somehow to the outbreak of war, he "skulked in the attic, and got two hundred French generals by name, from A to V – Augereau to Vandamme." Then he wrote a letter to President Roosevelt, his commander-in-chief. Politely he begged off, he refused to answer the draft. He was sentenced to a year and a day at a correctional centre where, having found a purpose and a place, he ended up as a conscientious objector yammering metaphysics in the morning on the jailhouse roof – taking the air in the company of Czar Louis Lepke of Murder Incorporated, talking to Lepke like he was *a human being*, even though Lepke,

Flabby, bald, lobotomized,
drifted in a sheepish calm,
where no agonizing reappraisal
jarred his concentration on the electric chair –
hanging like an oasis in his air
of lost connections . . .

Connections! Lost! Lowell was at swim so deep in his own mind that he was out of his mind, wanting not just connections but conclusions (his best poems seldom conclude!). A fellow jailbird, a Black Muslim, told him, Okay buster, here is a conclusion: take this – "Only man is miserable." That was too good. Lowell couldn't leave that alone. He had to add:

He was wrong though, he forgot the rats. A pair
in an enclosure kills the rest, then breeds a clan . . .

Someone rigged the enclosure with electric levers
that could give the rats an orgasm. Soon the rats learned
to press the levers, did nothing else – still on the trip,
they died of starvation in a litter of food.

Lowell took a trip. He enlarged his rooftop, he went across America with Senator Eugene McCarthy (the anti-war senator who was campaigning for the presidency), and he travelled as well to Mexico and Israel . . . as if he were trying to respond to Babel's grandmother . . .trying to know everything, to study . . . and he wrote poems – *Notebook 1967–68* – an enormous number of fourteen-lined unrhymed blank verse "sonnets" – sonnets that are a stringent conversation with himself, sometimes laconic, sometimes obscure, sometimes snippets of history, slogans, and pedantry, sometimes the gift of common room gab, all adding up to "words that seem right, though loosely in touch with reason" – his account of the destructive turn of his mind and the destructive turn of a decade, in which "man is thinning out his kind"and a civic fragging is underway:

. . . violence cracking on violence,
rock on rock, the corpse of the last
armed prophet
laid out on a sink in a shed, displayed
by flashlight.

He took part in the public March on the Pentagon:

lovely to lock arms, to march absurdly locked
(unlocking to keep my wet glasses from slipping)
to see the cigarette match quaking in my fingers,
then to step off like green Union Army recruits
for the first Bull Run, sped by photographers,

the notables, the girls . . . fear, glory, chaos, rout . . .
our green army staggered out on the miles-long green fields,
met by the other army, the Martian, the ape, the hero,
his new fangled rifle, his green new steel helmet.

The lines are clotted. They do not seize the ear, they are not memorable; none of the sonnets stick in the mind. What's memorable is what's always been memorable – watching Lowell watch himself, his barely repressed fury as he tries to do what is right only to wake up in the wrong bed in the wrong room, full of remorse:

The vague, dark new hallway, some darker rectangle:
The bathroom door, or a bedroom, someone else's;
saw of the wrong snoring, or, worse, the right –
each footstep a moral judgment, and the window
holds out its thin, black terminal disc of joy.

Black joy. A disc. A period.

"Angry, wrenlike," he still moves with "a greyhound's gentle tautness" across his internal borders . . . he is a kind of long-suffering Adrian Sulak who "bites his own lip to warm his icy tooth." He faces "the spineless vermin who slink stinking from the woodwork." He is vigilant. "Free-lancing on the razor's edge . . . he hears it, hears the clopping of the hundreds of horses unstopping . . . each hauls a coffin."

Clop.

The Telegram, 1969-71

STALIN SHRUGGED

No steel can piece the human heart so chillingly
as a period at the right moment.
—Babel

Tom Wolfe's *Esquire* epic on "The New Yellow Peril" is almost devoid of periods. It begins:

> suzie wong flower drum song no tickee no tong war no wonton no canton oriental pearly chop suey carry-out slanty-eyed family ties take care of our own Charlie Chan and his dragon dancers hoppy go bang-bang February red firecracker shredded Fu Manchu new year of rooster but none of your juvenile delinquency among our lilla fellas porcelain dolls almond-eye melon-seed miss chinatown my chinatown and then an odd thing happened. One of our young Chinese tigers over here threw a cherry bomb at the stage. The damn thing landed on the chest of Dr. Robert Jenkins, superintendent of schools for San Francisco and began rolling down his necktie . . . This particular cherry bomb is lit up with a weird silver flame, like a party match. You can't take your eyes off it . . . The moment begins to freeze . . . Jenkins . . . thrust back stiff in his seat with his eyes bulging and peering straight down his nose at the sizzling little doom ball on his necktie . . . His nose seems to have grown longer . . . enormous you might say . . . Such a variety of bulbs and tubers . . . long and pointed like carrots, gibbous like green peppers,

> puffy like cauliflowers, hooked like a squash, hanging off the face like a cucumber . . .

Tom Wolfe has never looked the doom ball in the eye. Doom – that black moment, that period between silences – is not his *shtick*. Bow-wow words are his *shtick*. Talking about bow-wow words, Sir Walter Scott said of Jane Austen (as if Tom Wolfe were talking about Raymond Carver): "She had a talent for describing the involvements and feelings and characters of ordinary life which is to me the most wonderful I have ever met with. The Big Bow-Wow strain I can do myself like any other now going; but the exquisite touch, which renders ordinary commonplace things and characters interesting, from the truth of the description and sentiment, is denied me."

Tom Wolfe's twenty thousand words on "The New Yellow Peril" are not about peril, not about newness or the nature of yellow. So, what is he – as a writer – trying to do?

In his collection *The Kandy-Kolored Tangerine-Flake Streamline Baby,* his Las Vegas piece begins with a variation on the "Yellow Peril" trick: he repeats the word *hernia* fifty-seven times:

> Hernia, hernia, hernia, hernia, hernia, hernia, hernia, hernia, hernia, hernia, hernia, hernia, hernia, HERNia; hernia, HERNia, hernia, hernia, hernia, hernia, HERNia, HERNia, HERNia, hernia, hernia, hernia, hernia, hernia, hernia, hernia, eight is the point, the point is eight; hernia, hernia, HERNia, hernia, hernia, hernia, hernia, all right, hernia, hernia, hernia, hernia, hard eight, hernia, hernia, hernia, HERNia, hernia, hernia, hernia, HERNia, hernia, hernia, hernia, HERNia, hernia, hernia, hernia, hernia

"What is all this *hernia, hernia* stuff?"

In "Girl of the Year" Baby Jane Holzer begins with the same studied mannered spontaneity:

> Bangs manes bouffants beehives Beatle caps butter faces brush-on lashes decal eyes puffy sweaters French thrust bras flailing leather blue jeans stretch pants stretch jeans honeydew bottoms éclair shanks elf boots ballerinas Knight slippers, hundreds of them, these flaming little buds, bobbing and screaming, rocketing around inside the Academy of Music Theater underneath that vast old mouldering cherub dome up there – aren't they super-marvelous!

Baby Jane is watching Mick Jagger as he "opens his giblet lips and begins to sing . . . with the voice of a bull Negro. Bo Diddley, you moving boo meb bee-uhtul, bah-bee, oh vona breemb you'honey snurks oh crim pulzy yo' mim down," and she goes:

> Eeeeeeeeeeeeeeeeeeeee

Wolfe knows how to turn a trick.

> Eeeeeeeeeeeeeeeeeeeee

Stalin would have listened for the period, heard *hernia, hernia,* and shrugged and forgotten him.

The Telegram 1970-71

"STAR, STAR, STAR, OH MY GOD"

The Beard, by Michael McClure, opens with Jean Harlow dressed in a slinky pale blue gown. She is snapping her hips at Billy the Kid. He is tough, he is cool in black stretch pants and boots. Billy grabs Harlow's arm, rolls her flesh between his fingers, and screams, "This is nothing but meat." Harlow threatens, "I'll cut your dumb brain open like a bag of meat." They dance, they slang each other, and then the Kid rips off Harlow's shoes and bites her foot. Harlow howls, "I suppose you'd like to bite my nipples off, you sadist pervert."

Harlow curls up at Billy's feet. She caresses his shiny black boots. Suddenly Billy is on his knees, kissing her feet, her calves, her thighs. Harlow, her head back, cries ecstatically, "Star, Star, Star, Oh My God . . ." The curtain comes down on the movie star and the gunslinger-turned-fey-bootlicker.

This one-act play is part of an emerging enthusiasm: the raunch-shock of sexual horror stories whose mechanics differ very little from the potboiler melodramas of the eighteenth century. Currently we have *The Beard,* Edward Albee's *Tiny Alice,* and Norman Mailer's *Why Are We in Vietnam*? These writers have forgotten what Horace told them long ago: *Nec pueros coram populo edea trucidet aut in avem Procne mutetui, Cadmus in anguem.*[1]

In late-eighteenth-century England, popular stories featured murderous monks, deformed noblemen, and the deflowering

[1] Medea should not devour her children in front of an audience; nor should Procne be changed into a bird, nor Cadmus into a snake.

of defenceless maidens. Diaries of the day tell us that sophisticated women and gentlemen after reading these stories lay awake drenched in cold sweat. With each new novel the devices of horror became more fantastic. On a given afternoon a young virgin was found wandering through a medieval charnel house, and there she saw, chained to a wall, a fallen nun. At the nun's feet were her illegitimate children, being eaten by worms. Then the gorged worms set upon the nun. As the delicate virgin fled down gloomy corridors from this scene, she passed statues that bled at the nose, and portraits of ancient tyrants leapt from their frames and pursued her.

The terror-stricken lady ran into the arms of the resident demoniac monk, who raped her, and then, on learning that the lady was his sister, gave himself over to the devil.

The stories of our time are similar in all respects but one: the virginal lady has been replaced by the virginal man. In Edward Albee's *Tiny Alice*, a defenceless, fey monk – Julian – struggles to preserve his virginity. He is prey to the richest woman in the world, Miss Alice. She has demoniac connections and arranges the seduction of the monk in her many-roomed mansion. The deflowering of Julian – his emasculation – comes at the second act curtain. It is raunch-shock, blending the mysteries of religion with carnality. Julian is on his knees, praying. The woman holds open her gown, baring her body. Seized by lust, the monk scrambles forward on his knees. I laughed. I couldn't help it. John Gielgud – playing Julian – seemed to be pigeon-toed even on his knees. He slammed headfirst into Alice and buried his head between her thighs. Like Jean Harlow, Alice is being licked on stage by a virginal man. She lifts her head and moans. She is ecstatic.

Norman Mailer's novel *Why Are We in Vietnam*? is hallucinatory. We are told the story of a sweetheart Texas disc jockey, another guileless man in search of purity. He seeks and finds not just God but also the devil, not just his father but also his lover, not just the negro but also the white – and he finds all of them in one place – up the accommodating anus of an Alaskan bear hunter. This is a novel of sordid devices and calculated hysteria.

In his preface to the second edition of *Lyrical Ballads* (1800), Wordsworth – trying to explain why his language "of a greater simplicity" had found no audience – wrote:

> A multitude of causes are now acting with a combined force to blunt the discriminating powers of the mind . . . to reduce it to a state of almost savage torpor. The most effective of these causes are the great national events, which are daily taking place [the war with France], and the increasing accumulation of men in cities, where the uniformity of their occupations produces a craving for extraordinary incident, which the rapid communication of intelligence hourly gratifies. The invaluable works of our elder writers . . . are driven into neglect by frantic novels, sickly and stupid German tragedies, and deluges of idle and extravagant stories . . . when I think upon this degrading thirst after outrageous stimulation . . . I should be oppressed with no dishonorable melancholy, had I not a deep impression of certain inherent and indestructible qualities of the human mind . . . and were there not added to this impression a belief, that the time is approaching when the evil will be systematically opposed, by men of greater powers . . .

As for "language of a greater simplicity," this note appeared in the *San Francisco Chronicle*:

> Sister Madelena said she is constantly surprised at the public response to her poems. "It shows," she smiled, "that what people want is simplicity. That's one of the reasons I always teach that 'Please pass the butter' is really a beautiful sentence.

The editor remarked: "We would rather have written that line, gentlemen, than take Québec tomorrow."

Mailer, Albee, and McClure have neither taken Québec nor ever had faith in a line of such simplicity.

Maclean's, 1969

TRUDEAU: THE 1968 CAMPAIGN

The Cadillac eased to a stop down a Chinatown alley in Vancouver. Pierre Trudeau, the Minister of Justice – running for Prime Minister – went in the back door of the Blue Eagle Café. Whitewash had been slapped on the roughcast walls but the backrooms were still dingy, little rat-tails of old paint hanging from the ceiling, and against one wall an old chenille stencilled chesterfield, the stuffing leaking out.

Chinese men and their wives shuffled into a receiving line, the men in Tip Top Tailors blue and brown business suits, the women in glossy satin dresses: red, cream, green. Trudeau shook their hands solicitously. After the airport hoopla, the motorcycle sirens, the roses wrapped in crinkly cellophane, the clatter of firecrackers in the alley, Trudeau moved with a silent, elegant, contained energy through the shabby rooms, nodding with a slight tuck of his chin under the glare of tubular fluorescent lights. The Chinese were soft-spoken. At the end of the receiving line Trudeau paused, as if something had skidded across his mind, as if there were more he might say to these people, but he was propelled by aides out the front door of the café, the overhead bell on the door tinkling as he went, propelled onto Pender Street.

The block between Abbot and Main streets was short but thousands were heaving forward and peeling apart for a procession of drummers, and firecrackers went off like distant guns in dry air. A policeman said: "Jesus, you could shoot him in a minute." An old woman crawled on her knees under a flatbed trailer, around the big wheels, and bobbed up on the other side, yelling with her hand out, "I'm eighty-five, Pierre, eighty-five goddamn years." She grinned, her black gums glowing.

Trudeau appeared entirely at ease, but behind his back he was stripping the petals from a rose. When only the stem and torn head were left, he snapped the stem in two and dropped the pieces. Scuffling and shoving broke out, and Trudeau, with a smirk, teased the hecklers, "Cut out that rough stuff or I'll get in there myself . . ."

Years ago the Montréal poet Abraham Moses Klein described the conventional Québec politician:

Worshipped and loved, their favourite visitor,
a country uncle with sunflower seeds in his pockets,
full of wonderful moods, tricks, imitative talk,
he is their idol: like themselves not handsome,
not snobbish, not of the Grande Allée! Un homme!
Intimate, informal, he makes bear's compliments
to the ladies; is gallant; and grins;
goes for the balloon, his opposition, with pins;
jokes also on himself, speaks of himself
in the third person, slings slang, and winks with folklore;
and he knows that he has them, kith and kin.

Trudeau darted into the crowd, letting himself be caressed, not just by girls, but by women and men. He had the passive manner only a man of self-confidence could afford; smiling coyly, he appeared limp before the pummelling, "like a dumb leper who had lost his bell, wandering the world, meaning no harm."

He had no sunflower seeds in his pockets.

He had his style, the feel about him – the high cheekbones, the narrowed eyes, the sensuous but slightly cruel turn to his lips – his disciplined, tempered body, his taste for delights. He had let it be known that he was bold and authoritarian, widely travelled, and amiably engaged in political philosophy. Because of a willingness to mix pragmatic wheeling and dealing with a diffident worldliness, his stern rigidity was seldom noted, but his response, when he had been left no room to manoeuvre, seemed tailored to Tyndall's description of the Jesuit: accuse him of murdering your mother, father, brothers and sisters, uncles and aunts, and the family dog . . . he would triumphantly produce the dog alive.

Once an old priest with years of administrative experience said to me, "You want to get the job done with class, get it done by a Jesuit . . . but don't trust him, don't take your eye off him for a minute."

I watched him. But as each day on the road ended he had the look of an innocent who had managed to come through unscathed. Or, to put it more colloquially, in the admiring complaint of his campaign bodyguards, "Go-Go Trudeau Dodo" – he was always on the go yet he always slept in the bed of an innocent (*dodo* being French for a child's cot or crib).

I had a conversation with him over supper in his airplane cabin. Chinese food. He was miffed because he had no chopsticks, but also he was amused at his own displeasure, a man acutely aware of himself. He had no trouble shifting a sweet-and-sour rib from his left to right jaw to make a clear, articulate point.

I suggested that by presenting himself as a decisive man ready to take control he was offering the people an illusion; that, as French historian Jacques Ellul had argued, a third apparatchik class, independent of both the public and politicians, now constituted the real political power. Public involvement with the prime minister was only a game –

There was no question about that, he said; the technicians, the civil service, had long since been developing political policy quite independently of politicians. But it was just this fact that necessitated the best men getting into government, to cope with complex subjects and, more importantly, to take control and give policy direction to the apparatchiks.

"What'll you do if the apparatchiks get you?"

"I'll probably be the last to know."

What was one to make of his admiration for the historian Lord Acton?

"I suppose my knowledge of Acton is out of one or two books: his essay on freedom and power, and another, the title of which I don't remember . . . I don't claim to know Acton in great depth. Though he's a rather conservative Catholic historian, I especially like his humanist approach. I find he is always trying to explain things. He's trying to look for the mainsprings in society. I just can't read history which is a description of events . . ."

"You mean stories?"

A natty steward appeared with a set of ivory chopsticks, apologizing because he had found only one set. Trudeau held them like twin batons as he repeated, "Description . . ."

"Stories."

"Have it your way," he said, rapping the batons on the edge of his plate.

"There's an opposition in you – just like there is a contradiction in Acton – between the rational and emotional; it's in your essays, and perhaps it's even an irrational fear of emotion, even a Jansenist thing. A faith in your own powers, the rational. I wonder if you're not drawn to Acton the absolutist."

"You are too hard on me," he said, deftly slipping the sticks into pincer position, "I am essentially a pragmatist. I think you are wrong."

"Absolutely?"

He laughed and plucked a morsel of chicken in lobster sauce from his plate.

"Absolutely."

What is this pragmatism that Trudeau so values in himself?

The authority is philosopher William James, who explained that pragmatism is a philosophical discipline, a method: The pragmatist "turns away from abstraction and insufficiency, from verbal solutions, from bad *a priori* reasons, from fixed principles, closed systems, and pretended absolutes and origins. He turns towards concreteness and adequacy, towards facts, towards action and towards power."

Lord Acton aside, this seems to be Trudeau's approach. Except there is a crucial contradiction between this method and that French expert on law and history whom Trudeau admires so much – Montesquieu. Montesquieu was not only a conservative and in some respects an idealist, he described his own method this way: "I have laid down the first principles, and have found that the particular cases follow naturally from them." Further, in *The Spirit of Laws* he attempted to discover the laws within laws – that is, some absolute system. As Minister of Justice, did Trudeau emulate Montesquieu or did he act pragmatically? He cannot have it both ways.

But he may try, and if he systematizes government (the arrival of computer specialists with their critical path flow charts in the Trudeau entourage suggests he will) and at the same time tries to run it pragmatically, his fate will be that of his friend Lord Acton.

For Acton, as a historian, was in exactly this impossible dilemma. What he admired about the American Revolution was the relentless pursuit of the absolute moral ideal of liberty. At the same time he had to condemn the American Constitution, for by its nature, its pragmatic method of checks and balances and countervailing forces, it denied the possibility of absolute liberty.

All his life Acton prepared himself to write his masterwork, *The History of Liberty*. It was to be definitive. But because revolutions – that is, human affairs – violated his ideals, he never completed it. Bitterly, in his later years he referred to it only as his Madonna of the Future (a reference to Henry James's story of an artist who devoted his life to the creation of a single masterpiece; after his death it was exposed as a blank canvas).

One hopes Trudeau, while erecting his Just Society, will not discover that his dedication to pragmatism, to countervailing forces, has left him with only a blank canvas.

Beyond the front line of Trudeaumania teenyboppers and housewives wielding Kresge autograph books, staid citizens stood becalmed, their hands on their hips or their arms folded, guarding their emotions. They lived in Irving Layton country:

A dull people, without charm
or ideas,
settling into the clean empty look
of a Mountie or a dairy farmer
as into a legacy.

Trudeau's speech to them was plain-spoken, sweetened by empty, trite phrases: "We are realizing in a basic way that this is a fabulous country." Watching Trudeau, I had to think of Mackenzie King, another bachelor Prime Minister, runty and bland, droning on, convincing the country that behind his pudding face there was a jackhammer will. Trudeau, of course, was neither pudding-faced nor blank, but when he wasn't speaking off-the-cuff – and he could be brilliantly concise in conversation – there was something flat in his prepared speeches, something dull; the words were bare, the images barren. Yet it was this very tone, with anecdotes of muscle and learning, that so impressed audiences. When talking of economic disparity, he retold a story by Saint-Exupéry. It was a good story – "The Assassination of Mozart" – about seeing a starving boy whose face was that of the child genius, but the narrator realizes with distress that the Mozart in the street urchin will have to die for want of food. Trudeau told the tale badly. He was right. He had no real interest in stories, the description of events. But it was this failure that worked in his favour. He didn't seem to be so much the intellectual. It allowed him to conclude solemnly, lamely, eliciting no laughter from the crowd: "We are our brother's keeper in the whole of Canada."

Trudeau hurried back through the café rooms, where several Chinese women were still sitting on the old chenille chesterfield. He went out into the alley, where a small group of men milled about his car. "What about the Vietnam War?" someone shouted. Trudeau muttered, "*Quand je parlerai aux Chinoises, je parlerai en français.*" What did he mean? Had he misunderstood? Was he answering the man or was he carrying on some intense conversation with himself? I suddenly wanted to ask whether he knew he had been tearing that flower to pieces while jibing with the crowd. The Cadillac raised cinders in the air as it sped away.

The Dog Alive

Eight generations
of Hungerfords, McGards and Staceys
have lived on this ridge
like incestuous kings.
Their blood is so pure
It will not clot.

This is the only
country they know.
There are men here
who have never heard of Canada.

—Alden Nowlan

On Beacon Hill ten thousand people are packed together, a great nubbly blanket of heads and shoulders, some standing stacked against each other and others determinedly sensible, enthroned in aluminum lawn chairs. The sunset dissipates, there is sea salt in the air. The crowd of ten thousand seems soundless. To the right, a totem pole, a drowsing mask with slitted eyes. The hill rises out of the Strait of Juan de Fuca, which is cobalt blue in the early evening light.

Moral Re-armament children are singing, doing little tap steps and salutes while in song. It is the mechanical military movement that so many associate with purity of purpose.

Trudeau's helicopter settles on the grass. Ducking the whirl of propeller blades, he stumbles. He is off stride. On the speaker's stand, because he gives talks that leave no gaps for applause, the crowd is not sure when to clap, and those on the far crest of the hill hear his voice late over the speakers. When they cheer, Trudeau is already in mid-sentence.

Once again he is stripping a flower behind his back, a blood red rose.

He is repeating himself, losing track.

The microphone goes dead.

Trudeau looks relieved and slips over to the side of the stage, drawing gawky cheerleaders with him. Who had the wit, I wonder, to pull the plug? His 'copter picks him up and darts to the other side of the hill.

Striding along in tweeds, a natty old fellow, his chin thrust out, stops and asks, "Well, what would you do if you could draw crowds like this?"

I shrug as if I were Trudeau. He snorts. Hunching his shoulders, he lets his left sleeve drop down so that it conceals his hand; he takes off his hat and cradles it in the crook he has made with this suddenly deformed arm; his eyes fill with supplication. He has become an old soldier.

"I'd get through that crowd like lightning," he says, and holds the hat out in his good hand.

I am taken aback. He laughs.

"Hah, I can tell," he says, "you'd like to befriend Trudeau. Not me. The trick is to find a guy like Trudeau, get those crowds out. That's what politics is all about. Let guys like Trudeau with their need for applause have the stage. Me? I just want to get my hand in there when they're feeling nice and friendly like tonight. He's a rare one, this Trudeau, just nice people looking to be entertained and some people want to be the entertainer and some want to be a part of the crowd, so to speak."

He gives me a wink, flips his hat back on his head, and ambles off. I want to kick him in the seat of his pants. I know that as a respectable citizen, he would have me arrested.

On a stand close to the South Saskatchewan River in Saskatoon a woman with long teeth is at the piano – each chord a hymnal roll. A young boy, no more than eleven, is huffing into a soprano sax.

Trudeau extends his arms to some four thousand people. From behind the stand, a scream: "Go on home, you faggot." Trudeau does not flinch. He hurries into his speech. "You faggot . . . go home, you lousy frog."

Then a fist fight breaks out. Police put an arm-lock on the battlers. Trudeau is silent, his hands on his hips. The police are twisting a young kid's right arm high over his head. The kid is screaming: "This is the Just Society!" Trudeau complains, "Oh dear. Come on, come on – let, let, leave him alone . . . what the hell."

Law in the Country of Cats

When two men meet for the first time in all
Eternity and outright hate each other,
Not as a beggar-man and a rich man,
Not as cuckold-maker and cuckold,
Not as bully and delicate boy, but
As dog and wolf . . .

A few days later we are at Place Ville-Marie in Montréal.

Twenty-five thousand people. Trudeau says, "I feel like a gypsy who has travelled all over the country and now has to sing at home for his supper." Then – *BANG-BANG* – the crowd sucks in, waiting for Trudeau to go down. It is only a firecracker. Pierre Bourgault, leader of the Rassemblement pour l'indépendance nationale, has promised violence. One thousand demonstrators were screaming revolution as he said, "Trudeau is a traitor to the French-Canadian nation . . ." He promised to be in the front line at the Saint-Jean-Baptiste Day parade. "If Trudeau doesn't show up it will be a victory for us." Only yesterday, while I was sitting in the bus close to Trudeau, two light bulbs crashed beside me. *POP POP.* Perhaps we are watching a ghost. The buildings are tall glass honeycombs, men and women sealed in amber.

Trudeau startles the crowd by singing "O Canada." He *is* singing for his supper. Amplified. His voice, unmusical and strained, falls from the honeycomb walls.

When two men at first meeting hate each other . . .
There will be that moment's horrible pause
As each looks into the gulf in the eye of the other,
Then a flash of violent incredible action,
Then one man letting his brains gently to the gutter,
And one man bursting into the police station
Crying: "let Justice be done. I did it. I."

I recall a conversation last year with the beautiful chanteuse Pauline Julien, a fierce *séparatiste,* and another singer, the travelled Jean-Pierre Ferland. That angry exchange went:

Julien: (wagging her finger) "You wait and see, you English. We will clean you out. We will bomb, we will burn, maybe even have to kill."

Callaghan: (waving her away) "Maybe not."

Julien: "Yes, you will see the blood."

Ferland: (with the air of a man who has known the violence of gangsters, the violence of street fighting in Europe) "You children . . . you bombers with words, who've never fought anyone. Go to Belgium, where they really try to kill each other. See if you still talk that way. Come have a drink, M. Callaghan."

Fixé, tel un oeil de verre dans la tête de robot: women in French-Canadian fiction are often without mystery; stripped of social distinction, their flesh stolen from them, they fall upon their own hearts. They glitter, fixed, like the glass eye in the head of a robot.

Visiting Quebec industrial communities with Trudeau. In Saint-Hyacinthe, a textile town east of Montréal, too many of the women had a wan look in their eyes, too many had blotchy skin and crust-like makeup, too many dressed garishly. I saw within the hour four women with abrasions on their noses.

The same was true in Joliette, another textile centre, and Hochelaga, in the east end of Montréal. Women expert in maternity, yet with the hostile look of dedicated virgins; women who appear consecrated to sacrifice, with candle flames in their eyes. Over these women hangs something twisted, the frustration of too little love. These women are the hard eye that stares accusingly out of Québec: abuse and hard labour and poverty and guilt. "*O mon pauvre pays,*" writes François Hertel:

> *Ou rien ne change jamais,*
> *Changer pourtant, c'est vivre, o mon pays! Et toi,*
> *Immobile, fixé, tel un oeil de verre dans la tête de Robot.*
> *Toi, immuable, avec ton estomac gave de viandes*
> *Et de promessess.*

Yet elsewhere in Montréal you can see that these unhappy women are already of the past; many of their daughters now stride as if they could swallow the sun.

These are not the ladies who have always been in the Ritz or in the antique stores along Sherbrooke Street. No, something has happened over the past ten years; these are the daughters of the lower middle-class and labouring families who have freed themselves in the universities; they have read and discovered their right to be mysterious, to question their fathers, their pastors, their politicians, and they have learned to eat nourishing food. In downtown Montréal they seem everywhere. They are like Manet's woman at lunch on the grass, eyes direct, noncommittal but alert, questioning but guarded, having cultivated an almost neo-classical formality and distance, yet inviting you to perceive who they are, confident they can stand the test. There is no place in the lives of such women for any orator uncle with sunflower seeds in his pockets.

The Battle at Lafontaine Park

The sun is down; it is the summer solstice, the evening of the annual Saint-Jean-Baptiste parade in Montreal, on the day before the federal election. *Séparatistes* in Montréal have warned Trudeau not to come to the parade. He is coming. I parked on rue Beaudry beside the Bibliothèque de la ville. Chairs have been placed on a reviewing deck, the stand draped in blue and white bunting.

Five hundred *séparatistes* have entered the crowded Parc Lafontaine from Cherrier and Amherst Streets, inching toward rue Beaudry, chanting: "*Trudeau aux poteaux* [to the gallows]." Hard-hatted cops with billies charge, punching and swinging. With a roar, cycle cops with sidecars swing into the park, leaving behind Chief Griffin looking like a natty dance band leader in his dark blue suit and hat with gold braid, the man who is in control, his right arm jerking back and forth, directing officers who are no longer there.

In attack, the leader of the Rassemblement, Pierre Bourgault, is boosted into the air. Immaculate in black suit, white shirt, and black tie, he rides the head of a single column. The chants go up: "*Québec aux Québécois* – "*en français*" – "*Trudeau aux poteaux*" –

and Bourgault is being hurtled forward so that he is hanging off the shoulders, screaming, shaking his fists. The column carries Bourgault to the police lines; his feet are in their faces; like a bird caught upon thorns, he is plucked by the police and carted away. An insane gesture by the *séparatistes*! (Is it possible the column was headed by infiltrators?)

As the Black Maria door slams on Bourgault, a broken road barrier sails like a huge bolt, a streak of yellow in the floodlights, and it crunches against a cop's head. He collapses. It's nine o'clock.

Two truckloads of police whirl into the mob, billies smashing anyone in their way.

Legs are wishboned and bent back. Cops stagger, their helmets torn off by thrown bottles. A cop half runs, half falls out of the crowd: a giant firecracker – a cherry bomb – has exploded in his face. Tearing at his eyes, he is led to an ambulance; lime has also been ground into his face. This is it, *la pomme coupée à l'équateur,* a riot.

Four palominos and one chestnut, huge rib cages and pumping legs, strike terror in kids who run blindly, banging head-first into trees, the horses plowing through cowering women, spurred on by the club-wielding cops, who scatter the rioters north toward the lagoon and east to a steel mesh fence. It is 9:34 – Trudeau has arrived, Archbishop Grégoire and Mayor Drapeau are already seated in their chairs on the balcony of the Bibliothèque. Trudeau appears unperturbed: he bows mockingly to a chorus of Bronx cheers; the others are shaken and white-faced. Paint bombs and pop bottles are hurled from the western knolls by the lagoon. Nightsticks are shattered; some cops wield broken tree branches.

Ten o'clock: the police are defenseless. Many have suffered gashed faces; women and children trying to get out of the park have been felled; a small boy running to a tree for cover has been smashed on the head; a pregnant woman, terrified by the horses, is on her knees screaming and pleading with the police to stop; a gentleman in a walking suit, accompanied by a younger fellow, strolls casually around the Black Maria, detached and engrossed in conversation; a long-haired boy, stripped to the waist, is dragged along a walkway through broken glass littering the ground, suffering lacerations to his back, his screams lost in the uproar. An unconscious cop, whose horse had been levelled by a crowbar, has had both legs broken. Most cops are running kids by choke-holds up to the Marias and heaving them through the door. Up the west side of the knoll, a huge fire has been built. Horses flash through the flames.

The Saint-Jean-Baptiste parade, a patchwork affair of no originality, has been under review for an hour. Trudeau, with one leg crossed over the other, hands linked around his knees, looks relaxed. The Bishop's hands are fluttering in abortive blessings. As bathing beauties roll by on a float, Trudeau blows them a kiss. Motorcycles and ambulances are weaving in and out of the floats and bugle bands. Trudeau acts, with a superb show of aplomb, as though he is at a country fair. This is *Le balcon. Séparatistes* break along the north sidewalk. Suddenly a bottle is up in the lights. An arc. A sliver of moon. It crashes behind Trudeau. It could have been a bomb, a Molotov cocktail. An RCMP guard tries to cocoon Trudeau's crouched body. The official party flees their chairs. The Premier's face is drained. He is not so much walking as being carried by his men.

Trudeau bounds to his feet, flushed with rage, pivots, shakes his fist, laughs, stands alone in the middle of a row of empty chairs, and then he sits down, spreading his elbows on the railing, holding his chin between his hands. Grimly he watches, making it clear that he is in control of his space, his place. Another bottle crashes. The police beat back the bottle-throwers. Trudeau smiles. As Premier Johnson returns he is already a forgotten, ridiculed man, though not a word had been spoken. The Bishop returns, fluttering. Trudeau's steadfastness has been seen across the country on television. His election is certain. A police car is burning. The tires burst with a screech of boiling air.

Thousands have swarmed from the east hill into Sherbrooke Street now that the parade is past. They are held at rue Beaudry.

Again they are chanting that Trudeau must go to the gallows. Once again police squads form and plod into action. As Trudeau departs the Bibliothèque balcony, deliberately making no effort to hurry, his effigy is held aloft by the rioters, a papier mâché head and body about the length and shape of a cricket bat. It is set afire and a roar rises from the *séparatistes*; unaccountably, it flickers and goes out. The spirit is sapped from the battlers. They have almost heard a meaning in their howls; they nearly broke through. But now they are strapped in confusion and failure and, following perfunctory scraps and some pacing about the beachhead at Montcalm Street, they go home to crouch in the darkness of this city not captured by assault.

It is two o'clock in the morning. Someone says a cop's throat has been slit. The Police Chief is holding a press conference. No writers I know go. I hear the sound of a motorcycle far away. The tinkling of church bells. St. Catherine Street is empty. On the corner there are two high-fashion queens in lace pantaloons, tweaking each other. The bulge behind my eyes breaks; there are tears. Those screams, the fires on the knolls and the children crumpled under horses' hooves, the park turned into Desolation Row, the will to kill on the air. How would the allotment be made? *L'heure prend place.*

I thought of that old woman with her black gums scrambling under the trailer . . . and Trudeau stripping the rose . . . Was there a story there? I had almost forgotten the rose. What would Trudeau make of my telling that story? What else had I forgotten, trying desperately to remember? That for a tiny moment, as Trudeau shook his fist into the howling mob, I saw a look of execration in his eyes, and I was swollen with grief and pride?

The Telegram, 1968-69

ERUPTION OF RAGE AGAINST THE SECOND-RATE

Hey, out there! – assistant professors, full,
associates – instructors – others – any –
I have a sing to shay.
We are assembled here in the capital
city for Dull – and one professor's wife is Mary . . .
forget your footnotes . . .
dance around Mary.

—JOHN BERRYMAN

There has been a lull in the literary life. There's been no cutting to the bone, no contemptuous curl of the lip for the second-rate. Instead we've had criticism that's been a plodding affair, a scholarly nod here, a footnote there, and a good deal of cheerleading. Out of this slough, certain scholars have fashioned formidable reputations. They've become powerful men in the increasingly powerful universities. Donkey researchers have vested themselves with authority, this one an authority on John Donne's sermons, that one on the juvenilia of Herman Melville. Most of this work has piled up uselessly in the cellars of huge campus libraries. At stake has been the establishment of pockets of power, a promotion and a position at this college and a chair at that college, with grants from the government along the way.

This is the peculiar world in which the second-rate is encouraged and thrives: shoddy writing and silly exercises in scholarship are tolerated so that no one will rock the boat, so that academic law and order will prevail. The rule is this: academic authority must not be sneered at. But something is in the wind. "Who has the authority?" delegates and intellectuals asked during the Chicago Democratic Convention. When they found out, they were enraged. They lit candles and marched to join the street riots. The quiet time of law and order was broken.

It is at first astonishing, but then seems quiet reasonable, that this same spirit of contempt and outrage should suddenly dominate the usually stodgy and academic *New York Review of Books*. In the current Special Fifth Anniversary Issue, Edmund Wilson, arguing at length, scornfully dismisses the whole university power structure, the PhD policemen, while William Styron just manages to contain within the elegance of his language his utter and complete loathing for the police and politicians he saw in Chicago. These two writers have suddenly and at the same time had a bellyful of the formidable band of second-rate people who've been paying lip service to each other over the years.

Wilson's angry outburst has been triggered by the political lobbying of the Modern Language Association, an organization to which almost every professor of literature or language in the U.S. belongs. It is a kind of Teamsters Union in that it intimidates nearly all the rolling stock (professors) moving from college to college. For some years Wilson has urged that the American government aid in financing a uniform edition of well-edited American literary classics. This is an important project, for the complete works of writers like Edgar Allan Poe are not available. But recently the MLA lobbied successfully and had Wilson's project "tabled" so that they could continue with their own clumsy industry along the same lines. It is this academic industry that Wilson describes and castigates.

The kind of useless scholarship that infuriates Wilson is this: at the present time there are eighteen workers doggedly reading *Tom Sawyer* backwards, word by word, in order to ascertain how many times *sst* is printed as *ssst* and how many times *Aunt*

Polly is printed as *aunt Polly*. They are reading backwards so that they will not be distracted by the story or style (in the academic business world this is known as boondoggling – being paid to do trivial or unnecessary work). This is the absurdity of the oppressive PhD system that so effectively tyrannizes letters and scholarship today, a system presided over to a large extent by Mr. Fredson Bowers of the University of Virginia, master bibliographer, of whom Wilson remarks tartly that Bowers is a thrilling lecturer on bibliography, but "I have found no reason to believe he is otherwise much interested in literature. It has been said in fact, I believe, by someone in the academic world that, in editing *Leaves of Grass*, he had done everything for it but read it."

This process results in editions like Hawthorne's *The Marble Faun*. Of its 610 pages, 467 are by Hawthorne, 143 are given over to textual notes (how many ink smudges Hawthorne made!), 89 to a textual introduction, and 44 to a historical introduction. Wilson's point is, Who, in his right mind, could want to read such an edition except the most impassioned bibliographer, and who could possibly enjoy it (the editions being overly expensive, overly large, and unbelievably heavy – *The Marble Faun* weighing in at nine pounds)?

The undeniable fact is that the university system of scholarship wastes time, talent, and money. Wilson's outrage is tempered only by his sense of the ridiculous.

The spirit that drives Wilson is forcefully evident in William Styron's description of the Chicago authorities. There, in that "indecent crush of ambitious flesh," he fastened his attention on the cops who were everywhere:

> Not only in the streets but in the hotel lobbies and in the dark bars and restaurants, in their baby-blue shirts, so ubiquitous that one would really not be surprised to find one in one's bed; yet it was not their sheer number that truly startled, as impressive as this was, but their peculiar personae, characterized by a beery obesity that made

> them look half again as big as New York policemen . . . and by a slovenly, brutish, intimidating manner . . . Constantly stamping out butts, their great beer guts drooping as they gunned their motorcycles, swatting their swollen thighs with their sticks, they gave me a chill, vulnerable feeling, and I winced at the way their necks went scarlet when the hippies yelled "Pigs!"

Styron's disgust is with a manifestly bogus and vulgar authority. Mayor Daley is denounced as a hoodlum suzerain obscenely lodged in the public eye howling "Kike!" at Senator Abe Ribicoff, and the MLA officials are treated by Wilson as if they are hard-working slack-minded buffoons. Yes, something altogether new is in the wind, stirring not only in the hippie compounds, but in places you would least suspect. Fredson Bowers and Mayor Daley getting their lumps at the same time in the same journal would have been inconceivable only one year ago.

The Telegram, 1968

DAVIES' DOUR ANGELS: *FIFTH BUSINESS*

Dunstable Ramsay, fascinated by saints, also has a feeling for evil, and in his own way he has slept with a she-devil. He also knows something about the mysteries attached to magic and ritual. And he certainly does know about killing, having come close to death in the war, where, in the trenches, he lost a leg. Legless, he still gets around, knowing many men of wealth and political position, fastidious Jesuits and fat old priests who have a proclivity for scampish talk. How is it, then, that he should seem in his memoirs to be so sour and small, so shrivelled in spirit ?

Dunstable, in his middle years, has been retired from a Toronto boys' school. Resentful, he feels he has been dismissed with disdainful ease, that the character and quality of his life is being overlooked. But, after all, he has led a life of much serious intent and interest, and if his headmaster and the boys he has taught don't know this, then in his memoirs – in their frankness – he will prove he is not just a dour old duffer who has been put out to pension.

All his life, Dunstable, his name changed to Dunstan, and known as Dunny to his few friends, has – like that peculiar stage character who is the odd man out, who has no opposite of the other sex, who knows the secret of the hero's birth, who assists the heroine when all seems lost, who succours the hermitess in her cell, who inadvertently causes someone's death – been exactly this kind of peripheral presence. He has been, and is, Fifth Business.

The hermitess in Dunstan's case is Mrs. Dempster, a woman of sweet temper who had once, in a dour, dismal Ontario town, been married to a dreadful parson. When Dunstan was a boy, the pregnant Mrs. Dempster was out taking a breath of air when Dunny, in front of her, ducked just as another boy, Staunton, fired a snowball at him. Struck by the snowball, Mrs. Dempster fell in a heap and, shortly after, out came her son Paul. Mrs. Dempster, left simple-minded from the shock of the blow of the snowball and the shock of the birth, became a burden to her husband, a burden to her town.

The scrupulous Dunstan is a scab-picker. He won't leave his soul alone. He's never forgiven himself for having ducked as a child in front of the woman, and he's fed on guilt all his life. Hence he has kept Mrs. Dempster through the later years of her madness, hence his need to believe that she really is a fool for Jesus, a singular woman, even a saint, because she has made miracles of love among a people who sucked on eggs and sin.

One such miracle was Mrs. Dempster giving herself sexually in the town pit (read Hell) to a tramp, not out of lust, but from charity. The public shame attendant upon such generosity drove her son Paul from her, but that act, as he understood it, has led Dunstan on a lifelong quasi-religious quest, a pursuit of angels and devils, with a pinch of evil along the way.

I say quasi-religious because Dunstan's life is all gestures amidst religious trappings. There is certainly a tone, a tenor to the story, what with a saint and much discourse about angels and the devil, but little depth of felt experience is in this talk. An old priest, learned in saint's lore, says to Dunstan: "The devil knows corners in us all of which Christ Himself is ignorant. Indeed I am sure Christ learned a great deal that was salutary about Himself when He met the devil in the wilderness. Of course, that was a meeting of brothers; people forget too readily that Satan is Christ's elder brother . . ." This could be interesting if the characters expressed any profound sense of engagement with the presence of evil, the presence of love – a pressure from within rather than information argued from without. Dunstan, in his hard, closed way, has character, but he is surrounded by ventriloquists' dummies, mere mouthpieces for discourse disguised as conversations about angels, God, Christ, etc., etc. Much of what they say is witty, a good deal of it is intelligent, but it is talk talk talk.

This is a shame. The first hundred pages of the novel are a honed and often engaging portrait of a small-minded Ontario man in an Ontario small town, a town where "it was not at all the proper thing for a pregnant woman to smile so much," a town on the cusp of Calvinism, a town given to wearing crepe on its nose, a town dominated by women like Dunstan's fierce, whip-wielding mother. Their hapless sons got away on troopships, going to war to go to war, with no clear idea of what the war was about. They were mutilated and died. Dunstan, because of a dumb act of heroism amongst the slaughter, was given a Victoria Cross. But he never became a giving man: "I was mean-spiritedly pleased that my mother had not lived to hear of my V.C.; how she would have paraded in mock-modesty as the mother of a hero . . ." He was pleasured by his own meanness, a man who wanted his life to be his own, and he ends by having his wish. He has been dismissed, he is alone.

The final pages of Dunstable's memoirs are marked by machinery – the machinery of characters moving nimbly around that dreary town, demonstrating not much emotion but a lot of learning, a good deal of it arcane. This is entertainment of a kind, affable and erudite, artificial and witty, but behind the stagecraft there is a sourness, and at the core there is only the mean little mind of Dunstable, neither evil nor ennobled, just mean.

The Telegram, 1970

A BEGGAR IN JERUSALEM: ELIE WIESEL

You encounter haunted faces in the stone alleyways of Jerusalem. The sun is white and the stones at the top of the walls are white, but down in the shadows, hurrying, hunched forward, are faces stricken with yearning, with wonder, with fear. Then you pass an old man who holds out his hand, begging, yet in his eyes you can see that he expects nothing, that there is nothing you can place in his white, vulnerable hand, which is a deeply lined hand, a map of what others have done to him and what he has done to himself.

The beggar is a figure of mystery. If he is a cripple curled up in a corner, men imagine him to be a great wanderer through evil cities; if he is sightless, then he must be a seer; if he is silent, then he is a messenger. His outstretched palm beckons, his upright hand wards off evil. His tale, if he tells it, looms up as both prophecy and private pain. Elie Wiesel went to Jerusalem, and there he found himself feeling like a beggar, haunted under the long shadow of the Wailing Wall.

Elie Wiesel was a child of Auschwitz – the death camp and the winter death march out of the camp – who settled after the war in France. He wrote in Yiddish and was translated into French, and French writers – especially François Mauriac – greeted his first novel, *Night,* with praise. It is a stark book. Cleanly told. Persuasive. But a stifling, smug piety then crept into the tone of his work – along with a proprietary air toward pain. Jewish pain: its singularity, its way of informing and shadowing other pain. In 1970, however, he has published in translation *A Beggar in Jerusalem,* and it is his most interesting novel since *Night.*

In 1967, during the house-to-house fighting of the Six Day War, Wiesel had broken through the Jordanian line, trailing the Jewish troops who had taken the Old City. He was not a soldier. He had just managed to find a place with one of the Israeli divisions. And so he'd run through the dank, narrow stone alleys toward the Wall, ignoring sniper fire from the Bedouin soldiers who were holed up in the stone houses. He was full of surging expectation, and then, suddenly, there it was, the Wall, those enormous piled stone blocks, the ragged joints and crevices, and, faces to the Wall, there were the weeping, rocking, moaning soldiers who stuffed the openings with scribbled messages to God. Wiesel, however, began to wonder about messages . . . and wonder about hope, and the forgotten, and he wondered why none of the messages put in that Wall over the centuries had ever been answered. Could his shtetl brethren – those who had died in the camps, those who could not be here in Jerusalem – could they end up forgotten, too, in the sweet rush of joy?

Also, he's no fool. Partisan, yes. But no fool. He knows that if there are victors then there are losers, "the vanquished who everywhere wear the same dark haunted look, the same pleading smile. Vanquished children are everywhere the same. In a world that is in ruins, selling ruins is all they have left." Dizzy with victory, he blushes each time a Mohammed or a Jamil pulls at his sleeve. The eyes hollowed, a haunted smile. A ruined childhood. He has not forgotten his own childhood, his stricken life in the camp and on the death-march road, he has not forgotten his first glimpse of himself in a mirror after escaping that camp ("From the depths of the mirror a corpse gazed back at me"), and he will not forget the little corpses he sees living in the eyes of Palestinian children. Victory after Six Days does not lose its significance, or its necessity; but victory does lose its taste of joy. His confusion in this swirl of memory is increased by a sabra soldier who tells him:

> God doesn't love us, and neither does the world. Too bad. It's no longer our problem, but theirs. From now on, they will not count in our calculations. We shall ignore them . . . I don't give a damn any more whether humanity has a conscience or not. It never had any, that's what I think. I think all the grandiloquent talk about humanity's soul and conscience was invented by persecuted Jews as a shield or alibi. So they wouldn't have to fight . . . Many persecuted Jews let themselves be massacred. They should have risen up in fury, they should have revolted.

A child with very dark eyes at Dung Gate smiles at him.

A beggar stares at him.

The beggar is not begging. He is watching.

The beggar is David, one of the mad Jewish mendicants of the city: "All of us are messengers, though we may not know for whom or for what purpose. If man be the messenger of man, why should a madman not be the messenger of God?" David, who is tormented by hope, is mad because he is unable to forget the past; and Jerusalem, the city of hope, is a mad city because it is a city where nothing is ever forgotten . . . Jerusalem is a city of holy men echoing holy men, scorpions mounting scorpions . . . stinging . . . and David, haunted as he is by the death camps and hardened as he is against joy, now finds himself in Jerusalem bursting with joy, so that he no longer knows how to be who he is – a man gratuitously chosen by God to live or a man who gratuitously betrays his dead every day by staying alive. In his stillness he remembers a soldier named Katriel, a big, silent man who seemed – before the six days of war – to be one of the dead who had come back to life to learn how to fight, a man who had prayed, "God, make me able to kill like the others do." Katriel, ready to kill, was optimistic – while David, riven by fear, was pessimistic – they were a twinning, and the two, going through the war, had reached the Wall together. But as the Wall was taken, Katriel disappeared – never to be seen again – and so hope, for David, had seemed to depart with victory, a hope not to be confused with light-headed exuberance, let alone the gloating remorselessness of so many sabras. David, sitting in stillness among the beggars, can find no hope in this war won over the Arabs, he can find no hope in the eyes of the vanquished children and no hope in the memories of his own shtetl dead. The resolution to this contradiction lies in the contradiction itself – for, as it is written that the divine presence never leaves Jerusalem, it is also written that the divine presence follows the Jews into exile. The divine presence is inherent in the contradiction, and that contradiction is life as it must be lived – haunted by death, bewildered by joy, bewildered by death, haunted by joy. (Though this is not explained by Wiesel, David's yearning and this spiritual tension are captured in the name itself, Katriel. In Hebrew the name comes from the word *keter*, meaning crown, and *el*, meaning God, and so *Katriel* suggests the plea "God, be my crown." On the other hand, in the language of exile the Yiddish word *kesrilovke* describes a town on the backside of God, a boondock shtetl filled with comic hicks and losers.) We have in Katriel, David, and Wiesel a deeply Jewish story, but not just a Jewish dilemma – we have the plight of man, fear-ridden, helpless, comic, in exile, yet alive with the need to wear God as his crown, to hope for more than survival, to pray for more than madness, to die with more than a sigh.

The Telegram, 1970-72

DESOLATION ROW: NEW YORK

It is ten-thirty at night on 42nd Street. Girls in satin miniskirts, old guys sour with the stink of sleeping in squalid movie houses, women with washboard fat on the backs of their necks are staring at a wall of blown-up movie stills: breasts, buttocks, and whips, rifles and pearl-handled pistols, two women on their knees kissing each other on the mouth, and, kitty-corner to the blow-ups, a FUN CITY amusement gallery – a fluorescent and neon-lit door and, inside the door, a tall mechanical gunslinger in black pants, black boots, black shirt, and a broad black cowboy hat on his head, a pink-faced sunburned white man.

About seven feet away from the gunslinger there are two holsters with six-guns welded to a concave steel bar. Standing at the bar is a finger-popping black boy who has a wide mouth and high, sloping cheekbones. He's been dropping dime after dime into the money slot. He is happy. For the last hour he's been killing this white cowboy man like he is all the white men of the world. He shifts his weight, hunches his left shoulder, loosening up, a southpaw, and then he grasps the gun butt, a skinny, long-legged boy-child talking at his dream:

I am the man who am,
in short I is,
John the Conqueroo Decatur,
born outa some hair-pie hustler
by Clarence Urreal, my daddy,
and I be no creeper

born to die
with a face full of frown

and never no more than
a mumbling word, no sir,
no nigger this kid
hobble-down hiding
in his grave; I got always
a big bag of goofer dust
and in my sleeping sack
my Molly sweet-sepia (her
percolator grind so fine
black coffee

for John the Conqueroo
Decatur); now this evening,
you and me, we's going to escalator on
into Farisee's Funland
through them double-doors plate glass,
to the mechanical
dude cowboy slung out in six-guns,
where they got him high-fashion
black, black boots high-heeled
and tooled leather,

and Levis black, and satin shirt,
and broad-brimmed hat,
and under that, his blue-eyed
coral carnival pink
sweet face, the fixed smiling
malice of your race,
and his right arm hang-down holding
his gun, waiting, serene,
for someone to feed that old slot,
a dime, three shots;

I gonne to satisfy his soul,
and do the whole rigmarole of his routine,
tie the holster on my hip, put up with all
that squawk box
recorded lip about my being a green horn
rube born for Boot Hill, and then,
there's only the silence
before the calm of the kill,
and he call Draw,

and never see that iron come off my hip,
cocking and firing,
and Bam-Bam, he wasted, and dying says,
yuh got me yuh badlands badman,
because you faster than I thought you was,
and I say, O Yeas, Yeas, sliding my shooter
on home to holster, You better believe it,
you white motherfucker,
Yeas, and I say, Yeas,
he dead, O Yeas, Yeas, Yeas.

Seventh Avenue South, the Actors Playhouse. *Futz* by Rochelle Owens has toured Europe and has won an Obie Award. The actors crouch down on all fours or stand on their heads or circle in a slow, high-stepping strut; they are sneering dirt farmers in blue denims, groaning, and one boy, his long blond bangs in his eyes, defiantly snaps the loose strings of a bass fiddle: *thlak – uhum, thlak – uhum.*

These are the neighbours of Cyrus Futz. He tends a garden of carrots and peas and potatoes and works a pig. These men and women hate Futz. They are hard-bitten and stern. He has an open, soft, eager sensuality. Marjorie Satz, the local slut who wants Futz, has hiked her skirt and is on her knees wagging her rump at him, running her tongue around her loose mouth. Futz will have none of her. He's in love with Amanda, and Amanda is his pig.

Futz has tried being social, taking his beloved Amanda to church service to hear the preachifying, but he was driven from the church door and now he asks only to be left alone to live on his farm and feed himself and his pig, wanting to harm no one.

The townspeople are a mean breed. They have a meeting place. It is the jailhouse. Waiting in a cell to die is Oscar Loop, a sensual, mystical half-wit. One afternoon while courting his girl, he was drawn to Futz's barn by human and animal sounds; peeping through the slats he saw Futz astride his Amanda, and in a blood rage he had strangled his own girlfriend. Now, waiting to hang, he tells what he saw to the jail warden. Futz is arrested, he is imprisoned, and since hell hath no fury like a woman scorned for a pig, Marjorie, the scorned woman – and her brother, mother, and father – become a hairball of revenge, killing Futz, killing Amanda.

This is a ritual fantasy from the sordid backwoods of the mind. In its craftless staging and the forced music of its language, *Futz* suggests celebration, but these slavering folk are the husk of human experience: righteous men who turn women into pigs and pigs into women, and their sons into cops and hangmen. Futz had a strange innocence (Billy Budd as Li'l Abner) but his love in its celebration was hateful, swinish. He was fucking a pig.

Near Madison Square Garden there is a news vendor's wooden hut; once it was painted an ebony green, now it is ashen; it is a box with a window and a ledge, and the vendor has a pale, puffy face half-hidden behind newspaper and magazine headlines that are strung across the window like washing on a wire line:

THE NEW BARBARIANS
Daniel J. Boorstein
THE POLITICS OF ASSASSINATION
William F. Buckley Jr.

It is early evening. Governor George Corley Wallace of Alabama is going to speak in the Garden. On 34th Street, off Eighth Avenue, mounted policemen sidle into line, pulling their reins short, the bits making the horses snort and bare their long yellow teeth. These horsemen canter along the north sidewalk, iron shoes clattering like small-arms fire heard from afar, and they are leaning out of the saddle, swinging and slashing with their nightsticks at clusters of guileless kids and New Left old pros who are wearing construction safety helmets. The kids are howling: "Oink, oink, oink."

Pop bottles explode against the walls.

A chartered school bus has backed in by the curb: Wallace supporters from Long Island. The kids pound their fists against the Permaglass windows: "*Sieg heil*, you bastards, *Sieg heil*." Behind the glass, blue-collar workers, their mouths moving in astonished sullen curses that cannot be heard, show a strange satisfaction in their eyes; they are seeing for the first time hippies as they had always imagined them to be. These northeastern Long Island patriots are wearing Wallace hats and waving Southern Confederate flags. There is a silence trapped between the double sheets of Permaglass, as there is a silence between these small businessmen and union card carriers and civil servants who are angry because their institutions have failed them – and these hippies and yippies and students and leftists who are angry and out on the street because their institutions have failed them.

The Wallace people step from the bus, their flags are torn out of their hands by several kids and turned into torches: "Burn, baby, burn." There are very few blacks protesting in the street, but a woman with big round Wallace buttons on each ample breast yells: "Them goddamn niggers . . . Wallace'll get 'em." And she confides: "If God had made 'em equal he wouldn't have made 'em black."

The police beat a white kid with their batons. Dazed, his blood congealing in his hair and a senseless grin on his face, he is given a push by a laughing cop and he stumbles face forward into a wall. Kids chant: "Pig, pig, pig." A placard with Wallace riding a pig's back is waved in the cop's face and he bellows: "We're all for Wallace, and you watch it, 'cause you're gonna catch it." Policemen wear Wallace badges on the flip side of their uniform lapels. A hippie, his hair dragging in the wind as he runs, screams, "Don't feed the pigs, don't feed the pigs."

A kid shrugs and says, "Fuck the pigs, baby, this must be Desolation Row."

Sixteen thousand men and women stand inside the Garden to hail George Wallace. They sing "Yankee Doodle Dandy," an old Jimmy Cagney song about a feisty man who came to town riding on a pony, and they punch and jab at thousands of balloons dumped on their heads as Wallace, secure within a bulletproof steel-plated podium, feeds their rancour, their fear, promising retribution after a punitive maelstrom. Cupping his ear because he's hard of hearing, and with a slack little salesman's smile, he harkens to a cluster of hecklers, and then he says with a sneer, in a drawl that lends his toneless voice an air of gentility: "Y'awl better have your say now, I can tell you thet. After November 5 you anarchists are through in this country." His supporters, who are good but bewildered people, gleefully clap their hands. Little George Wallace, in his pinstripe suit and his iridescent grey undertaker's tie, is their poultice, he is coaxing their deep sense of injury – their deep-set feeling that they've been overlooked – to the surface:

Black snake is evil, black snake is all I see,
Black snake is evil, black snake is all I see,
I woke up this morning he was moved in on me.

Seventh Avenue and 44th Street: the clatter of steel wheels on cement, a legless man riding his board, laughing, a singing mouth down among the legs, gone, a wind-driven face, gone, and only the sound of his laughing voice: "If you were the only girl in the world and I was the only boy . . ."

Along 47th Street, the American Tribal Love-Rock Musical *Hair.* A lady wearing pearls and silver-beaded slippers is standing in the centre aisle, taking her ease, aloof among the usherettes and paunchy men checking ticket stubs. Creeping up behind her, a boy in bell-bottom trousers torn at the cuffs. His feet are bare and there are tufts of black hair on his toes. He covers her slipper with his big bare foot and she tries to pull away, but he roots her to the floor with his foot, and through the hair hanging over his face he whispers: "Baby, baby, do your own thing." Then he whirls away in laughter and a rattle of wooden beads. More actors come down the aisle.

They line up in a chorus and there is crowing about acid and shacking up and a boy goes prancing by with a sign: SEE ETHEL MERMAN IN *HAIR*. Everyone laughs at the cosy old musicals. The noise and clatter fade and a narrow-chested Jewish boy stands with hands clasped (a child at elocution class), his kinky brown hair an Afro-bush, and he croons a love song about muff-diving as the boss of this band of merry trippers, fags, and coloured studs appears. He is a long-haired, earnest man with a childish whine who has been inducted into the army. In boot camp he loses his locks. The blue-eyed stare of the well-drilled soldier comes into his eyes. He has been transformed by the regimental haircut into a conventional killer. He is the figure around whom all the action revolves. As a character he's no more than a prop for a series of skits calculated to puncture current prejudices and loyalties. Three beautiful soul sisters wearing blonde bouffant wigs sing:

White boys are so pretty
Skin as smooth as milk
Hair like Chinese silk

I tell you that white boys
give me goose bumps . . .

Then mockery is made of the folding of the flag and even old Abe Lincoln gets his lumps: a very hip, very cool black girl wearing a stovepipe hat and sideburns pasted on her cheeks, her hair in tight piccaninny pigtails, sings to the syncopation of the blues:

Four score, I said four score
and seven years ago
(sock it to 'em baby
you're getting better all the time)
our forefathers brought forth
upon this here continent
a new nation
(O come on, it's too wokely-Stokely)
conceived, conceived like we all was
in liberty
and dedicated to the one I love . . .

Three boys and three girls stand stone-naked, stand in a dusky light for twenty seconds and then disappear. In the old days Sally Rand and Gypsy Rose Lee called this "flashing" – they flipped a last fan for just a moment and the men in the front row had a blurred glimpse of a bare breast. On Broadway, *Hair* and this glimmer of nudity are said to be revolutionary.

There is nothing revolutionary about *Hair*. The play's excellently produced and acted, but in terms of staging, the techniques are already conventional in the experimental theatres. The score, for all its gaiety, is ordinary if not trite. The lyrics are flat and banal. The quality of the pain that haunts our children is strained until it has become pleasant entertainment. You are persuaded that the street kids who so bedevil authority are no more than unwashed in their ways. Undeniably there is goodness among the incense children, but *Hair* is pure pastry; neither the emotions nor the situations are authentic. As the hippies gather in campfire fashion to shout a foot-stomping gospel finale about the "dying nation," they seem to be charming children on the verge of coming home. *Hair* is no threat to the audience; nothing said or done is so outrageous that it can't be assimilated in under twenty minutes. As an experience, it is a meringue neatly lifted from the body of what is a dangerous and compelling social condition.

One of the town's few peaceful places: Gramercy Park, at the foot of Lexington Avenue. It is the only private park in the city, enclosed by a high ornate iron fence. I have a key, so I am able to sit on one of the benches. It is almost pastoral. I've brought James T. Farrell's essays, *The Frightened Philistines*, to the park. The so-called New Morality has been on my mind; morals are in fashion – a media-savvy theologian can be much in demand these days.

In 1944 Farrell wrote about the wartime fashion for morals:

> Where in it can you find that energy of mind of Augustine, the intellectual scope of Aquinas, the anger of Luther, the consistent bleak logic of Calvin, the wonderful love and gentleness of Saint Francis, the womanly dignity and intelligence of Saint Teresa, the soldierly ability and genius of Ignatius, the simplicity of devotion of Thomas à Kempis, the real gentlemanliness of Cardinal Newman, the burning sincerity and indignation and exquisite pride of Leo Tolstoy? Where? If one had known religion, and known it, too, in rejecting it, one is not impressed by morals which masquerade as religion, moral density based on fear of living in the present and facing the future.

It is a time for space-travelling moralists and space salesmen, horoscope prophets and holy men: Marshall McLuhan and

Maharishi Mahesh Yogi suffer little children to come unto them, and a hippie sporting a Nazi Iron Cross cries out, "May the baby Jesus open your mind and shut your mouth," while Timothy Leary, high on acid, puts on white robes and enters Detroit as the reincarnation of Father Divine and Herbert Marcuse bleeds the optimism out of Marx and, like nimble cockroaches, GI Joes come home from Nam sporting belts strung with the cut-off ears of Charlie Cong, and K-Mart kids brought up with the Bible in their jumpers drift like lost angels on angel dust singing the songs of Howlin' Wolf. It is a time for Tiny Tim, alias Julian Foxglove, alias Derry Dover, alias Herbert Khaury, alias Larry Love – a talentless singer rescued from freak-show obscurity – to declare that he takes a shower six times a day because cleanliness is next to godliness. He believes in the "pure moral virtues" and carries a copy of the New Testament, and the pages of St. Paul are marked for reading: "Now concerning the things whereof ye wrote: It is good for a man not to touch a woman. But, because of fornications, let each man have his own wife, and let each woman have her own husband." There he is, a fluttering falsetto, Tiny Tim, the ugly icon of celibate purity, to sing of tip-toeing through the tulips on the Carson show as he marries – *live on air* – the most beautiful virgin in the United States, Miss Vicky – *live on air* – as we suffer a demoralization not experienced since the Depression.

In 1932, at the height of the Depression, Walter Lippmann wrote:

> A demoralized people is one in which the individual has become isolated . . . He trusts nobody and nothing, not even himself. He believes nothing, except the worst of everybody and everything. He sees only confusion in himself and conspiracies in other men. That is panic. That is disintegration. That is what comes when in some sudden emergency of their lives, men find themselves unsupported by clear convictions that transcend their immediate and personal desires.

Henry was not a coward. Much.
He never deserted anything; instead
He stuck, when things like pity were thinning.
So maybe Henry was a human being.
Let's investigate that.

—JOHN BERRYMAN

It's been raining, and down among the warehouses of Wooster and Canal streets it is desolate. A garage has been made into a theatre for the performance of *Dionysus in '69.* There are no seats and the audience sits cross-legged on the floor around a set of mats, and on the mats are young men and women performing shoulder rolls and back bends and headstands, all in slow motion, as if their controlled movements bespoke an inner serenity. There are scaffolds built against the wall and, shinnying up a two-by-four to a platform, I watch the performance.

Five nude men are lying stomach down in a row on the mats. Five women stand over them with their legs spread apart and their spread legs form an archway. The women writhe and caress the thighs of their men. They knead the bodies of their men. Then a long, skinny fellow with a moustache enters the archway and he is pulled over the buttocks of the men and through the legs of the groaning women. It is the ritual birth of Dionysus, ancient god of blowing your mind.

Prowling on the outskirts of the audience is Penthius the lawman. With his cropped hair and muscled body he seems a disciplined marine out on patrol. Pausing by a scaffold he executes an exercise: balancing on one foot, he curls his forearms in against his chest. It is a self-satisfied gesture. Penthius is arrogant, shallow, and rational. He believes in punishment and the efficacy of jails.

The women rattle their tambourines and enter the audience. There is something comic and lovely about the way they pluck out young boys and bring them gently to the dancing mats. When the women strip off their red shirts and dance bare-breasted with the boys there is nothing lewd about them. It has all been done with so little pretension, without warning.

A round-faced girl sitting by the edge of the mats has broken into shrill laughter: a naked male dancer is crouched before her. He holds her head in his hands and he soothes her. She smiles and takes his arm and they rise up. The girl pulls her sweater over her head and folds her hands back to unclasp her brassiere. But Penthius leaps between them and cups his hand over her mouth. He stares at her sternly and she remains motionless, caught up in the performance. Penthius moves from dancer to dancer, touching their mouths, halting the Bacchanalian rites. He moves with the desperation of the righteously indignant and he drives the dancers to the walls, where they creep about, caressing and fondling the spectators. Dionysus the young god and Penthius the young ruler are left alone and they confront each other on the mats. Penthius is outwitted, humiliated, and scorned by the clever and glib Dionysus. He is stripped of his righteousness and self-confidence and he is sent off to the fields where the women dance.

The actor who has been playing Dionysus has now taken upon himself a second role, that of a hectoring New Left agitator. His real name, he says is William Finley, and he proposes to marshal the irrational emotion of the aroused Bacchanalians behind his political pursuit of power. This transformation of Dionysus from priest to politician puts Penthius in an altogether new light: he becomes more than a victim from ancient myth. He suddenly looms up as the representative of those wounded citizens who had pledged themselves to Mayor Daley, Richard Nixon, and George Wallace. William Finley promises these "law and order" people the death he has reserved for Penthius. For Penthius, once he is in the fields, is seized by the ecstatic women and they form the birth arch once more and drag him through, and cut him as he passes, and finally the women stand triumphant, their arms upraised, and the blood from Penthius runs down their bodies.

Finley, having made a scaffold his speaker's platform, calls for Dionysian power in '69. Something compelling happens here, for as Dionysus he was a fairly harmless fellow, shallow, but preferable to Penthius the cop. But now it is Finley's very shallowness as an agitator that lends his figure a chilling reality. As he screams, "I love assassinations," and as the garage doors open and the audience herds out into the street, Finley is recognizable.

With his hoarse pitilessness and his wagging, accusing arm, he embodies the sterile lunge for power that characterizes so many of the agitators in the streets today. These ruthless men have been cashing in on the moment, substituting crudity for needed criticism, irresponsibility for revolt, indifference for purpose. The politics of assassination and the jailhouse have cut down the Kennedys, Martin Luther King, Malcolm X, and in their place we now have men made narrow by their paucity of ideas and emotion. We have rid ourselves of intelligent, feeling rebels and are now confronted by men who have gained prominence only through the shrillness of their rhetoric.

Each dissident taken from us by death or by enforced silence has been replaced by another, always more violent, more shallow, more appalling voice. As Stokely Carmichael warned the whites who wanted to crush him, "If you think I'm bad, wait 'til you get Rap Brown." Consider that Malcolm X, once hated and reviled, was an introspective, accommodating man who left behind a body of writing and commentary remarkable in its depth of feeling. What did his successor have to say about human affairs? Only that "violence is as American as cherry pie." William Finley is the priest turned political criminal, twisting the faith of his followers to his own ends, making them his tools of power.

It is Sunday morning: the air is very clear. I get into a cab and give directions to a little old man wearing a peaked cap: 333 East 34th Street. He drives directly west. He has a thick Yiddish accent and waves his hands at me as he is driving, his hands doing a dance on the wheel.

"Listen," he says, "I should be in Israel fighting Arabs, so if I'm gonna fight it should be with the Arabs and not in my own car. Here I turn into a gangster; all of a sudden I'm a sixty-seven-year-old gangster."

We are at Eighth Avenue and he throws up his hands apologetically. "Me, I'm a talker driving west the whole time. I'm supposed to be driving east." He turns the cab around. He doesn't turn the meter off.

"I get mugged by a nigger," he says, "and I have a heart attack, like I need a heart attack. I was born in 1901, so I should get a heart attack in New York from a nigger? So now I got a butcher knife, an eighteen-inch butcher knife, a very kosher knife. You know what that means?" He turns and smiles and he has gaps between all his upper teeth. I recall that Chaucer believed gaps were a mark of sensuality. "A kosher knife," he explains, "is a very sharp knife. Listen, I'm a very touchy old guy," he goes on, "and when I see niggers in the street I got my knife wrapped in newspaper. They make me, an old man, they make me a gangster. You know what? I vote for Nixon, a nothing, but Wallace, he would be tough on the niggers."

We are parked at the apartment house. He sizes it up. "Very classy," he says. "Listen," as I get out of the door, "I'm from Bessarabia, and where I'm from they're the kind who go out with a rope and come back with a horse. I don't get mugged no more. I carry that knife in the newspaper, and the cops, they see me and they don't say nothing, 'cause they know an old guy's got to protect himself. Those goddamn niggers, they make me, an old man, a gangster . . ."

You may be right, Friend Bones.
Indeed you is . . .
Bit by bit
our immemorial moans
brown down to all dere moans . . .
Who gonna win?
– I wouldn't predict.
But I do guess mos peoples gonna lose.

—John Berryman

In 1910 Jack Johnson loped around the ring in Reno, Nevada, chasing Rabbit Jim Jeffries, pleading, "Come on now, Mr. Jeff. Let me see what you got. Do something man. This is for the champeenship." After he beat Jeffries to a pulp, whites streamed into the black ghettos looking for nigger blood, and while these riots were going on, Johnson drove his white ofay wife, Etta, through the streets of Reno in an open car (he knew how to fly the white flag, but it was not the flag of surrender). Etta was only the first of his Wishbone Sally wives.

The massive Johnson, reared by a pious janitor who had been a slave, shaved his big head skeeter clean and he lived high on the snoot as owner of the Café de Champion. He had a loose lip, a happy, sneering unawareness, and he refused to dance on eggs among whites. He battered any and all of the big white farm boys the promoters pushed at him, but it never dawned on him that he might try to advance the cause of blacks. He didn't give a pig's arse for the freedom of blacks. He never fought a black boxer. "Bloodsuckers," he called them. If there were black brothers who suffered – even got killed – because of his success and self-indulgence, he was too busy crowing from the top of a dung-hill salted with gold, taunting the big-time sporting men who were looking everywhere for a white hope, "A goddamn fucking white hope."

Howard Sackler's play *The Great White Hope* begins with Jack Johnson defeating Rabbit Jim Jeffries. He is harassed and hunted; every legal angle is played out in an attempt to get him into jail. Finally he is charged with violating the Mann Act and sentenced to three years in prison. He jumps bail and hightails his "black ass" to Canada and then to England and then to the Continent. Everywhere bigots, prudes, and the piety-stricken cut him off from his boxing livelihood; he becomes an Uncle Tom for a Hungarian travelling troupe, a hambone song-and-dance man. He is humiliated, scorned, and belittled and is told he should take a dive to save his skin, but he will not relinquish his title. Deals, double deals, and side deals are put to him by patriotic American promoters (patriotism is equated with nigger-hunting). He still refuses to take a dive. Not for any price. He turns up in Mexico and then stands on the Texas border, carrying on like one bad coon, swaggering, waving his champion's belt, taunting, insulting white America, an over-age, overweight, paunchy black man, demanding that someone – anyone, old or young, any bag of white bones – fight him. His plight is laid on with a trowel. There is little attempt by Sackler to make Johnson anything more than a *champeen* who, because of his bumptious, unthinking champeen prowess, ends up as a chump. What makes him attractive (and James Earl Jones is responsible for this attraction: he plays the part dangerously – eye-rolling and mugging for all he is worth) is his insistence that those whites who want his crown must take it from him personally; no cut deal, no bent law can make him deny who and what he is.

Of course the backbeat to the story is the role of the heavyweight champion in American mythology. Eldridge Cleaver, the ex-jailbird and Black Panther candidate for president, has put it this way:

> The heavyweight champion is a symbol of masculinity to the American male . . . Through a curious psychic mechanism the puniest white man experiences himself as a giant killer, as a superman, a great white hunter leading a gigantic ape

> ... But when the ape breaks away from the leash, beats with deadly fists upon his massive chest and starts talking to boot, proclaiming himself to be the greatest ... and annihilating every gunbearer the white Hunter sics on him ... a very serious slippage takes place in the white man's self-image – because that by which he defined himself no longer has recognizable identity. "If that black ape is a man," the white hunter asks himself, "then what am I?"

Johnson beats his fists on his chest but he is out of shape, dead broke, and at last he settles for a fight.

Jess Willard defeats him in 1915.

Johnson stands in the ring in Havana with his teeth busted, choking on his blood. The white Willard is carried past him on the shoulders of his supporters; he is rigid, his arm thrust out in a dumb salute, his eyes swollen like grapes, his mouth a bulbous welt. Johnson, about to be forgotten, calls out, "Let 'em pass by."

At Gerdy's Folk City in the Village, Brownie McGhee and Sonny Terry come through the swinging kitchen doors, deftly sidestepping the straddlers on the barstools, and Brownie on stage assumes the expository tones of a country barrister, thrusting his jaw forward, the tendons in his neck and forearms catching the light, a slight curl at the corner of his lip, the curl of contained animosity underneath the high tone of his haughty air, and he turns to Sonny – ebony black and burly, sitting on his stool, arms hanging limp, staring unperturbed into the glare of the spotlight.

Brownie asks, "What you doing, Sonny?"

Sonny replies, "Just relaxin' my mind, man, just relaxin' my mind."

"How you relax your mind?"

"Fattening frogs for snakes."

A tiny white girl with cropped hair has followed Brownie and Sonny out of the kitchen, and she is standing at the end of the bar, four coloured felt pens and a sketching pad in her hand, and as Brownie and Sonny sing, she sketches. She is so small and she works with so little flair that no one notices her. She sings along as she sketches. After the set, when Brownie and Sonny are closeted again in the cramped dressing room downstairs below the kitchen, she appears with a stringy black boy of about nineteen. He has a straggle beard and wears a patterned skullcap. She says, "Meet a friend, Sonny. He be from Chicago." Sonny jabs his heavy hand into the blind man's nowhere space in the centre of the room and the boy grasps it. She adds, "He also be a artist." Sonny shakes his hand again. After friendly but awkward and broken banter about the violence in Chicago, the boy departs. She says, "He be coming apart, bad . . . he be messed up, man."

Laura Brown, the white girl, had come alone to the dressing room one night. Since then she has looked after Sonny whenever he is playing in the club. Sitting with her in a corner of the tiny room, sharing bar Scotch in a paper Dixie cup, she tells me that at sixteen she had received a Guggenheim fellowship and had gone to study in Paris. Returning to New York, she "was sickened, man. Really, I be so sickened of this town where the people be more like the roaches they trying to kill. It be a sewer town, man. Happy time in rat town." Each evening she looks after Sonny, guiding him up narrow stairways, taking him home to his old and dying wife, sometimes helping Sonny's wife sew Sonny's clothes. Her sketch book was filled with portraits, in brown, black, red, and yellow, of Sonny.

The next day I go around in the early evening to have supper with Sonny. He has just moved to the Eighties west of Central Park, a brownstone full of boosters and bootleggers. He lived with his wife for more than twenty years in a two-room Harlem flat; but after the Harlem rent riots and all the junkie killings, no one – not even Brownie – will go into Harlem for a drink and supper with Sonny. Harlem, certainly Sonny's old streets, reeks of decay and dying, and rats play hopscotch in the gutters. Stores, particularly the Jewish delicatessens, are boarded up, the broken glass of the looted windows catching the pale sun that shines on the late winter days. The afternoon that Sonny left Harlem, four young boys from a nearby building were struggling along the sidewalk with a mattress, trying to carry it home without it flopping over, but then, shrugging with exasperation, they just dropped it and left it on the sidewalk, the vermin inside scurrying for cover in the torn quilting. The music Sonny could hear as he stood in the street, the music from inside the Pabst Blue Ribbon bars and the open piss-smelling doorways, was grinding, tough electric blues, electric, like he said he felt sometimes, felt *like drinking me some gasoline, striking me a match and blow my fool self up in steam.* Street singers like himself, he says, have come out of the south "where the water tastes like cherry wine" and they have moved from corner to corner singing for nickels and dimes and there has been shared whisky, but none of those singer friends ever goes onto the streets now, not where "the water tastes like turpentine" and some strung-out dude might cut them with a razor, not only for nickels and dimes, but for their guitars, their rings, anything off their bodies that might fetch a few dollars at the pawn shops or through a fence, a few dollars put down for a doobie. So Sonny has just moved to West 85th Street, into big rooms down a dimly lit long hall, what they used to call a railroad hall, that stinks of pork fat and cabbage. The bleak light at the top of the stairs is a small bare bulb in the ceiling. Sonny has brought a young man and wife out of Harlem. They have made an agreement. The rent will be free for them and Sonny will teach the young man to play the mouth harp if the girl cooks, sweeps up, and helps Sonny's wife around the house while Sonny is singing on the road.

The girl, dark and shy and delicately boned, seems to enjoy deep frying the chicken and rice and collard greens. It is Sunday, and Sonny is full of the expansiveness of a man at ease in his home. He sends the boy downstairs to bang on the door of the house bootlegger to get more Scotch. After supper Sonny stomps his feet on the hardwood and flaps his hands across his harp as he sings. "I got my eye on you, woman, there ain't nothing in the world you can do." He reaches out, his eyes wide open, unseeing, his big hand beckoning. His wife, emaciated, her skin looking as if it has been brushed with wood ash, her hair grey and deep lines around her mouth, begins to hum, watching to see if Sonny will encourage her, and Sonny says, "Yeah," and then he tells me that she had been churched as a child and had once sung church songs at Town Hall. Uncertain of the words, she starts "Didn't It Rain, Children" – but loses the beat, and Sonny speaks gruffly to her. He stomps out the beat, making sure she gets it, and she swings in, her aged voice deep and husky from sickness but strangely sensual as she throws her head back and tries to roar – "see them coming in, two by two . . ." Her thin arms, the flesh hanging loose under her arms, are lifted in the air and she is pat-patting with her feet, her felt slippers flapping against the floor, but her memory fails, she loses the words. We clap. Sonny lets out a fox-call whoop and speaks about the night she sang at Town Hall. Then Laura Brown, the white girl, takes Sonny's bony and rangy wife by the elbow and helps her to her sickbed, a narrow bed under a window, under burglar bars in the window.

There's a light drizzle in the air. James T. Farrell and I are taking a taxi to his home. The driver has a hooked nose. And a moustache. I'm with him in the front seat because Farrell, a jaunty blue beret on his head, wants to stretch out after supper, and he is in the back seat and there is a bulletproof barrier between the seats. It's insane. We talk through a small oblong opening. After Jimmy tells me about a feisty lady who had made her dying husband's bedside nurse her lover, I ask, "God, what in the world would you do with a woman like that? Dykedom in the land of the dying." The driver has slipped a black-and-white canister from his pocket and he says, "I'd know what to do with her." Then he asks,

"You know what this is?" Casually, I say, "Looks like Mace to me." He wags his head in approval and then blurts out: "I'm an arsenal." He has a seven-inch knife and, in a snug shoulder holster, he has a snub-nosed gun.

I tell him about the old Jewish driver who had shown me an eighteen-inch butcher knife, and he says, "That guy'll get caught and they'll take away his licence. I only drive cab on the side to pay for my daughter's wedding. I got the gun 'cause, you see, I'm actually a federal narcotics investigator."

"Really?"

"Yeah . . . I been everywhere with them goddamn hippies and niggers in the streets. I listen to you and the gentleman when you get in and I can tell you're common-sense people, so you appreciate what I'm talking about. They're pigs, those kids. They're swine."

"You were in Chicago?"

"From the first days, and you better believe that Mayor Daley's right. You should believe that, 'cause I tell you, he was right. I was there."

Farrell asks through the bulletproof shield, "What was it like in the streets?"

"Sir, they should be in prison, all of them. Them hippies – they're ugly, filthy people. Do you know they expose themselves and the girls don't wear brassieres, and do you know they threw offal in the faces of the police, and bags, sir, of urine."

At Tudor City on the East River the driver sits like an overgrown wounded child, staring through the methodical cranking of the windshield wipers, and when I pay him he mutters, "Thanks." He is clenching his canister of Mace.

⁂

. . . be seated at the piano.
. . . If they throw stones upon the roof
While you practice arpeggios,

It is because they carry down the stairs
A body in rags.
Be seated at the piano

—WALLACE STEVENS

Charlotte Moorman, a comely woman with a pouting mouth, is a cellist. Of an evening she has come to play her cello naked to the waist at the Cinematheque on 41st Street. She plays Brahms. Several in the audience say that watching her play bare-breasted is fun. The police arrest her for performing an obscene act in a public place.

"Maybe what we need," a policeman says, "is someone to bridge the gap between generations."

There is, of course, another perspective. "What America needs," Robert Benchley said, "is fewer bridges and more fun." Certainly the bridges are there: the Triborough Bridge, Bridgeport, the George Washington Bridge, Hart Crane's *The Bridge*, the Golden Gate Bridge, Arthur Miller's *A View from the Bridge*, contract bridge, and the Bridge of Sighs and the Bridge on the River Kwai. But as one wag asked plaintively, "Where's the fun?"

He is a blond boy who says he is from a farming family. He is a student at Columbia who wears a black beret with a Black Power button pinned to the beret. He is angry. He speaks with a curl to his lip, saying, "You don't understand, man. The pigs are committing genocide. They're genociding blacks and the students, and the administrators of the universities are just like Eichmann, they just boxcar the students into the arms of the pigs every time there's a demo, and they're genociding us, man. I mean, this is a genocide country, the evillest country in the world, 'cause we're genociding in Vietnam and genociding in our own streets."

"Genocide!" I say.

"Yeah, genocide."

Later that night, walking with James T. Farrell, I tell him about the student and he snorts, "They're entirely ignorant of history. I knew Leon Trotsky; yes, I once bought him a typewriter. Yes, he was a great man. He was one of the eight men I've known who was the victim of a political murder (and a great writer, too). Ahh, the New Left . . . they want confrontation, get somebody else's head beat in. It would be a very good idea for them to have a confrontation with knowledge, you know. If you riot, you should riot for a tactical reason or a strategic purpose. All they do is make hooligans out of a lot of people. And, of course, everything was changed by the murder of Robert Kennedy. That had a deadening effect."

"Do you realize where we are?" I ask. "Where you've taken me again?"

"Sure."

"The underground steam room . . . the furnace room for a hotel!"

"It's my shortcut through this part of New York."

We are walking side by side between rows of boilers, and overhead there are thin pipes and fat pipes and insulated pipes, all painted a battleship grey . . . it is like being in the belly of a ship, a low thudding of motors, a pulse beat, felt as much as heard . . .

"Is it true, when you lived at the Beaux Arts Hotel, that the hookers gave you a typewriter?"

"I used to protect them. I wouldn't let anyone swear in front of them . . ."

"Not swear in front of the hookers?"

"My son came to visit me; he got all upset, and I said: 'Now, these girls are from the sisterhood of the streets. If I were their customer, do you think they'd give me a present?' They were, to coin a platitude, human, except it's a profession in which most who go into it are stupid. The same like criminals. Largely stupid."

"What about politics – the profession?"

"Politics is the easiest way to have power over somebody else. It is naturally attractive to stupid men."

"And the police, the pigs . . . ?"

"A cop is a cop, a pig's a pig . . ."

"Okay . . ."

"Look, the students at Columbia . . . they broke into the president's office. This is their revolution. But defecating on the president's desk is no more than vulgar. And occupying the dormitories . . . A revolution? I happen to know the difference between the taking of a dormitory and the taking of the Winter Palace."

❧

The Brooklyn Music Academy is forlorn and shabby, the seats and aisles are crowded. I am on stage with perhaps a hundred loitering people, waiting for the final performance of Julian Beck's *Paradise Now.*

I had seen Beck's innovative and energetic work in the early sixties. He had directed Jean Genet's *The Balcony.* Then he and his wife, Judith Malina, had formed a nomad company called the Living Theater, outfitting themselves in the theories of Antonin Artaud, the French actor and director. Artaud had written, "It is the *mise en scène* that is the theatre much more than the written and spoken play . . . preoccupation with personal problems disgusts me . . . the theatre is the time of evil, the triumph of dark powers . . . It releases conflicts, disengages powers, liberates possibilities . . . like the plague, the theatre has been created to drain abscesses collectively."

The Becks, by stripping their plays of dialogue and concentrating on chants, groans, howls, eruptions of rage, and stark silence, by concentrating on "pantomime, mimicry, gesticulation, intonation, architecture, lighting and scenery," hope to "crap" on the theatre as "a Solemn Ceremony just as an Arab does at the foot of a Pyramid." Beck, Artaud's American high priest, intends – through the Living Theater – to provide new and terrible visions, he intends to make the theatre a dangerous arena in which the audience – "greedy for mystery" – will be compelled to engage in "an extreme purification."

There is a fraternity air on stage: several college boys wearing campesino straw hats, and a man wearing a cradleboard on his back, with a baby strapped into the cradle, are handing back and forth a paper bag stuffed with fat purple grapes, and following it, a plastic bag of Hershey chocolate drops. A woman in a poncho says wisely, "Be careful, we don't know how them things are laced."

The college-boy campesinos, slugging back cheap muscatel, are drunk. A grown woman with a child's pouty face is turning, turning, turning in a tight circle in front of them. She wears a wine-coloured velvet floor-length gown and her thick flaxen hair hangs down her back, and she looks impressively dismayed as she contemplates the drunken boys. She is the first member of the cast to appear.

Almost everyone on stage is sitting cross-legged, knee to knee, elbow to elbow. Tattered clouds of hashish smoke hover three and four feet from the floor. A woman in bikini panties, breasts bare under a mesh top, leans into my face: "I can't travel without a passport." She slips away, confronts another man. The cast is dispersed throughout the crowded theatre. They are pushing through the aisles, leaping up onto the balcony railings, yelling: "I can't travel without a passport."

A slouching man with liverish pouches under his eyes stumbles to centre stage. He has a drawl. He is drunk and waves his fist and he screams: "You goddamn nigger lovers . . . you're on a subway ride, a . . . down into the hole . . . line 'em up, line 'em up, gimme my gun and I'll ride that subway ride . . . and I'll get 'em. I'll get 'em – you and all the nigger lovers . . ." The campesinos shoulder him from side to side, bounce him back and forth. He foolishly thinks he's among friends. They hook his feet and he hurtles into the wall, falls, smacking his head against the floor.

There is blood on the floor.

A girl wails: "I don't know how to stop the wars . . . I don't know how to stop the wars."

One of the campesinos has taken off all his clothes and he has folded them into a hitchhiker's bundle. He strides bow-legged to the apron of the stage, naked, and he snaps his hips to a burlesque house bump and grind only he hears, fondling himself. He gets a hard-on.

An actor, a man, protests: "I'm not allowed to smoke marijuana." The boy beside me, in a husky voice, says to the actor: "Have some hash, baby." There is derisive laughter. The actor repeats his line. Hash smoke hangs around his hips; his line is redundant. He is the only one not smoking. The baby in the cradleboard has begun to cry.

The campesinos, stumbling out of their trousers, looking gawkish for a moment because they're all wearing baggy boxer shorts, have stripped clear down to their peckers and are posing *à la* Charles Atlas, flexing and pumping air for the audience. The actors, now clustered on stage, partially strip – the men to G-strings and the women to bikinis. Someone in the audience yells mockingly, "Aw, come on, you uptight people, get all your clothes off."

An actress cries: "Do your own thing." And a campesino yells: "I am, I am," hop-dancing, his dick flopping, and then he fondles up an erection and begins, with his back arched, to strum off for the audience. About fifteen rows along the right aisle a middle-aged woman rises and yells: "Julian Beck, you'll kill us all. Julian Beck, you'll kill us all. This place is a fire hazard. We'll all burn, we'll burn, Julian Beck . . ."

Near a side exit to the back, against the dark oak panelling, Allen Ginsberg appears, his bald head catching the light, his white teeth shining in his black rabbinical beard. He struggles with his clothes, pulling and tugging, until he stands against the wall naked. "I'm not allowed to take my clothes off," he shouts, and beams, trying for irony.

On the other side of the house a man yells at his wife, "I don't care, I don't care . . . taking your clothes off don't mean shit." Stand-ing out in the aisle naked – all rib cage, hip angles, and knobby knees – arms upraised, he is enormously pleased with himself, as if at a revivalist camp meeting he had stepped into healing waters.

"This is a fire hazard, Julian Beck. We'll burn in here."

The actors and actresses spiral on their toes and collapse to the stage, lying on their sides or bellies; they are joined by the drunken campesinos, who lie down beside them, but not one woman in the cast or in the audience has taken her clothes off completely. Only men are naked. Black bushes, stubby little cocks. The performance has been stolen from the actors. The purging abscess is open, the stage has degenerated into a stag party, so

Drink deep to Uncle Ugleg,
That early heroic human –
The first to marry a woman –
Had only he eaten the woman,
Had only he married the oyster

—OGDEN NASH

As men and boys parade for each other, prancing as they paw each actress who passes, they shout obscenities. "Motherfucka." "Do your own thing." Two of the college boys are whacking off, facing the audience, fist and cock, fist and cock. To a roar, one of them comes and slumps to the floor. Someone pours wine over his head. Another offers a sign of the cross. The actors are herding people back against the stage wall, clearing a space, a silence, leaving room for a wiry little man who screams: "The revolution . . . guerillas in the hills of Bolivia . . . there are the hills . . ." And he points up to the balcony. "How many CIA agents are up there in the hills . . . how many?"

"Two," someone says dryly.

"Then get up there and kill the fuckers, kill them, kill them, get the fuckers and kill them."

"This is the death of the theatre. Julian Beck, this is the death of the theatre."

Beck, narrow-hipped, with a beaked head, seizes the woman by the shoulders, shaking her, screaming, "I want to make love to you . . . I want to make love to you . . . What about the killings in Vietnam? . . . What about Vietnam? . . . I want to make love to you."

Allen Ginsberg, now that he has buttoned up and is fully clothed again, looks very much like a Lower East Side storefront lawyer, and he has asked people to link arms and form a circle, and the circle widens. They chant: *Om . . . om . . . om . . . – Om . . . om . . . om . . . om . . . om . . . om . . . – Om . . . om . . . om . . . – Om . . . om . . . om . . . om . . . om . . . om . . .*

A lull settles on the theatre. A welcomed stillness. Then a girl holding her head in her hands cries, "They raped her. The sons of bitches raped her. Those college boys raped her." The actress in the velvet gown is guarding Judith Malina's dressing room door. Half the cast has quit the stage, giving way to drunken slovenliness, the hopheads. Six or seven actors stand in the hall, suddenly stricken: "Did anyone call a doctor . . . ?" No one answers. *Om . . . om . . .* – the lullaby of *om . . . om . . .* Judith Malina has been raped. That is said. And said again. A shriek. "Raped." Another cry. But no one leaves Malina's room, no one speaks with authority. I have the feeling that these actors, whether Malina was raped or not, need to believe that it is so; the necessity of violence is in their eyes. The man wearing the cradleboard says, "I can't travel without a passport." One of the actors says, "Shut up." I leave the theatre, a depression driving in on me, and as I go out the stage door into the street and into a musty after-rain silence, that silence is a sudden refuge against this war on lucidity, this war on the word.

War! *Ev'rybody's talkin' 'bout war, Lord.* "The cold war is the real warm front," Marshall McLuhan says – "a surround – involving everybody – all the time – everywhere. Wherever hot wars are necessary . . . we conduct them in the backyards of the world with the old technologies." This is cant, no different in kind from the generals telling their soldiers to *sanitize* . . . to kill every living thing . . . now that's a *surround.* McLuhan, a conservative, prattles on the way the kids prattle. He instructs, he probes, seeking impact . . . often an impact containing its own obsolescence. When language loses its validity, rape can become recreation. I wonder, walking now in a drizzle, how I will give the slip to so much twisted emotion in this plummeting time.

At Cooper Union it is about eleven at night. Though the sidewalk is very wide, I have to step around the bodies of young boys and girls stretched out and huddled together on the pavement, grey and tattered children. Someone has propped up a sign that says LOVE IS REDEMPTION. I can hear only whispers from them and sometimes low laughter, and then a pale-faced girl with round black eyes lifts her head and asks: "Say, man, do you for five bucks . . ." The bare-footed boys and girls lying in one another's arms have tied long strings to their toes, and there, floating high in the air, are white balloons, and it is hard to know whether they are distress signals or gestures of contempt, or both.

The leech's kiss, the squid's embrace
The prurient ape's defiling touch.
And do you like the human race?
No, not much.

The Telegram, 1968
("John, the Conqueroo" poem, 1974)

CLAUDE MONET'S MAGPIE: A SONNET

The magpie pecked at the snow, he spat orange
On the black locust gate rail, sitting out in plain
View among the black apple trees. A sheen, strange
As any oscillating sea lamp as it sustains
Its flame, steeps the day in coral light, a flange
Torn along the mother of pearl that now retains,
Now strews oriental pink and grey on that grange
Tilted back against the sky, ashen, and its flames
Fed not by a cold fire but the combustible
Wintering of mistletoe, ivy, a seed pod
Green ground to paste in someone's palm, inedible
Except perhaps by the bird or the outcast god
Quailing on the bottom stair, incompatible
Among embers, out on the prowl, alone abroad.

• Translated from the French of Robert Marteau

Translator's note: In Celtic lore magpies are associated with the Christian incursion into tribal lands; in Christian lore they are birds of evil omen; in Chinese myth the magpie signifies marital bliss; in Roman myth sexual exaltation. In Canada a lone magpie means impending sorrow. Several magpies in a circle signify that these birds peck out the eyes of newborn lambs, making them responsible for a race of blind sheep:

One for sorrow, two for mirth, three for a wedding,
Four for a birth, five for a christening, six for a dearth,
Seven for heaven, eight for hell, nine for the devil himself.

Exile, 1988

SONG MY: MY LAI

Old men, old women, and children in arms were shot down in ditches at Song My [My Lai], and many were then scalped or their ears were cut off, and some were raped. Soldiers now talk calmly of how this was done, and some are surprised that attention is being paid to the slaughter at Song My. It was, they say, only one among many such operations in Vietnam. It is, they say, a habit of the war.

That habit was at the heart of conversations with several soldiers from Company C who, led by Captain "Mad Dog" Medina, were at My Lai 4, one of nine numbered hamlets clustered near the village of Song My. Company C soldiers called the area Pinkville because it was coloured rose on their military maps.

Two or three weeks before March 16, 1968 – when the massacre took place – sniper fire from across the Pinkville river had killed a Company C grunt, and his buddies believed the fire had come from My Lai 4. Some two weeks earlier enemy land mines had killed five men and wounded twenty-two, and in a hamlet near My Lai 4 a booby trap made from an unexploded artillery shell had killed one of the GIs' favourite squad leaders, Sergeant George Cox.

"I was his assistant squad leader," Charles West told the *Sunday Times.* "On the way back to camp I was crying. Everybody was deeply hurt, right up to Captain Medina." At the briefing, West says, "Captain Medina told us we might get a chance to revenge the deaths of our fellow GIs."

Shortly after sunrise, on a bright, clear, warm day, the helicopters lifted approximately eighty Company C men from the base camp at landing zone Dottie and delivered them seven miles away at the paddies west of My Lai 4.

"We landed about nine or nine-thirty in a field of elephant grass," said Varnado Simpson, a nineteen-year-old assistant platoon leader from Jackson, Mississippi. "There were about twenty-five of us and we went directly into the village. There wasn't any enemy fire.

"We'd come up on a hootch, we'd torch it to see if there was someone in it. If there was no one in it, we'd burn it down. Some people ran; we tried to tell them not to run. There were about fifteen. Some stopped. About five or six were killed."

Sergeant Ron Haeberle, a photographer, moved through the rice fields toward a hill at the back of the village area. "Off to the right," Haeberle said, "a woman's form, a head, appeared from some brush. All the other GIs started firing at her over and over again. She had slumped over one of those things that stick out of the rice paddies so that her head was a propped-up target. There was no attempt to question her or anything. They just keep shooting. You could see bones flying in the air, chip by chip."

Sergeant Charles West led his squad of thirteen men through the rice paddies and heard gunfire. He was coming down a hairpin winding trail and he was keeping a close watch for booby traps. He turned a curve in the trail and there, twenty-five feet ahead of him, were six Vietnamese, some with baskets, coming toward them. "These people were running into us," he said, "away from us, running every which way. It's hard to distinguish a mama-san from a papa-san when everybody has on black pajamas." He and his squad opened fire with their M-16s. Then he and his men kept going down the road toward the sound of the gunfire in the village.

"There was a little boy walking toward us in a daze," Haeberle said. "He'd been shot in the arm and leg. He wasn't crying or making any noise." Haeberle knelt down to photograph the boy. A GI knelt down next to him. "The GI fired three shots into the child. The first shot knocked him back, the second shot lifted him into the air. The third shot put him down and the body fluids came out. The GI just simply got up and walked away. It was a stroboscopic effect. We were so close to him it was blurred."

Lieutenant William Calley Jr.'s platoon was the first to arrive in the centre of My Lai. "There was about forty, forty-five people that we gathered in the centre of the village," Private Paul Meadlo said. "And we placed them in there and it was like a little island, right there in the centre of the village, I'd say.

"Men, women, children. Babies. And we all huddled them up. We made them squat down, and Lieutenant Calley came over and said, 'You know what to do with them, don't you?' And I said yes. And he left, and came back about ten or fifteen minutes later and said, 'How come you ain't killed them yet?' And I told him that I didn't think you wanted us to kill them, just to guard them. He said, 'No, I want them dead.' He stepped back about ten, fifteen feet, and he started shooting them. And he told me to start shooting. So I started shooting. I poured about four clips into the group. I fired them on automatic – you just spray the area so you can't know how many you killed, 'cause they were going fast.

"We're rounding up more, and we had about seven or eight people. And, well, we put them in the hootch and then we dropped a hand grenade down there with them. And somebody told us to bring them over to the ravine, so we took them back out and led them over, too, and by that time they had about seventy, seventy-five people all gathered up. So we threw ours in with them and Lieutenant Calley told me, he said, 'Meadlo, we got another job to do.' And so we walked over to the people and he started pushing them off and started shooting . . . off into the ravine. It was a ditch. And so we started pushing them off and we started shooting them, so altogether we just pushed them all off, and just started using automatics on them. Men, women, and children. And babies."

"Just outside the village," says SP5 Jay Roberts, "there was this big pile of bodies. This really tiny little kid – he only had a shirt on, nothing else – he came over to the pile and held the hand of one of the dead. One of the GIs behind me dropped into a kneeling position, thirty metres from this kid, and killed him with a single shot."

A black GI told Haeberle he couldn't stomach it, he had to get out of there. Later Haeberle and Roberts were sitting near a ditch, a clump of bodies off to the left, when they heard a shot. They hit the ground, thinking it was a sniper. The black soldier who had wanted to get out of there had shot himself in the foot with a forty-five. Accidentally, he said.

Sergeant John Kinch was the point man for the heavy-weapons squad. "We moved into Pinkville and found another stack of bodies in a ditch. It must have been six or seven feet deep, and they were level with the top of it. One body, an old man, had a C carved on his chest.

"Captain Medina was right in front of us. Colonel Barker, the task force commander, was overhead in his helicopter. He came through over the radio saying he had got word from the medevac chopper [medical evacuation helicopter] there were bodies lying everywhere, and what was going on. I heard Captain Medina tell him, 'I don't know what they are doing. The first platoon's in the lead. I am trying to stop it.' Just after that he called the first platoon and said, 'That's enough shooting for today.' Colonel Barker called down for a body count and Medina got back on the horn and said, 'I have a body count of 310.'"

"That day I was thinking military," said Charles West, "thinking about the security of my own men. I said to myself, This is a bad thing that all these people had to be killed. But if I was to say that I actually felt a whole lot of sorrow for the people, then I'd be lying."

"We thought about My Lai a lot after we got back to Duc Pho," said Roberts. "But neither one of us was very much of a banner carrier." When he wrote about it for the brigade newspaper, Roberts says, "I played it up like it was a big success."

Telford Taylor was the chief prosecutor for the United States at the post–World War II Nuremberg trials. Squarely set, he has steady but kindly eyes, a tight mouth, and iron-grey closely cropped hair. He is a man of presence who appears to be unflinching yet reflective, a man who is amiably at ease with himself because he knows what he knows and is not inclined to doubt, a man of the law, of principle, of patrician sternness. With resolve and yet a certain sadness he says that the people of America must now, in light of Song My, examine the conduct of their armed forces under the same principles that they – and he, as a prosecutor – applied to the Germans and Japanese. "When we sent hundreds of thousands of troops to South Vietnam, bombed North Vietnam, and moved into Cambodia, were our national leaders as guilty of launching a war of aggression as were Hitler and his generals when they invaded Poland or Belgium or Greece, or other countries that were way-stations on the Nazi march of conquest? Will Song My go down in the history of man's inhumanity bracketed with Katyn, Lidice, Oradour, Malmédy . . . ?"

Before answering these questions Taylor says that in his book *Nuremberg and Vietnam* he has conducted a careful survey of the history of the laws of war, their development and articulation through medieval theologians, through the Hague and Geneva conventions and the Nuremberg trials. He wants it clearly understood that much excellent judicial thought has gone into definitions of just and unjust wars, superior orders and legitimate reprisals, the treatment of prisoners and the movement of civilian populations. In fact, his book is an expertly argued brief on international military law. But there is more to it than that, for the ultimate question raised by such a discussion is whether or not American armed forces are guilty of war crimes, and if they are, should not the generals and government policy makers be held liable and prosecuted by tribunals like the one at Nuremberg as war criminals?

Taylor argues in his book, and insists to me, that it is impossible to answer the first crucial question – that is, to determine who the aggressive force is in Vietnam, who is waging the unjust war. On this issue, there was no debate at Nuremberg. The Germans were quite clearly the aggressive invaders. One of the fruits of the total Allied military victory was the capture of documents to prove it. But in Vietnam there is no such clear evidence. The American position itself is muddled, so if the question were ever put before an international tribunal, there would be much debate.

But as for war crimes, the second crucial issue, this much is clear. The United States maintains that its position in Vietnam is based in the principles of Nuremberg. That is, the Americans regard the Viet Cong as the aggressors waging an unjust war. If, Taylor says, one takes the American government and armed forces at their word on this, then they cannot turn around and maintain that in order to win the war they must violate the principles of Nuremberg. They cannot commit what are quite plainly war crimes.

This, however, is the very position that many soldiers take: that to battle a guerrilla army, the laws of war must be broken. Mr. Taylor will have none of this, and the areas of conduct he cites as possible American war crimes are "forced resettlement of millions of rural families with utterly inadequate provision for their health and human dignity; complicity in the torture of prisoners by our wards, the South Vietnamese; enthusiasm for body counts overriding the laws of war on the taking of prisoners; devastation of large areas of the country in order to expose the insurgents; outlawry of every visible human being in the free-fire zones; slaughter of the villagers of Song My, even to infants-in-arms." Mr. Taylor then goes on to ask, "Are these things a terrible mad aberration, or can cause and responsibility be traced?"

Mr. Taylor carries this point forward, saying, "Soldiers are bound to be powerfully influenced by the examples set by their commanders. That is why . . . the only way in which the behavior of the German troops in the recent war can be made comprehensible as the behavior of human beings is by a full exposure of the criminal doctrines and orders pressed on them from above."

Which raises the case of General Tomayuki Yamashita, tried by a tribunal of American generals, a trial that set a legal precedent. General Yamashita was the commander of the Japanese army in the Philippine Islands during the closing months of the war. His troops, fleeing before the advancing Americans, massacred prisoners of war, slaughtered civilians, and burned and looted villages. The General's systems of communications with his troops had broken down completely and "there was no charge that General Yamashita had approved, much less ordered these barbarities, and no evidence that he knew of them." Nevertheless, the tribunal found Yamashita guilty on the grounds that he had "failed to provide effective control of his troops as required by the circumstances." He was sentenced to death and was hanged.

Now, the American troops committed what certainly appear to be war crimes at Song My, and there is much evidence that Song My is not an isolated case but represents the habit of the war. If this is true, then the generals are responsible for that habit – just as General Yamashita was responsible for his troops – and even more, the American generals, unlike the Japanese, are in constant contact with their troops all over Vietnam. There are no mitigating circumstances. The conclusion, then, is that a very good case could be brought against the American generals and the government policy makers, a case in which they would be charged as war criminals. As Mr. Taylor puts it, "If the principles that were applied in the Yamashita case were applied to our own commanders, of whom General Westmoreland is one, if they were applied with the same rigor, a conviction would be possible."

The issues raised are far-reaching. Not only is the whole conduct of the American presence in Vietnam brought into question, not only are American citizens and soldiers forced to stand in the dock beside Nazis, but Taylor himself, the former prosecutor, says unequivocally that the Allied actions at Dresden and Nagasaki were war crimes.

The debate is enjoined: should the Nuremberg trials ever have taken place? Could the politicians and generals who ordered the obliteration of civilian populations in Germany and Japan sit in judgement of other politicians and generals who ordered the obliteration of civilian populations? Is it possible that the Nuremberg trials proved only, as some generals have said, that military men can no longer afford to lose a war because the victorious generals will prosecute and hang the opposing generals as war criminals? The law has its ironic ways, for now we watch Lieutenant Calley as he stands trial for Song My. Nuremberg is biting the hand that fed it – except it is a lieutenant and not General Westmoreland who is charged. At Nuremberg there were no foot soldiers in the dock, there was no hapless Lieutenant Schmidt staring into the hangman's noose.

In the burrows of the Nightmare
Where Justice naked is,
Time watches from the shadow
And coughs when you would kiss.

CBC's *Weekend; The Telegram,* 1971-72

ON THE LINE WITH THE OLD BRIGADE

Historians have treated Donald Creighton's *Canada's First Century* with a fondness and respect that leaves me bemused. He is a writer of a certain narrative ease, but as a historian he has been ingrown rather than outgoing, irascible rather than ingratiating, embattled when young, embattled and embittered when old. *Canada's First Century* is an old man's book, and I wonder if it is being taken up for its scholarship or as a grouchy fable for the boys of the Old Brigade.

Steady shoulder by shoulder,
steadily blade by blade,
marching along,
steady and strong,
the boys of the Old Brigade.

These stalwart fellows have been reduced in recent years to afternoon outings on Farley Mowat's little British boat that won't float, but now suddenly – out of the azure blue of Tory lost causes – we have Professor Creighton's wrathful screed.

In common rooms across the country, Professor Creighton is said to be our most graceful narrative historian, but narrative means more than tying events together in a progression, more than giving events an accessible shape. There must be some sense of the ambiguous confusion of human experience, the baffling thrust for power by cowled monks, and criminals, too; the plight of men and women passing through the mirror of conformity into individual greatness while men born for greatness stare dumbly into the same mirror, looking for a place to die; and the wonder of men putting aside principle so that – pushed beyond expediency – they can do what is right. This is the distinction of Toynbee, of Hume, of Michelet . . . but there is none of this in Creighton's recent work. (I admit that a decade ago, as an undergraduate, I read his biography of Sir John A. Macdonald and admired his clarity of storytelling purpose, a purpose achieved.) Instead he has given us a bad-tempered, spiteful polemic, and to do this he has grouped certain events and names into patterns, like lily pads on the Canadian pond, and he has leapt from one to the next, full of croaking vituperation, disdain, and high moral intent.

Creighton's tract for the times is simple enough. In 1867 Sir John A. Macdonald became our first prime minister by forging a national federation out of fractured local ambitions. The federation was to be held together by a protective tariff, immigration, a transcontinental railway, by provinces who would take their places subservient to federal power, by an understanding that no minority group had special cultural rights, and by nesting in the military (and moral) bosom of the British Empire.

Of course, in the Creighton scheme of things the Québécois and other Catholics queered this covenant early in the game by insisting on bilingualism and separate schools. The Liberals, opportunists and carpetbaggers lacking higher purpose, led us south down the garden path, across the forty-ninth parallel, and into the Valley of Death, the United States.

This is not only a tired argument (*pace* George Grant and his anti-Lockeian anti-Americans), it has the simplicity of a medieval sense of morality at play: the British imperial powers of light vs. the American manifest powers of dark. Creighton snarls and snarks at any notion that the natural flow of Canadian interests – economic, cultural, and political – is north and south on this continent. He hearkens back to the Confederation Fathers who "preferred the public order and private restraint of the Canadian community to what they believed was the anarchy and license of the neighbouring republic."

Eschewing anarchy and republican licence, Canada was privileged, Creighton says, to participate "in a great providential mission for the elevation of mankind," the dissemination of imperial standards among backward peoples. So, for that reason, I am left to suppose, we went into the South African Boer War and carried the light for General "Butcher" Kitchener as he invented the concentration camp. He neglects to mention that to defeat the Boer the Canadian army aided and abetted in the starvation and murder of twenty-seven thousand women and children in those camps.

Not surprisingly, he disposes of Louis Riel's half-breed (Métis) rebellion in the West with a curl of his lip, but he points out that there was a pleasing symmetry to the way it worked out: the first days of the rebellion ensured the completion of the transcontinental railway, and then the new rails were proved efficient by moving troops out west to put an end to the rebellion. "Donald Smith drove home that last spike in the completed transcontinental line; and nine days later Louis Riel dropped to his death in the prison at Regina." Creighton finds this "magnificent."

His view of British-Canadian history, for that is what he is writing, verges on silly when he discusses the English and Americans at Suez in the Middle East war of 1956. He derides Nasser, a mere dictator who had a "darling nationalist project" called the High Dam at Aswan. The Americans are vulgar, "interfering" in a traditional sphere of English and French influence. They had no right to do so, he says, because the English were partners to a legal lease on the canal. The Americans had no basis for a position of moral superiority during the crisis – after all, they had come into control of the Panama Canal through obvious and crude political bullying, while England had gained her position in the Suez through "ordinary commercial methods." And anyway, if England was guilty of chicanery in Egypt, then America was guilty of chicanery in Guatemala. So how dare the Canadian Liberal government – how dare Lester Pearson and his small-change wheelers and dealers from Québec – undercut the Empire by supporting the coarse Americans while rejecting the fastidious English?

This is a preposterous grouchy whine.

One wonders, Why the reverent attention? Or is it reverence, all the editorial space accorded Creighton? Isn't the reading of this book like finding yourself with nothing to do out on Yonge Street, applauding because there's a fine old fellow on a sway-back white horse, his chest out, and some straggling troops are marching behind him? You realize it's the Old Brigade parade: there they are – shoulder to shoulder, blade by blade – and they used to compel fear, if not respect, but now they're quaint of an afternoon. Years ago, so many years ago, they were a force – but now they're charming in their bluff aggressiveness, out on the line, out on parade.

The Telegram, 1971

POINTS OF REBELLION: JUSTICE WILLIAM O. DOUGLAS

There comes a time in the life of a man when prudence is no longer the great virtue, when he feels he can say what he believes. This is a rare freedom. It can come in old age, when caution seems pointless in the proximity of death, or it can come when, no matter your years, you feel only the ambition to serve the truth that you believe is in you. In either case, it is a stage beyond the quest for preferment.

I was thinking this while watching in New York last week a puckish performance by Justice William O. Douglas of the United States Supreme Court. Douglas is seventy-one, intelligent, cantankerous, and willful, and he has written a broadside political pamphlet in which he speaks on behalf of rebellion in his country. So pointed is his position – that violence may prove to be "the only effective response" to the lies and half-truths from government and the military – that there's a move afoot to impeach him. His response to this caterwauling in Congress has been to dismiss it as the bland leading the bland.

I saw him at a Brooklyn Law School symposium. Douglas, white hair grown long, sat with disdain as Sidney Hook and other prominent professors dissected his polemic. "Sheer caricature," sneered Hook, who then harrumphed, "Exaggeration, thy name is Justice Douglas." Douglas got to his feet and warned that if anyone was upset by this book, he'd better not read the next one. The discussion, he said, proved a tired truth, that the old academic generation was politically bankrupt. Then the Justice said, "But it's such a beautiful day . . . a beautiful day for a hike." He went on in wistful cornpone fashion and concluded by introducing his lovely young wife, Catherine. She smiled. Professor Hook shook his head in earnest.

Justice Douglas's troublesome thesis is that the people of the United States are living in "a black silence of fear," a state of fear nurtured by Truman, a fear promoted by Johnson, a fear that now wears the face of common sense and conformity, that "ready acceptance" of what H. L. Mencken called "received opinion" – Mencken's prescription for mediocrity. Mediocrity and the military mind find their Siamese mandate in a silent majority; the silent majority manifests its will through the rule of law, and it is through the increasing rule of the law that old people confirm their values and themselves; it is only the young, says Justice Douglas, who will have none of this.

They insist on their freedom of speech, on the resurrection of human values, on quality in the environment.

> The dissent we witness is a reaffirmation of faith in man; it is a protest against living under rules and prejudices and attitudes that produce the extremes of wealth and poverty and that make us dedicated to the destruction of people through arms, bombs, and gases, and that prepare us to think alike and be submissive objects for the regime of the computer. The dissent we witness is a protest against the belittling of man, against his debasement, against a society that makes lawful the exploitation of humans.

Then, with a burst of enthusiasm he declares, "This period will indeed be our great renaissance." The older generation, Douglas concludes, are doomed in their dullness to resist this renaissance. So there will be violence.

At no time in his short book *Points of Rebellion* does Douglas speak out of a carefully reasoned judicial position. Not at all.

He has whipped off his wig and come down from the bench snapping his braces, talking recklessly, as men do when they reveal what is in their hearts. What Douglas abhors is the curse of like-thinking, conformity.

> When the university does not sit apart, critical of industry, the Pentagon, and the government, there is no fermentive force at work in our society. The university becomes a collection of technicians in a service station . . . The result is a form of goose-stepping and the installation of conformity as king . . . We are witnessing, I think, a new American phenomenon. The two parties have become almost indistinguishable and each is controlled by the Establishment. The modern day dissenters and protesters are functioning as the Loyal Opposition functions in England. They are the mounting voice of political opposition to the status quo, calling for revolutionary changes in our institutions. Yet the powers-that-be faintly echo Adolf Hitler, who said in 1932:
>
> "The streets of our country are in turmoil. The universities are filled with students rebelling and rioting.
>
> "Communists are seeking to destroy our country. Russia is threatening us with her might and the republic is in danger. Yes, danger from within and without.
>
> "We need law and order."

Douglas wants a vast restructuring of American society: an end to the dominance of the military mind; an end to the dubious leadership of the political parties; an end to lawmakers who would condone wiretapping and electronic surveillance – not just of criminals – but of men like Martin Luther King, deemed a Communist security risk by J. Edgar Hoover; an end to secret dossiers compiled by companies and the happy acceptance of invasions of privacy through so-called psychological tests; an end to the presence of the CIA and the FBI on campuses; an end to universities that would exploit black slum land; an end to repressive responses to protest; an end to governmental deals that allow businessmen to pollute the land and water for their own personal profit; an end to the political effectiveness of lobbies in Washington, lobbies that have stolen the voice of the people; an end, an end, an end . . . and an endorsement of individual integrity.

"People march and protest but they are not heard . . . Violence has no constitutional sanction . . . but where grievances pile high . . . violence may be the only effective response . . . Few youngsters want to destroy the system. The aim of most of them is to regain the freedom of choice that their ancestors lost, to be free, to be masters of their destiny."

There he is, Justice Douglas, white hair long, his arm around his fourth wife, excerpts from his book appearing alongside sex photographs in the *Evergreen Review*, threatened with impeachment by braying senators, scorned by professors – there he is, snapping his braces at noisome power-brokers, inviting us to take a hike on a fine spring day, as imprudent as Wordsworth's happy warrior,

. . . whose powers shed round him
in the common strife,
or mild concerns of ordinary life,
a constant influence, a peculiar grace.

The Telegram, 1971

MOVING

Snow: Cold fleece on a black day. He found
her at the table playing the piano on a paper
keyboard –

"The world is ripe with unsolved problems,"
she said. Paint scaled off the walls. There
was a knock on the door, men wearing coveralls.
"We are the movers.

We've come to move the piano."

Hogg, 2001

THE HEART OF THE WORLD: YEHUDA AMICHAI

Leprous, I sit among potsherds and nettles,
at the foot of a wall eaten by the sun.
—RIMBAUD

When God created the world He placed the waters of the ocean around the earth. And in the heart of the inhabited world God placed Jerusalem . . . This is the heart of the world.

Jerusalem has a heart as crooked as ecclesiastical sheets, as crooked as yellow thorn branches, dry in their silence. In the alleyways there is no sound of water. By a wrought-iron window in a stone house on a rise called Yemin Moshe, looking across a gully to Jaffa Gate, Yehuda Amichai the poet sits hunched forward, solid and fleshy through the shoulders, and his face is red from the sun. "And what about love?" I ask.

"It goes without saying," he says.

"It goes?"

"Sometimes it goes, sometimes it doesn't come."

He lives with his wife, Hana, in a stone house outside the city walls. She is smoking a pipe so small it fits in the palm of her hand. She has an open face, big eyes. There is big sorrow in her eyes, and big love, too, for him. In his eyes there is a melancholy stillness, the stillness of the house as he says, "When you live in a house here, it's like living in the skins of all the men who've owned the house, maybe not friends, maybe enemies. It's very tiring to walk around naked in your own house wearing so many different skins." Desert winds pass over the house, over the gravel hills and twisted olive trees and thorn bushes. The winds never soothe the city: it is too much a stone boat of bloodshed and benedictions, it is too weighed down to ever be soothed. To get away, to escape, prophets and holy men have always gone out into the desert where they could be alone in the harsh light with their harsh desert god:

And I'm like someone standing in
the Judean desert, looking at a sign:
"Sea Level."
He cannot see the sea, but he knows.

Amichai and I sit in the cooling shadows and talk of Yeats and Ted Hughes, Lowell and Agnon, and we eat dates. "The place you are staying," he says, "Abu Tor . . . it means Father of the Ox. Named after an old man who lived there on that hill. Agnon has written a story about Abu Tor, but I forget it. There are too many stories here." As a storyteller, as a poet, he has been forced to go to war and then limp back to his solitude, and then go to war and then come back, telling stories about the wars, smuggling arms from the Sinai Desert, scouting in the Negev Desert. "Poets are like foot soldiers, all by themselves out there. They get wounded." He is a man who thinks with a limp, the way Adam couldn't count his ribs without thinking of Eve. That's the way his mind works, analogically. He moves from the thing to the idea. He can't help himself. He can't let a thing just be a thing. He has to embody in it an idea. In his eye it is the flesh that is made the Word, the reverse of the Christian mystery of the Word made flesh. This leads not to death on a cross but to poetry as death at swim in the mystery of life:

Broken by the sea,
my head a broken tin
sea water fills it
and drains out . . .
Broken by the sea,
My lament.

During the battle for Jerusalem he said: ". . . everything is dry and there is no ocean of water, yet the Sea of Jerusalem is the most terrible sea of all." When he walks he walks the stone alleys of the old city like a sailor on board a ship. He feels a swell underfoot. He is not alone. Walking with him I have seen the sea in the faces of men on their way to the Wailing Wall, men who believe they can sit in a stone boat and enter eternity. Even the postal contraction for Jerusalem on envelopes is י – ם , (that is, Sea) .

"They think," Amichai says with an impish smile, "that Jerusalem is the Venice of God."

"In the beginning, God said – let there be light," he laughs, "but there was too much light. There is still too much light. We're not from here. We never get used to the hard light. We're forest people. We dream of the dark (every now and then someone says, even after forty or fifty years, 'The sun is killing me')." Shtetl Jews, forest Jews (like Amichai's people, farmers from the Würzburg forests in southern Germany), when they are here they dream of dark groves of trees, medieval cities, and Slavic knights who've been turned to stone and covered with forest moss, and forest streams running through the moss. Yet there is a dream in the old city that is of dark groves, too, of underground grottoes, of cooling dark vacancies, a dream of water. But in Jerusalem it is always the taunting dream of the absence of water, because in Jerusalem men want to be healed, to begin again, blessed by water. The problem is, men carry too much of the desert in their hearts. Men with the desert in their heart walk on stone believing it is water. So it is a city where men fall in the water and break their knees, but somehow Amichai has not fallen:

> *Every day I know the miracle of*
> *Jesus walking upon the waters,*
> *I walk through my life without drowning.*

Still, there is something dangerous in the air, like the taste of brass on the tongue.

"People can lose their minds here," Amichai says, "you better be careful."

Yes. The sun strafes everything in sight.

Yes.

There are

> *rapists in a deep slumber in the forest*
> *dreaming about real love.*

He says that lots of people among the settlers lost their minds before the war of 1948, that the seeds of their failure have been hidden. This is after I tell him that a kibbutznik from Galilee, a man named Muki Tsur (the son, I believe, of the ambassador to Paris), has told me that the settlers back in the twenties kept public books in each kibbutz dining hall and every night the men and women wrote down their small joys, and a lot of pain . . . accusing each other and themselves of fear, cowardice, crimes, despair . . . and he said there were many suicides. These books were then hidden away, as so much since 1948 has been hidden away, which was a kind of betrayal, because fathers then told their sons lies so that their children's children wouldn't know about the suicides, told them that the early years had been as green with hope as the sea, and so their sons, needing to look only to the future, all turned their backs on the sea.

"Betrayal has become a kind of necessity," he says.

He knows that I have been talking to Ygal Allon, Deputy Prime Minister, commander of the southern front in 1948.

"Yes, it's our attitude now that we didn't chase the villagers out of their villages so they could never come back. Allon knows. But not now. Now is not the time for what he knows."

He gives me a mournful smile, not apologetic, just wryly saddened.

"You do what you can with what has been done," Amichai says.

"Times have taught us you can run bankrupt, but anyway you go on. You collapse, yet everything is normal. We are paying the price of pragmatic thinking. We have had to change our attitude so many times that by now the problems are empty. Our first feeling about the Holocaust was revenge, but we are security-haunted. So whoever helps us to go on living physically is our friend, and so the Germans helped us and they are our friends. Again and again we have made such changes; it breaks you, makes you collapse, but in order not to break you just put yourself into little pieces, because it's much harder to break little pieces than to break one big piece." A little later I ask: "You and your friends, you're a little mad, you're coming apart at the seams?" He laughs, his laughter always muffled. "Yes, yes. I think it is one of the deep feelings one has in this country."

Walking slowly arm in arm we glide along the stones. The alley takes on a softness, a fluidity. "It's easy to create madness," he says, "if you take away memory from the man who is remembering . . ."

Everything is too close here, too intense, dream piled on dream. The holy men are the great pilers. They believe they possess the Navel of the World, an omphaloid stone that they say was measured by Christ's own hand, and they say that they've got the tomb of Adam, too, buried beneath Christ's gibbet, and they say that Adam was granted absolution because the divine blood shed on the gibbet fell on his bones, and they are sure that they've got the print of Adam's footbone in stone and, close by, the seven footprints of Abraham and Isaac, and they say that from exactly the same stone Mohammed leapt off his horse into heaven, the hoofprint of the horse only a stone's throw from the grotto of Mary, who also leapt into heaven, her grotto close to another chamber where the blood of the crucified Christ stains a stone that was also the altar upon which Abraham offered Isaac, before it became the altar on which Melchizedek cut through sinew and bone to get blood and more blood for the altars of the great temple that must have been a slophouse full of blood . . . bodies tangled and piled on each other:

God's hand in the world
like my mother's
in the guts of a slaughtered hen . . .

There is no distance in Jerusalem. It is a walled city, melancholic, ecstatic. It holds heat during the day, it holds a chill at night; like a snake cut in two it goes on twisting,

full of tired Jews
Always whipped into memorial days and feasts
Like bears dancing on aching legs.
What does Jerusalem need? It doesn't need a mayor,
It needs a ringmaster with a whip in his hand
To tame prophecies and to train prophets to gallop
Round and round in a circle . . .

"So much prophecy," he says, "so much sadness."

He says he has seen sadness, too, in the eyes of "the Joint Chiefs of Staff, consisting of Job, his friends, Satan, and God." So much sadness in his own eyes, too:

My child still unborn is also a war orphan
of three wars in which I was not killed,
but he is a war orphan of all of them.

It is eight-thirty on a Thursday evening in the square that faces the Wall. The army is bulldozing Arab homes to open up more of the Wall. The Arabs are wailing. At the Wall the night before, brought there by an actress who knew Amichai, I had watched a swearing-in ceremony for paratroopers, the stride of the troopers (very British), the abrasive nasal harangue of the company commander over the loudspeakers, and then the burning of their "insignia" – letters on fire in the dark night sky, unsettling to the actress as it was to me, as if we were looking through the lens-eye of Leni Riefenstahl.

"Anyway," she said defensively, "they are giving the Arabs better homes than they've ever had before."

"Right."

"No, it's wrong, but sometimes you have to do something wrong so that you can do what's right."

To do what is right by doing something wrong, to believe you are right while you know you are wrong, means learning how to forget, though

forgetting someone is like
forgetting to put out the light in the back yard
and leaving it on all day:
it's this light, though,
that makes you remember.

Sons and fathers wrapped in fringed prayer shawls stand face to the Wall . . . that curious white-faced rocking of the men, a furtive pent-up sensuality in their bodies, pitching forward as if in pain on the balls of their feet, tilting on their heels, like men trying to hold to the deck of a ship in a heavy sea.

I speak of this rocking to Amichai.

"Rocking soothes a baby," he says, "but it's the circumcision of the baby that does it to us. Pain. We never forget the pain. We live with the memory of pain all our lives."

Men among men, sharing the severed hood. It is their bond as they shed blood and as they hunger for water. They know women are the water carriers as they know the covenant is sealed by blood, the knife. The blood is the bond, but women, the water carriers, are unclean in their blood. It's a lot of confusion. So confusing that men who lack the confidence of their confusions sometimes howl in their dreams and wake up sopping wet, their mouth dry.

I am wakened by the howling of dogs in the night, dogs down in the valley, and then I hear them howling during the day. Amichai tells me that there is a canine insane asylum in the valley for dogs driven mad during the khamsin, a time of breath-eating heat and desert winds.

"This city," I tell him, feeling dread, "this city is like being trapped inside somebody's story that is all honey and bees, and you get stung and you eat sweet and you get stung and you eat sweet, and I woke up the other night because I was freezing with a fever and I wanted out of here, but I not only didn't know how to get out, I forgot right away as soon as I warmed up that I wanted out . . ."

"You sound like someone crazy . . ."

"I sound like I gotta stop hanging around with you . . ."

We are tired.

We are tired from walking in the sun. When we get back to the house we will wash our

> *eyes with a lot of water*
> *so as to see the world once more*
> *through the wet and hurt.*

Cats lie slumped in the roof gutters waiting for rain. Someone is playing an oboe. An old beard of brown grass hanging from a stone window ledge. A Chassid in his hot fur hat, wheeling an empty baby carriage down the stairs of the Dolorosa, says defiantly, touching a soldier with his long, pale hand, that the Messiah will come only when there is springwater:

> *And it is said that the Sea of Ezekiel is under Jerusalem, and that sea is sealed off. The Chassidim say they are the waters of the Abyss; when the spring is discovered, then the Messiah will come. Until that time of trembling, Jerusalem is a sea of stone, a golden basin filled with scorpions.*

In 326 the Emperor Constantine's mother, Helena, discovered a cistern close by a demolished temple to Venus, and in the cistern, the three crosses and the holy nails. The cross was true, she said, because of its power to raise the dead . . . a sign of the Messiah. A section of the cross was kept on the holy site; slivers were scattered among the Empire's churches. The nails were forged into the bridle of Constantine's warhorse and set on his helmet.

He rode his horse into the world brandishing the cross.

Christ came to the city on a donkey, looking for his cross.

On Palm Sunday, the beginning of Holy Week, I walk out of a cypress grove close to the Garden of Gethsemane, the garden of the kiss, holding a small braided cross of palm. I am in a long procession of schoolgirls, black-robed and bearded priests, older women carrying umbrellas to shield themselves from the sun, with Jewish graves on the hillside, and an army helicopter, cracking the air open with its pulsing *thwack-thwack*, swoops over the Valley of Hinom, where Abraham is said to lie in a tomb, and then swings out toward Jericho and the road to the Dead Sea, and then back across the Vale of Gihon (where the builders of Baal placated their priests by impaling their firstborn):

> *The air above Jerusalem is saturated with*
> *prayers*

and dreams.
Like the air above industrial towns
It is hard to breathe.

Again and again the helicopter angles down toward us, clattering over the hillside seeded with sepulchres. At the Tomb of David – a great long stone box – the guide tells a group of Jews from Newark that the archeologists have an actual hair from David's beard; and close by, in another room, the walls are bricked as if they are ovens – a tidy chamber to commemorate the dead in the death camps – I cannot bring myself to tell the guide that the ovens in Auschwitz are fake, too; the real ones were destroyed and then, later, faux ovens were built, a protective lie, so that pilgrims would have something to look at in their need to be appalled . . .

The dead in the ovens in the camps, David's whisker in a tweezer . . . the mind goes blank. The sun is white, the stones at the top of the walls are white, stones that once were sealed with molten lead, and what seems to be the shadow of a bird is only a dry yellow thorn bush. In the bend of a wall the snout of a lion's-head fountain is stopped up with cement.

Stoppage.

"We, those of my generation," Amichai says, "believed that still, through politics, there was a way out, out of this entrapment. Your generation still believed a little bit. But your son, he has no interest in politics because he knows there is no way out."

Yet Amichai writes:

An Arab shepherd is seeking a kid
on Mount Zion,
And on the opposite hill I seek my little son.
An Arab shepherd and a Jewish father
Both in their temporary failure.
Our two voices meet above
The Sultan's Pool in the valley between . . .

Afterwards we found them between the bushes,
And our voices returned to us
And we wept and laughed deep inside ourselves.
Searches for a kid or for a son were always
The beginning of a new religion in these mountains.

Near the ninth Station of the Cross a soldier sits in the gutter between roofs, overseeing strolling pilgrims. Two black-hatted Jews – Neturei Karta Chassids ("the black crow people from Meah Sh'earim," as Amichai has called them) – hurrying white-faced along the alley, the wind flapping in their long black surcoats, do not look up at the soldier. They refuse to recognize the soldier. The Messiah, they say, has not come. The State is stillborn. They spit when the State is mentioned. They are anti-Zionist (does that make them self-hating Jews, does that make them anti-Semitic, as non-Jews are said to be if they are anti-Zionist?). They are true believers. In Meah Sh'earim they have their signs: "The Nazis used our bodies for soap, the Israelis use our bodies for money." No wonder prophets saw scorpions inside wheels of fire in the air and no wonder that these men, stung by those scorpions and hungering for the sound of water as they headed out into the desert to dream of the sea, found that the desert hills have the sensuous roll of a woman's hips and thighs, and it is no wonder that they – in their wild aloneness – dreamed of stuffing her

bed with apples
(as it is written in the Song of Songs*)*
so we'd roll smoothly
on a red, apple-bearing bed.

Under the Dome of the Rock is a remarkable limestone; it occupies, with its regular form, the greater part of the area beneath; and is surrounded by a gilt iron railing, to keep it

> from the touch of the numerous pilgrims. It appears to be the natural surface of the rock of Mount Moriah . . . At the south-east corner of this rock is an excavated chamber, called by Mahomedans the Noble Cave, to which there is a descent by a flight of stone steps. This chamber is irregular in form, and its superficial area is about six hundred feet, the average height seven feet; it derives a peculiar sanctity from having been, successively (according to Mahomedan tradition), the praying-place of Abraham, David, Solomon, and Jesus: its surface is quite plain, and there are a few small altars. In the centre of the rocky pavement is a circular slab of marble, which being struck, returns a hollow sound, clearly showing that there is a well or excavation beneath; this is called, by the Mahomedans, 'Bir arruah,' the well of souls – the well of wicked messengers we must suppose, this being the narrow entrance to the Mahomedan hell.

As for the well of messengers and their resurrection, Amichai says,

> *Afterward they'll get up*
> *all at once, and with a sound of moving chairs*
> *face the narrow exit.*
>
> *And their clothes are wrinkled*
> *and clods of soil and cigarette ash*
> *are scattered over them*
> *and fingers will uncover in an inside pocket*
> *a theatre ticket from a long-gone season . . .*
>
> *And their eyes are red from so much sleeplessness*
> *underground.*
> *And immediately – questions:*
> *What time is it?*

Where did you put mine?
When? When?

Good Friday. The day of the Wounds of Light. Crowds gather at St. Stephen's Gate under four stone lions, men and women shoulder large dark brown varnished crosses and begin a slow, stumbling processional along the Way of Sorrows, stopping first at a broad courtyard, the Place of Judgement – and there, in the polished, almost translucent paving stones, are a carved star, a carved sword, a spiked crown with the letter B, a scorpion . . . the games, we are told, played by bored soldiers, incising their signs in stone . . . except this is not the place of the Judgement Hall. This is a section of Hadrian's forum where the "guardrooms" were actually shops; and across the Dolorosa is the Church of the Flagellation and the Place of Condemnation, and they say that this is where Christ received his cross . . . except he did not shoulder it here, not in this Roman temple yard. Still, the crowd moves on through the cobbled alleyways of the market, past tray upon tray of Arab sweets soaked in honey, and leather purses, meats, worry beads, the crowd chanting prayers, lunging forward, led by brown-robed Franciscans, and I let the foot of their huge cross rest on my shoulder, for this ritual has become a devotional Way of Sorrows in my mind, too . . . a pilgrimage toward death and resurrection, because the truth is in the story, not in the details . . . stopping where Christ was helped by Simon the Cyrene, where Veronica wiped his face, where he fell, and fell again, and fell for the third time at the Ninth Station, where the best baklava in the old city is sold, not far from where Amichai shops for vegetables, and little Palestinian schoolgirls in maroon dresses sing in Armenian as the cross is twirled like a huge propeller, bruising my neck. This is done so that it will fit through a narrow passage into the sepulchre forecourt, the crowd bulging and surging toward the tomb within the church, a shabby little roundhouse tomb with a litter of paper currency and coins on the stone slab scooped up by a bearded priest, eyes drowsy with a dulled sensuality, dulled by too much candle smoke in the cramped, sweaty chamber. I want air and spin out of the tomb, past women wrapped in black and a blind man whose eyes are bleached white, an old dream of apocalypse in his eyes, and outside, up on Olivet Hill, close to where Christ spoke to the Apostles of the Last Things, there is the Church of Dominus Flevit, "The Lord Wept."

The church is shaped as a tear.

"The wine did not end," Amichai says, "but the eyes ran out of tears."

He has his father's eyes and his mother's greying hair on his head as he makes his way home with his vegetables to sit

in a house that belonged to an Arab
who bought it from an Englishman
who took it from a German
who hewed it from the stones
of Jerusalem, my city:
I look upon God's world of others
who received it from others.
I am composed of many things
I have been collected many times
I am constructed of spare parts
of decomposing materials
of disintegrating words. And already
in the middle of my life, I begin,
gradually, to return them,
for I wish to be a decent and orderly person
when I'm asked at the border,
"Have you anything to declare?"

"What I've got to declare is what I talk about over and over. Maybe I am a little boring, but my story of me sits at the middle of me, and everything around it – like a sleepless lover who leaves cigarette butts on the floor all around his bed – is an interpretation, a different version, Midrashim – some foolish, some sad – it's how my life goes on, it's what I have to declare."

"Bounce the ball. Bounce."

"Hup, one two three four . . ."

"Shoot . . ."

"Hup, one two three four . . ."

We are on a patio surrounded by bushes on a terraced slope outside the old city, the home of a painter. The patio backs on to a house wall. There's a German shepherd sitting under a round table (is it just me? why do I find it strange to see more and more Jews who own German shepherds?) and five or six red kitchen chairs and a netless basketball hoop are up on the wall. Hana and Amichai's old friend Dennis Silk are at the table. He is a poet, a man of doleful eyes, a sweet smile, and a shoulder always bent toward the sadness he feels for his "angelology of puppets – puppets lowered from heaven, dripping light, engaged in a *coup d'état* on behalf of magic." There's wine and water on the table, no need there for magic, a miracle. Hana is smoking her pipe.

I am bouncing a basketball, firing it up at the hoop. Amichai, in jeans and a loose shirt, is marching with mock military sternness, carrying a rod like a rifle over his shoulder.

"Shoot . . . shoot . . ."

Bump bump bump, dribbling the ball on stone paving.

"The last war," he says, "they put me in charge of the Mount of Olives, in a hotel. I had an office. And my men brought in a man who wouldn't obey the curfew, and I said, I know you from somewhere, and he said he was Burt Lancaster, he was playing Moses or somebody who I knew, so I was a big military man in the war in charge of Moses on the Mount of Olives."

Bump

"Shoot."

He is still marching back and forth.

Everyone is laughing. Hana says, "He is trying to take Amichai Hill," puffing on her pipe.

"Which hill is that?" I ask.

"It's a hill where women go to restore their virginity . . ." he says, a mischievous light in his eyes.

"Opposite Mount Zion," Hana says.

". . . the women crouch on their haunches over the stone at night, flapping their bent arms like wings."

The ball caroms off the side of the rim and rolls away. Amichai stops marching and sits down, holding his side as if he were counting his ribs. There are sandwiches, salad in Styrofoam boxes. And bottles of water.

"I'll tell you how things have changed," he says. "The poor, the impoverished, no longer turn to the left. Here they are right wing . . . no one will deal with what has to be done here."

"Meantime, we can do nothing," Hana says.

"Pray," I say, laughing, because sardonically he has written that there are Hebrew prayers for everything, even prayers that are to be said after defecating, a prayer thanking God for having created man with orifices, a prayer to God, knowing full well that

> *He who created man*
> *and filled him full of holes*
> *will do the same to soldiers*
> *afterwards, in war.*

After lunch, as we are leaving the patio, I hand him his soldiering rod, his rifle, but he hunches forward and taps the stone walk, turning the rod into a cane. "Me, already I'm an old man," he says.

"You're not old, you're middle-aged. My father is in old age: he has three girlfriends in their thirties who take him to supper, and the proof that he is in his old age is that his real pleasure is that they pay the bill."

Amichai laughs as loud as I've ever heard him laugh.

"Your father is not bored?" he asks. "He doesn't look back?"

"No, never. Hardly ever."

"I knew an old couple," he says conspiratorially. "They concentrated on their beginning, how they began, telling each other the same old story over and over until they were so bored that they badgered and badgered each other all day about how happy they were."

He tosses the rod into the bushes.

"There has been this rumour," he says. "It's about God, that He has gone missing. Several men said this; Theodor Adorno said this, he said that after Auschwitz it was no longer possible to talk about God. But anyway we have started talking about God again." And Amichai asks:

> *My God, my god, why? Have you forsaken me?*
> *My God, my god. Even then you had to call him twice.*
> *The second time already a question, a first doubt: my God?*

At Easter in 1697, Henry Maundrell wrote:

> Thus, if you would see the place where St. Anne was delivered of the Blessed Virgin, you are carried to a Grotto; if the place where the Blessed Virgin selected Elizabeth, if that of the Baptist's . . . if that of the Agony, or that of St. Peter's Repentance, or that where the Apostles made the creed . . . all these places are also Grottoes. And in a word, wherever you go, you find almost everything is represented as done underground . . .

Skulls are underground.

The small hill where Christ was crucified was called Golgotha – Skull Hill.

Skull Hill is now buried within the walls of the Church of the Holy Sepulchre, and Herman Melville, the old pilgrim sailor, haunted by Ahab and the leprous white whale, came to the Holy Sepulchre in 1857:

> Ruined dome – confused and half-ruinous pile. Labyrinths and terraces of mouldy grottoes, tombs, and shrines. Smells like a dead-house, dingy light. At the entrance, in a sort of grotto in the wall, a divan for Turkish policemen, where they sit cross-legged and smoking, scornfully observing the continuous troop of pilgrims entering and prostrating themselves before the anointing-stone of Christ, which veined streaks of a mouldy red looks like a butcher's slab. Nearby is a blind stair of worn marble ascending to the reputed Calvary . . . and the hole in which the cross was fixed and through a narrow grating as over a cole-cellar, the rent in the rock!

Outside of the Sepulchre, Amichai, in a moss brown suit jacket, all three buttons buttoned, self-enclosed, puts his hand to his eyes, a shielding hand:

> *Many a sailor has seen a cross on the water.*
> *A cross of blood.*
> *A sign.*
> *To be made in blood.*

After supper in his house with Hana and their boy and girl, he walks me halfway to Abu Tor, and startles me as we go down stone stairs in the dark. He asks a question no writer has ever asked me: "Do you believe Jesus was the Messiah?"

"He was like everything else in this city," I say. "Nothing is what it seems."

"Yes?"

"The Messiah," I say "was supposed to be from the line of David, right? – that's what they said – and David, he was of

Joseph's house, except Jesus wasn't Joseph's son." And I put my arm around him, trying to keep a stern believer's face. "His father was a bird who whispered into his mother Mary's ear, and that's why seventeenth-century Puritans, who covered their women from chin to toe, thought ears are so sexy."

On July 15, 1099, Fulcher de Chartres, a Crusader, came clanking across a stone courtyard in Jerusalem wearing his iron suit, looking for the Holy Sepulchre, and he wrote:

> With drawn swords, our people ran through the city; nor did they spare anyone, not even those pleading for mercy. The crowd was struck to the ground, just as rotten fruit falls from shaken branches, and across from windblown oak . . . On top of Solomon's Temple, to which they had climbed in fleeing, many were shot to death with arrows and cast down headlong from the roof. Within the Temple about ten thousand were beheaded. If you had been there, your feet would have been stained up to the ankles with the blood of the slain . . . it was an extraordinary thing to see our squires and poorer people split the bellies of those dead Saracens, so that they might pick out the besants from their intestines, which they had swallowed down their horrible gullets while alive. After several days, they made a great heap of their bodies and burned them to ashes, and in these ashes they found the gold more easily . . . It was pleasing to God at that time, that a small piece of the Lord's Cross was found in a hidden place. From ancient times until now it had been concealed by religious men, and now, God willing, it was revealed by a certain Syrian. He, with his father as conspirator, had carefully concealed and guarded it there. This particle, reshaped in the style of the cross and artistically decorated

with gold and silver, was first carried to the Lord's Sepulchre and then to the Temple joyfully, with singing and giving thanks to God, who for so many days had preserved this treasure, His own and ours.

A patrimony reclaimed. A city reclaimed every hour:

The city plays hide-and-seek among her names:
Yerushalayim, al-Quds, Salem, Jeru, Yeru, all the while
Whispering her first, Jebusite name: U'vus,
Y'vus, Y'vus, in the dark. She weeps
with longing: Aelia Capitolina, Aelie, Aelia.
She comes to any man who calls her at night . . .

There is a great cave that echoes under the city. It is dry at the mouth and made of liquid stone along the roof, and in this vacant darkness, this musk-reeking womb of the city, a woman

at night is naked and alone.
And sometimes she's naked and not alone.

This is where

You can hear the sound of bare feet
running away: and it was death.

And afterwards the sound of a kiss
like the fluttering of a moth
caught between two panes of glass.

In the Holy Sepulchre, crowds are waiting for the first sign of the resurrection of the shed blood. There are two small windows in the tomb and fire bursts out of the windows . . . hand-held candles snatch the flame . . . Little has changed since Claude Reignier Conder wrote in the 1870s:

> Torches were passed out of the fire-hole, and the fire spread over the church, as the roar grew louder and louder. The flame spread, seeming to roll over the whole crowd, till the church was a sea of fire, which extended over the roof to the chapel, and ran up the galleries and along the choir. Meantime a dreadful bell was clanging away . . . A dense blue fog, made by the smoke, and a smell of burning wax rose up, and above all, a quiet gleam of light shone down from the roof.

Black Abyssinian monks who live on the roof, who live a contemplative village life in small plastered hutches and cells built on top of the sepulchre, have come out of their crow's nests and are down in the square parading under a large multicoloured tent to the beat of small drums. Their bishop, in a glittering robe, carries a jewelled umbrella. Boys in white galabiyahs leap around him . . . They are hunting, as they do every year, for the body of Christ as the sun goes down.

"Everybody," Amichai says, "is a sailor in Jerusalem without knowing it, sailors or passengers, mechanics or captains, everyone according to the pattern of his life or character." And among them, Amichai says, he remembers the pattern of his father's life by putting a little stone boat or two on his father's gravestone:

> *I put little stones on his tomb:*
> *a sign I was here,*
> *the calling card of one alive*
> *on the big stone of my father. My father,*
> *causer and affected,*
> *your alarm clock breaks my body.*

All the bells ring on Easter Sunday. The sun shines and all the bells ring. The dead body has not been found by the Abyssinians. In a sepulchre chapel, squat women in black dresses and black shawls crowd onto the altar, bullying one another, shoving and squirming, stubborn in their joy, pitiless in their grasp of it, as they let out a joyous shout tinged by pain . . .

Is it the sound of stone becoming water?

The city that has been in dry-dock is set sail:
And there are days here when everything is
sails and more sails,
even though there's no sea in Jerusalem,
not even a river.
Everything is sails: the flags, the prayer
shawls, the black coats,
the monks' robes, the kaftans and kaffiyehs,
young women's dresses and headdresses,
Torah mantles and prayer rugs, feelings
that swell in the wind
and hopes that set them sailing in other directions.
Even my father's hands, spread out in blessing,
my mother's broad face and Ruth's far-away death
are sails, all of them sails in the splendid regatta
on the two seas of Jerusalem:
the sea of memory and the sea of forgetting.

Soldiers, who never forget, stand on the city roofs, cradling their guns.

Amichai, done with his shopping, has all the vegetables he needs for his family. There are tourists crowded into the Arab alleys, tourists who have bought filigreed Arab jewellery, and they have put on grave faces at the Wailing Wall and they have had their pictures taken among the famous dead at Rachel's

Tomb and Herzl's Tomb and on top of Ammunition Hill, making – as Amichai says – visits of condolence before heading to their air-conditioned hotels, just as he is heading home to his stone house in Yemin Moshe.

"Once," he says, "I sat on the steps by a gate at David's Tower; I placed my two heavy baskets at my side. A group of tourists was standing around their guide and I became a target marker. 'You see that man with the baskets? Just right of his head there's an arch from the Roman period. Just right of his head.' But he's moving, he's moving – I said to myself: redemption will come only if they're told, You see that arch from the Roman period? It's not important; but next to it, left a little and down a bit, there sits a man who's bought fruit and vegetables for his family."

The Eye in the Thicket, 2002

I WISH TO EXPRESS MY GRATITUDE TO:

At *The Telegram*: Tom Hedley, Ron Evans

At the CBC: John Kennedy, Robert Patchel, Richard Nielsen, Terrence Gibbs, Robert Weaver, Bill Casselman

At CTV: Tom Gould, David Sobelman

At *Toronto Life*: Tom Hedley, Marq de Villiers

At *Weekend:* John Macfarlane, Gary Ross

At *Leisure Ways:* Jerry Tutunjian

At *il cannocchiale:* Brunella Antomarini

At *The National Post:* Noah Richler.

ACKNOWLEDGEMENTS:

Most of the selections in this book first appeared in the following periodicals and books. Grateful acknowledgement is made to:

The Toronto Telegram, Maclean's, Weekend, Books in Canada, Leisure Ways, The National Post, Toronto Life, Exile, il cannocchiale, The Eye in the Thicket, Tamarack Review, The David Annesley Drawings.

About the dating of the selections: as I said in "On the Prowl on Rue Morgue Avenue," oftentimes after a piece was published, I tinkered with lines, honed a paragraph, added, deleted – while never changing the spirit of judgement – especially in 1971-1973. Some pieces just naturally grew according to demand. For example, one of my first radio talks in 1964 on CBC's *Audio* was about the poet W.W.E. Ross; I then published, as a free-lancer for the first time in *The Telegram*, 400 words on Ross; that grew, in 1966, into a memoir/introduction to a Selected edition of his poems; by 2003, that piece reached its present expanded form as the introduction to an expanded Selected edition. On the other hand, I have condensed both the very long *Trudeau 1968* journal – which appeared as three full folio pages one Saturday morning in *The Telegram* to its present length, and *Desolation Row: New York*, which appeared as four full folio pages on subsequent Saturdays to its present length. Those essays or poems with dates but no journal attribution, are appearing in print for the first time.

B.C.